Rethinking Private Authority

Rethinking Private Authority

AGENTS AND ENTREPRENEURS IN GLOBAL
ENVIRONMENTAL GOVERNANCE

Jessica F. Green

PRINCETON UNIVERSITY PRESS

PRINCETON AND OXFORD

Library of Congress Cataloging-in-Publication Data
Green, Jessica F.
   Rethinking private authority : agents and entrepreneurs in global environmental governance / Jessica F. Green.
      pages cm
   Summary: "Rethinking Private Authority examines the role of non-state actors in global environmental politics, arguing that a fuller understanding of their role requires a new way of conceptualizing private authority. Jessica Green identifies two distinct forms of private authority—one in which states delegate authority to private actors, and another in which entrepreneurial actors generate their own rules, persuading others to adopt them. Drawing on a wealth of empirical evidence spanning a century of environmental rule making, Green shows how the delegation of authority to private actors has played a small but consistent role in multilateral environmental agreements over the past fifty years, largely in the area of treaty implementation. This contrasts with entrepreneurial authority, where most private environmental rules have been created in the past two decades. Green traces how this dynamic and fast-growing form of private authority is becoming increasingly common in areas ranging from organic food to green building practices to sustainable tourism. She persuasively argues that the configuration of state preferences and the existing institutional landscape are paramount to explaining why private authority emerges and assumes the form that it does. In-depth cases on climate change provide evidence for her arguments. Groundbreaking in scope, Rethinking Private Authority demonstrates that authority in world politics is diffused across multiple levels and diverse actors, and it offers a more complete picture of how private actors are helping to shape our response to today's most pressing environmental problems"— Provided by publisher.
   Includes bibliographical references and index.
   ISBN 978-0-691-15758-0 (hardback) — ISBN 978-0-691-15759-7 (paperback)
1. Environmental policy—International cooperation. 2. Public-private sector cooperation. 3. Non-governmental organizations. 4. Environmental law, International. 5. Industrial management—Environmental aspects. 6. Corporations—Environmental aspects. 7. Business enterprises—Environmental aspects. I. Title.
   GE170.G7326 2013
   333.7—dc23   2013016011

British Library Cataloging-in-Publication Data is available

To John

Contents

List of Illustrations

Acknowledgments

THIS BOOK WAS INITIALLY borne out of the questions I formulated during my time working at United Nations University. Faced with the policy challenges of promoting sustainable development, governments and international organizations alike voiced great optimism in the "power of partnerships." I began to wonder, Why do governments need nonstate actors? What could they accomplish that governments and the UN system could not? I began investigating these questions from a policy perspective at UNU, and I am thankful to my former colleagues there, in particular Hamid Zakri, Sam Johnston, and Bradnee Chambers, for allowing me to pursue them.

Upon arriving at the Woodrow Wilson School at Princeton, I received generous support from the institution and wonderful training from its faculty. Bob Keohane has been an incredible mentor from the very first. I am a lucky beneficiary of Bob's tireless dedication to scholarship and to teaching. My other graduate advisers, Christina Davis and Emilie Hafner-Burton were, and continue to be, generous with their time and guidance. Their input has improved this book, and my scholarship, tremendously. Other faculty at Princeton, including Joanne Gowa, Helen Milner, Andy Moravcsik, Michael Oppenheimer, and Anne-Marie Slaughter, provided feedback on the earlier incarnation of this work (as my dissertation) and challenged me with big questions about the role of private authority in world politics.

In addition to sharing the battle scars of graduate school, other colleagues from Princeton have been sounding boards, editors, critics, and cheerleaders, including Sarah Bermeo, Sarah Bush, Tom Hale, David Hsu, Gwyneth McClendon, Eri Saikawa, Jordan Tama, and Dustin Tingley. Jeff Colgan and Mareike Kleine have read so many versions of this manuscript that they are undoubtedly relieved it is finally in print.

Beyond the halls of Princeton, I have benefited from the generosity of Ron Mitchell, whose data form the basis of my analysis in chapter 2. Stu Shulman helped me through the various beta versions of the Coding Analysis Toolkit with which I coded and analyzed Ron's data. I would also like to thank the many people I interviewed for this book, who patiently answered my questions about what is now ancient history concerning the climate change regime.

I have been fortunate to have supportive colleagues at Case Western Reserve University, who have all been extremely helpful in transforming this into a book project, both intellectually and logistically, including Joe White, Karen Beckwith, Justin Buchler, Katie Lavelle, Kelly McMann,

Vince McHale, Pete Moore, and, in particular, Elliot Posner. I was able to complete the manuscript during my time at the Institute for International Law and Justice at the School of Law at New York University, thanks to Dick Stewart and its director, Robert Howse. For other helpful comments, suggestions, and critiques throughout the research process, I would also like to thank Ken Abbott, Liliana Andonova, Graeme Auld, Tim Büthe, Josh Busby, Ben Cashore, Burkard Eberlein, Jen Hadden, Virginia Haufler, Christer Jönsson, Jibecke Jonsson, Benedict Kingsbury, Duncan Snidal, Dick Stewart, Jonas Tallberg, Bryce Rudyk, David Victor, David Vogel, and Stepan Wood.

Some parts of this book have been published elsewhere. An early version of chapter 2 appeared in *Transnational Actors in Global Governance*, edited by Christer Jönsson and Jonas Tallberg. Chapter 5 draws from my 2010 article "Private Standards in the Climate Regime: The Greenhouse Gas Protocol," which was published in *Business and Politics*. I thank Palgrave Macmillan and De Gruyter and for permission to use these materials.

It has been a pleasure working with Chuck Myers at Princeton University Press, who has supported this project from the outset and capably guided me through the editorial and production process. His comments on the manuscript have improved it markedly.

Finally, none of this would be possible without the support of my wonderful family—my parents, Madeleine and Stephen, and my sister Julia, who all have cracked jokes when I despaired of ever finishing, and helped me keep things in perspective. More than anyone, my deepest thanks go to my husband John, whose love and patience are without parallel. He has been my intellectual partner, my best friend, and my most ardent supporter from the very beginning, believing in me when I did not, and doing so with incredible grace. I cannot begin to express my gratitude for his gifts of love and support.

Acronyms

AIJ	activities implemented jointly
CDM	clean development mechanism
CITES	Convention on International Trade in Endangered Species of Wild Fauna and Flora
FSC	Forest Stewardship Council
G-77	Group of 77 and China
GHG	greenhouse gas
IO	international organization
IPCC	Intergovernmental Panel on Climate Change
ISO	International Organization for Standardization
JUSCANNZ	negotiating bloc of Japan, the United States, Switzerland, Canada, Australia, Norway, and New Zealand
MEA	multilateral environmental agreement
NGO	nongovernmental organization
REDD	reducing emissions from deforestation and forest degradation
SCAR	Scientific Committee on Antarctic Research
SGS	Société Générale de Surveillance
TRAFFIC	Trade Records Analysis of Flora and Fauna in Commerce
UNFCCC	United Nations Framework Convention on Climate Change
EPA	Environmental Protection Agency (United States)
UN	United Nations
UNDP	United Nations Development Programme
WBCSD	World Business Council on Sustainable Development
WRI	World Resources Institute

Rethinking Private Authority

Introduction

THIS BOOK IS ABOUT how the global environment is regulated and, in particular, the diversity of actors involved in addressing the problem of climate change. But it is not only, or indeed mostly, a book about climate change. Rather, it is about how private actors—including nongovernmental organizations, firms, transnational networks, and others—exercise authority in world politics. Increasingly, private actors assume duties normally considered the province of governments. They are taking on the role of regulators, as they create, implement, and enforce rules to manage global environmental problems. This book asks when and why private actors perform these regulatory roles. Three examples show the diversity of private authority and the ways in which nonstate actors are serving as rule makers.

In 2005 Walmart decided it was time to go green. It outlined three long-term goals to guide its sustainability efforts: zero waste, 100 percent renewable energy sourcing, and sustainable sourcing of its products. Since then, it has taken additional steps to achieve these goals. To promote "sustainable sourcing," Walmart has created an index that helps its suppliers evaluate the sustainability of their production and performance.

When Walmart decides on a new set of practices, the world has to listen. It has 200 million visits *per week*—roughly equivalent to having every citizen of Brazil shop at Walmart on a weekly basis. In 2011 it had nearly nine thousand retail units in fifteen nations and did roughly half a trillion dollars in sales.[1] And that's only the retail end of the story. To keep all of these consumers in low-price goods, Walmart relies on more than 100,000 suppliers across the globe; roughly one-tenth of these are in China.[2] Indeed, if Walmart were a country, it would be China's fifth- or sixth-largest export market.[3] Walmart's commercial reach—and its environmental impact—are truly global.

So a new sustainability index for Walmart potentially means big changes all along the supply chain. Walmart has become, in effect, a global regulator of production practices. Its rules require suppliers to change their behavior or lose a major source of revenue. For instance, Walmart recently announced it would cut 20 million metric tons of carbon emissions from

---

[1] Walmart 2011 Annual Report. http://www.walmartstores.com/sites/annualreport/2011/financials/Walmart_2011_Annual_Report.pdf.

[2] Dauvergne and Lister 2012.

[3] Mufson 2010.

its supply chain by 2015.[4] Suppliers must therefore find ways to reduce their carbon intensity—lowering their emissions while maintaining current production levels. Although the measure is voluntary, the signal is clear: Walmart will buy from those who achieve the goal and stop doing business with the laggards. Some defenders of industry have renounced the measure as coercive.[5] But many suppliers have simply accepted this new reality and have started making the requisite adjustments to ensure Walmart's continued business. One representative of a Chinese company noted: "We heard that in the future, to become a Wal-Mart supplier, you have to be an environmentally friendly company. So we switched some of our products and the way we produced them."[6]

Sustainability is no longer a future goal of Walmart but a present requirement. Although Walmart cannot physically audit all of its suppliers, it has begun to evaluate systematically the extent to which they are in compliance with the newly created sustainability criteria. Companies that receive a "disapproved" ranking are banned from selling to Walmart for a year. Those found to be in egregious violation can be permanently barred from doing business with Walmart. Of course, the system is new, and inspections are still incomplete; less than 4 percent of all audited Chinese suppliers fell into these bottom two tiers in 2011.[7] However, the threat of losing the ability to sell to the second-largest corporation in the world is enough to make many suppliers "go green"—whether they want to or not. For better or worse, Walmart is now a global rule maker for sustainability.

* * *

Varecia variegata, commonly known as the ruffed lemur, is a primate found only in Madagascar. There are approximately ten thousand left in the wild, and about six hundred in captivity. The remaining wild lemurs are under threat, primarily due to habitat destruction and hunting. These surprisingly humanlike creatures are protected by the Convention on the International Trade in Endangered Species (CITES). As a regulated species, commercial trade in ruffed lemurs is prohibited. Approximately one thousand of the world's most endangered species are similarly protected

---

[4] http://www.nytimes.com/2010/02/26/business/energy-environment/26walmart.html?_r=1.

[5] http://www.prnewswire.com/news-releases/corporate-ethics-group-blasts-wal-mart-for-forcing-its-politics-on-suppliers-through-new-environmental-mandates-58278977.html.

[6] http://www.washingtonpost.com/wp-dyn/content/article/2010/02/26/AR2010022606757.html. As quoted in Dauvergne and Lister 2012.

[7] Lister and LeBaron 2012.

by CITES: trade is prohibited, with limited exceptions for research and education.

What is surprising about the ruffed lemur and other endangered species facing a similar fate is not their protection under CITES, but who actually does the protecting. In 1975 states created a global treaty to help stem the trade in endangered species, but since then, they have delegated key aspects of running the treaty to an international nongovernmental organization (NGO), called TRAFFIC. TRAFFIC (or Trade Records Analysis of Flora and Fauna in Commerce) was created in 1979 by two large conservation NGOs and quickly became the largest and most respected organization for monitoring wildlife trade. For two decades, TRAFFIC has been an authoritative source of data on trade in endangered species. It often contributes reports to CITES that serve as the basis of debate and decision making among states.

Then, in 1999, the Secretariat of CITES—the administrative body that oversees the treaty—entered into a formal relationship with TRAFFIC. Now, TRAFFIC helps police the treaty. It has been delegated the important task of detecting noncompliance. It issues regular bulletins reporting on threats to species protected by the treaty. In 2010 it reported a surge in illegal hunting of lemurs in Madagascar to provide meat to local restaurants which serve lemur as a delicacy.[8] It also maintains two key databases that track the illegal trade in ivory. Information gathered from TRAFFIC has led to in-depth investigations of state practice. More generally, when suspected violations of the terms of the treaty arise, states often delegate the task of investigation to TRAFFIC.

The fates of the ruffed lemur, the elephant, and hundreds of other endangered species rest not only in the hands of states and their policies but also in the actions of nonstate actors like TRAFFIC. Armed with authority delegated by states, this NGO helps decide who is following the rules and who is not.

* * *

As I finish this book, states have just completed yet another round of negotiations on the future of the Kyoto Protocol—the centerpiece of their efforts to address climate change. The global legal process has been bumpy, but most agree that the Kyoto Protocol has not worked. It's true that some developed countries have reduced their emissions, but the consensus is that this is not sufficient to change the perilous trajectory that we are on. Many countries have said they will not commit to "hard targets" into the future and instead have focused on nonbinding

[8] TRAFFIC 2010.

"pledges" to reduce their emissions. Collectively, states are focused on an agreement that will take effect in 2020, leaving a gap in efforts over the next eight years. Arriving at this underwhelming state of affairs has taken two decades, innumerable meetings and negotiations, and a great deal of resources.

At the same time, nonstate actors of all stripes have begun to take decisive action—sometimes on a surprising scale. Firms like Walmart are preparing for a carbon-restricted world by creating their own targets and timetables for emissions reductions. The ripple effects of their decisions reverberate throughout the global economy. There is also a burgeoning private market for carbon offsets; well-meaning actors can reduce their carbon footprint by buying offsets from private retailers. In 2011 this produced almost 100 million tons of reductions, valued at more than half a billion dollars.[9] There is even a new umbrella association—the International Carbon Reduction and Offset Alliance—that polices the quality of these private offsets. Institutional investors representing US$10 trillion now participate in the Investor Network on Climate Risk, which seeks to reduce their exposure to climate risks through investment practices.[10] All of these activities are happening independently of government regulation.

* * *

Why is Walmart becoming a standard-bearer of sustainability? Why do states entrust NGOs with the fate of the ruffed lemur? Why would firms choose to report their carbon emissions—let alone spend money to offset them—without being compelled to do so by regulation? The goal of this book is to answer these questions. I develop a theoretical account of private authority, which I define as situations in which private actors make rules or set standards that others in world politics adopt. But I also argue that there is much legwork to be done before grand theories can be presented. For instance, we need more conceptual clarity on what, exactly, constitutes private authority. We also need a better understanding of the importance of this phenomenon by determining how frequently each type of private authority occurs and if this has changed over time.

The book makes three key contributions to understanding the role of private actors in global environmental politics. First, I offer a new typology of the concept, which distinguishes between two different types of private authority—delegated and entrepreneurial. I show that this distinction is crucial not only to understand the breadth of private authority in global environmental politics but also to formulate a complete explanation of

[9] Peters-Stanley et al. 2011.
[10] http://www.ceres.org/incr/about.

why it emerges. The three examples show very different ways that private actors are contributing to the production of global public goods. If we are to understand fully their role in environmental governance—and, indeed, in world politics more generally—then we must examine *each type* of private authority, while also considering them jointly.

Second, I provide a much-needed empirical assessment, which includes some of the first longitudinal data on private authority. Certainly, Walmart's foray into sustainability could potentially have a huge impact on both local and global environmental quality. And yes, endangered lemurs, elephants, and toads would be worse off without TRAFFIC carefully watching states' efforts to protect these species. But beyond these examples, we know surprisingly little about how often private actors are acting as rule makers and whether this has changed over time. So the second key contribution of this book is to provide one of very few elaborations of the extent of private authority, both quantitatively and longitudinally.

The third contribution is to explain why this is happening. Only with a clear typology of private authority, and a much bigger picture of its breadth and variation over time, can we turn to understanding the conditions under which private authority emerges. Here, the book engages with a question broadly applicable to the study of international relations: What does private authority mean for the authority of the state? Some have argued that the state is waning, as the power of nonstate actors grows. This book shows that such a story is an oversimplification of reality. Private authority is definitely a fixture of contemporary world politics. But this fact does not imply a zero-sum relationship with the authority of states.

Indeed, despite its focus on private authority, this book is as much about governments as it is about private actors. Instead of arguing, as many have, about *the* locus of authority in world politics (i.e., states), I show that there are multiple loci of authority in the international system—some of which include private actors. These private actors (which I also refer to as nonstate actors) include NGOs, firms, and transnational networks.[11] By focusing on policy outputs—the effective governance of transnational environmental problems—this approach does not privilege the public or private sphere. I purposefully sidestep what I believe to be misleading juxtapositions of private versus state authority. Rather, I maintain that private authority is one of many sources of governance in world politics and seek to specify the conditions under which we should expect the private sphere to serve as one, among many, loci of authority.

---

[11] Because they are created, governed, and funded by states, I do not include international organizations in the category of nonstate actors.

THE ARGUMENT

A clear conceptualization of private authority is the first step toward assessing the conditions under which it occurs. Thus, the first part of the argument is conceptual, distinguishing between two different types of private authority. Second, because there are multiple loci of authority to address a given global environmental problem, I turn to an explanation of the relationship among them. I argue that private authority does not occur in a vacuum, and so a theory of private authority must necessarily examine the role of the state. The final piece of the argument sets out when we should expect to see private authority emerge and, importantly, which type—delegated or entrepreneurial—it will be.

Laying the Conceptual Foundations: What Is Private Authority?

Definitions matter. One of the themes of the book is that definitions of private authority have been underspecified and incomplete. As a consequence, investigations into the incidence and effects of private authority have been correspondingly flawed. Chapter 1 seeks to redress these conceptual shortcomings by identifying two distinct types of private authority. But before turning to this discussion, a more general conceptualization of authority in world politics is needed.

Authority is a slippery concept. Like pornography, most would agree that we know it when we see it, even if it is difficult to define. In world politics, states are the only actors with the legal right to coerce, but coercion is generally costly. As a result, authority—whether projected by states or other actors—is generally based on consent. *Somebody* must consent to following the rules, or else there is no authority. In this sense, authority is "a social relationship between authority and subject," because it is mutually constituted, requiring that the subject acknowledge and consent to the claim of authority.[12]

Private authority shares these attributes. It is relational and requires the consent of those who are subject to it. Formally, it can be understood as *situations in which nonstate actors make rules or set standards that other actors in world politics adopt.* To be clear, private authority is distinct from efforts by nonstate actors to influence states; it does not include activities like lobbying or agenda setting. Nor does it include the creation of norms. Rather, this definition restricts private authority to the creation of actual rules, standards, guidelines, or practices that other actors adopt.

---

[12] Pauly 2002, 6.

In this book, I distinguish between two types of private authority: delegated private authority and what I call "entrepreneurial private authority" (or, more briefly, delegated and entrepreneurial authority). In both types, the rule maker is recognized as legitimate—that is, it has the right to rule.[13] Because of the perceived legitimacy of the rule maker, the targets of rules consent to change their behavior. Yet the origins of authority differ in each.

Claims of delegated authority are ultimately derived from the state. States, acting collectively, are the principal. They delegate a circumscribed set of tasks to a private actor, which serves as the states' agent. If the source of authority does not originate with the state, then private authority is entrepreneurial. In this mode, any private actor that projects authority must persuade others to adopt its rules or practices. If the private actor is successful in its persuasion, entrepreneurial private authority occurs. Entrepreneurial authority moves beyond traditional conceptions of nonstate actors as lobbyists, seeking to influence the rules made by states.[14] Rather, in entrepreneurial authority, private actors strike out on their own, serving as *de facto* rule makers in world politics. The rules, standards, or practices created by private actors "can become authoritative" owing to the expertise of the private actors or to other tactics that they use to cultivate legitimacy.[15] Other tactics might include persuasion through moral arguments, or by leveraging market pressure, whereby the adoption of entrepreneurial authority facilitates entry into new markets. In other words, entrepreneurial authority is the translation of claims of authority by private actors into actual control.[16] Often, the timing of consent can also help distinguish between the two forms. In general, the governed grant their consent *ex ante* in the case of delegated authority, whereas it tends to be *ex post* in entrepreneurial authority.[17] In sum, delegated authority is *de jure*, while entrepreneurial authority is *de facto*.

This first piece of the argument—the expansion and refinement of the concept of private authority—is a key contribution of this book because it allows consideration of the full range of ways that private actors serve as rule makers in world politics. Research on global environmental

[13] Hobbes 1996, 112.

[14] The question of when nonstate actors are successful at influencing the policies of states at the multilateral level is addressed by the literature on global civil society and transnational advocacy networks. See, e.g., Keck and Sikkink 1998; Tarrow 1998; Florini 2000; O'Brien et al. 2000.

[15] Cutler, Haufler, and Porter 1999a, 5.

[16] On the useful distinction between theoretical conceptions of authority and empirical mechanisms of control, see McDougal and Lasswell 1970, 364.

[17] In practice, the timing distinction may be blurred by the fact that the private actor can (and often does) lobby for such delegation to occur before the transfer of authority takes place; however, it does not have authority to act until delegation occurs.

governance, with its focus on entrepreneurial authority,[18] has largely overlooked the role of private actors as agents. The international relations literature has focused on delegation to international organizations rather than private actors.[19] However, if we are to understand the ways that private actors are contributing to solving environmental problems, then we must examine *both types* of private authority. While it is critical to recognize that delegated and entrepreneurial authority are distinct phenomena—they occur at different rates for different reasons—we must consider them in tandem. Excluding one of the two types fundamentally skews the picture not only of private authority but also of public authority.

The Relational Story: Private Authority Does Not Occur in a Vacuum

As should be clear from the definitions outlined above, any account of private authority is invariably one of public authority as well, because the distinction between the two types rests in part on the involvement of the state.[20] Yet many studies to date have failed to make this fact explicit or even to recognize it. Early discussions view private authority as a regulatory force that emerges in the interstices of global governance, where the state does not regulate.[21] Although the causal accounts vary, many attribute the emergence of private authority to globalization, as manifested by the growth in size and power of multinational corporations.[22] Others see the rise of private authority as reflection of the neoliberal turn in world politics, where private-sector solutions are privileged over government policy.[23]

A related interpretation views public and private authority in a zero-sum relationship: to the extent that private actors are exercising authority, states are losing their ability to govern. Thus, Jessica Mathews refers to a "power shift" from states to nonstate actors.[24] This view implies only one set of actors can be in charge. In a similar fashion, some have suggested that private authority is "a functional equivalent" to public

---

[18] Garcia-Johnson 2000; Lipschutz and Fogel 2002; Falkner 2003; Cashore, Auld, and Newsom 2004; Prakash and Potoski 2006; Pattberg 2007.

[19] For exceptions, see Avant 2005; Wolf 2005; Green 2008; Koremenos 2008; Cooley 2010; Büthe and Mattli 2011; Green and Colgan 2013.

[20] In the context of global governance, public authority can be understood as cooperative efforts among states; this includes intergovernmental treaties as well as the activities of international organizations.

[21] Cutler, Haufler, and Porter 1999a; Spar 1999; Kobrin 2002; Pattberg 2005; Betsill and Bulkeley 2006.

[22] Cerny 1995; Strange 1996; Ohmae 1995; Cutler 2003.

[23] Bernstein 2002; Bartley 2003.

[24] Mathews 1997; Cerny 1995; Strange 1996.

authority.[25] This statement suggests that private authority exists only as a substitute for public forms of regulation. In one of the earliest studies of private authority, Cutler and colleagues acknowledge the role of the state but suggest that it can be replaced, noting that substitutability is a key feature of private authority: "The degree to which private arrangements can substitute for the regulatory functions usually associated with states is often not recognized."[26] Contrary to these depictions, I find no evidence that public and private authority exist solely in an either-or configuration.

Indeed, these views are incomplete; they are overly stylized versions of a much more intricate reality. The increasing complexity of global governance arrangements demonstrates that authority is "polycentric," diffusing across multiple venues and through a variety of actors.[27] As Avant and colleagues succinctly note: "No governor governs alone."[28] Private authority is imbricated in a larger constellation of governing institutions, comprising many different types of actors. The findings of this book show the many ways in which this is the case.

In sum, private authority in world politics does not exist in a vacuum. Rather, it is linked to public authority in different and complex ways. In the case of delegated private authority, the relationship is clear and explicit. States serve as principals and as the source of legitimacy for private agents. Moreover, public and private authority are not in conflict; rather, as the next section shows, they have expanded together. This is not evidence of a retreat of the state, as Susan Strange famously claimed, but rather a change in the actors that constitute the public domain.[29]

In the case of entrepreneurial authority, the role of the state is implicit but still paramount: the absence of the state as a source of legitimacy is a defining characteristic. Moreover, as chapters 3 and 5 demonstrate, entrepreneurial authority often exists in tandem with other public arrangements. These findings illustrate that the relationship between the two is most certainly not zero-sum.[30] Instead, the two enable and constrain each other in important and varying ways. Finally, public authority is an important factor in explaining which form of private authority emerges.

This book seeks to remedy earlier incomplete representations of the concept of private authority. Private authority is not just "out there" in

[25] Pattberg 2005, 593. See also Börzel and Risse 2010.

[26] Cutler, Haufler, and Porter 1999a, 16.

[27] Ostrom 2010. This has been well documented in the literature on environmental governance. See, e.g., Biermann and Dingwerth 2004; Betsill and Corell 2008; Biermann and Pattberg 2008; Dingwerth and Pattberg 2009; Haufler 2009; Andonova 2010; Andonova and Mitchell 2010.

[28] Avant, Finnemore, and Sell 2010b, 7.

[29] Strange 1996; on the changing nature of the public domain, see Ruggie 2004.

[30] Avant, Finnemore, and Sell 2010b, 357.

the ether, nor does it always occur at the behest of states. Rather, multiple sites of authority coexist. The relevant line of inquiry is to understand how and when they do, and under what conditions.

Delegated and Entrepreneurial Authority: Two Empirical Stories

This book provides an expansive picture of what private authority in the environmental arena looks like now, and how it has changed over the past one hundred years, offering much needed context for the case studies presented in the second half of the book.[31] The new data presented in chapters 2 and 3 show two very different ways in which private actors are exercising authority. Delegated authority is a small but consistent phenomenon in which states tap private actors for their expertise. Entrepreneurial authority, by contrast, is new and growing rapidly, with an increasing amount of overlap among standards.

There are now more than a thousand multilateral agreements and thirteen hundred bilateral agreements related to environmental issues.[32] And yet we have little notion of the role that private actors play in them. For almost sixty years, states have called on private actors to aid in the implementation of multilateral environmental treaties. They asked the International Union for Conservation of Nature to compile lists of endangered species. They tapped the Scientific Committee on Antarctic Research to compile and analyze data and make recommendations to states about how to manage fragile ecosystems. And they empowered numerous technical and scientific experts to provide advice, help arbitrate disputes, and review treaty implementation.

Interestingly, the role of delegated private authority has largely been overlooked in the work on environmental governance. This work tends to focus on nonstate actors either as advocates, trying to influence interstate bargaining, or as sources of entrepreneurial authority, creating their own rules outside the intergovernmental arena. The few contributions that examine private actors as states' agents in international politics are largely outside the environmental realm.[33] For this reason, it is not surprising that a recent work on international delegation identified research on the role of NGOs as agents as "the research frontier."[34]

---

[31] Ragin 2004.

[32] Mitchell 2002–13. For a slightly different count, see ecolex.org.

[33] See e.g. Mattli and Büthe 2005; Koremenos 2007; Koremenos 2008. The International Accounting Standards Board is an example of a private standard setter that is now an agent. Exceptions in the environmental arena are Green 2008; Lund 2010.

[34] Lake and McCubbins 2006, 341.

Consequently, the data presented in this book provide important new insights about how private actors serve as sources of authority in multilateral environmental treaties. I find that they have a small but consistent role, though this has mostly occurred in the last two decades. In general, states delegate to private actors because of their expertise. In the 1998 Dolphin Conservation Treaty, states delegated to an international review panel—composed of states, NGOs, and industry representatives—to monitor the performance of member states, notify parties to the agreement about potential infractions, and make recommendations about ways to improve the treaty's implementation. In the North American Agreement on Environmental Cooperation, a side agreement to the North American Free Trade Agreement, states delegate to private legal experts to serve as potential arbiters in cases of dispute. Other treaties tap private agents to serve as arbiters or to evaluate scientific data. Thus, the authority delegated to these private actors is rather narrow—generally limited to a few tasks in which their expertise can be of explicit use to states.[35]

The data yield another important finding: once they have been delegated authority, private actors rarely govern on their own. That is, there are usually other actors, either IOs or states, that are responsible for the same tasks. This fact has two important implications. First, the authority of private actors is doubly constrained—by their principals and by other agents. Private actors not only must stay within the bounds of the authority delegated by the principals but must coordinate and contend with other agents. Second, the governance landscape is becoming increasingly complex, as more actors are responsible for the same task. The relationship between public and private authority is not zero-sum. Rather, the loci of authority are at once expanding and increasingly overlapping.

The relatively limited role for delegated private authority raises a question: If private actors are increasingly serving as global governors, as many claim, where, exactly is this phenomenon occurring? The answer is evidenced by the data on entrepreneurial authority. In contrast to the rather small and auxiliary role that private actors play in environmental treaty making, they are increasingly active in the realm of "civil regulation," where privately created rules govern the social and environmental practices of firms and their supply chains.[36] Civil regulations can be understood as a form of entrepreneurial private authority. As I show in chapter 3, there has been a veritable explosion in the number of these private rules over the past decade. Eco-conscious consumers and

---

[35] This does not mean that agents are always perfectly controlled by their principals. The issue of agency slack and shirking is addressed in greater detail in chapters 1 and 2.

[36] Vogel 2008.

health-obsessed citizens of developed nations have been able to purchase food products certified as organically grown since the 1970s. But now one can also purchase sustainably harvested timber, cruelty-free clothes and beauty products, and environmentally friendly appliances and even go on holidays that promote sustainable development in some far corner of the world. Private actors are also deciding about what constitutes carbon neutrality, environmental safety, and social justice and creating systems of environmental management and disclosure. All of these are examples of entrepreneurial authority.

Of course, authority is a two-way street, and entrepreneurial authority is no exception. Not only are private actors creating rules, but many different types of actors, firms in particular, are increasingly adopting their rules. In 2007, 7.6 percent of the world's forest cover was certified as sustainable according to private environmental codes.[37] For some leading nations, the percentage climbs from 20 percent to as much as 40 percent of total forested lands. Sales of Fairtrade products, which aim to level the playing field between producers and consumers, approached five billion dollars in 2009.[38] Starbucks now sells Fairtrade certified coffee in every store in the United States.[39] The Marine Stewardship Council certifies the sustainability of fish sold in retail giants such as McDonalds, Walmart, Carrefour, and Whole Foods.[40] An array of firms, NGOs, and other organizations purchased almost a half a billion dollars' worth of carbon offsets on the voluntary carbon market, which is governed entirely by private rules.[41] These data show that entrepreneurial authority is credible and useful to a sizable swath of the private sector.

Whereas the picture of delegated authority is relatively straightforward and simple, the survey of entrepreneurial authority is complex and messy. Several interesting findings stand out. First, the data above suggest that entrepreneurial authority is growing rapidly and diffusing across the globe. The longitudinal data bear this out: almost 60 percent of all civil regulations were created in the past decade.

Second, the content of these schemes is changing. Instead of creating their own rules, civil regulations are increasingly drawing on existing ones (both public and private) and incorporating them into their own "new" rules.[42] This shows yet another way in which private authority

---

[37] Auld, Gulbrandsen, and McDermott 2008.

[38] Fairtrade International n.d., "Facts and Figures." Available from http://www.fairtrade.net/facts_and_figures.html.

[39] Conroy 2007, 2.

[40] See http://www.nytimes.com/2011/06/09/business/global/09fish.html and http://www.msc.org/where-to-buy/product-finder.

[41] Peters-Stanley et al. 2011.

[42] Green 2013a.

does not occur in a vacuum: private rule makers frequently build on extant rules to establish their own entrepreneurial authority. This finding also suggests a potential pathway for the diffusion of entrepreneurial authority: by embedding older private standards into newer ones. The Greenhouse Gas Protocol, described in chapter 5 provides a useful illustration of how private authority can become embedded in others' rules. The protocol provides a system for organizations to account for and report their greenhouse gas emissions—a "corporate accounting" tool. This system not only has been widely adopted by firms around the world but also serves as the basis for virtually all other corporate accounting tools, both public and private. The International Organization for Standardization based its accounting framework on the Greenhouse Gas Protocol, as did the Climate Registry. The former is the oldest and largest international standard-setting organization in the world. The latter is an emissions reporting registry used by firms and local, city, state, and provincial governments in North America.

Third, the majority of certification schemes are "hard" schemes, requiring a third party to verify compliance. For example, timber companies cannot simply say that they meet all of the requirements for sustainable logging set forth by the Forest Stewardship Council (FSC); they must hire an FSC-approved third party to verify that this is in fact the case. Thus, most certification schemes (with the notable exception of those that promote corporate social responsibility) are concerned about compliance and the perceived legitimacy of their rules. These instances of entrepreneurial authority are not just nice ideas about improving environmental quality; they have been created as real governance tools for achieving this goal.

Moreover, hard rules require verifiers, which are in turn another source of private authority. The firm that certifies a timber producer as FSC-compliant is itself a source of entrepreneurial authority. It does not have any authority delegated by the state but decides what constitutes compliance with privately created rules. In other words, some forms of entrepreneurial authority have created the need for even more private authority, in the form of those NGOs and firms charged with verifying compliance.

In short, the data provide important issue-wide, longitudinal data about how private authority *really* operates and how it has changed (and not changed) over time. The conceptual distinction between entrepreneurial and delegated authority is of pivotal importance in this regard, allowing the disaggregation of different phenomena that tell fundamentally different stories. In one story, private delegated authority, though relatively small, is consistent and long-standing; private actors are lending their expertise at the request of the state. However, it is a relatively untold story, with most work focusing on how nonstate actors influence the environmental law-making process. It is noteworthy that these private actors have been helping to regulate environmental problems for six decades—beginning well before any arguments about the demise of the state in the face of globalization.

The other story, that of entrepreneurial authority, is a relatively new one—and it continues to grow rapidly in breadth and importance. Here, private actors are largely targeting other private and subnational actors in a variety of environmental areas. They are creating standards of environmental quality, in many cases leveraging the power of the market to project authority.[43] The data here paint a much more complex picture of global governance. Although these rules are ostensibly "soft law," most require some third-party verification of compliance. There are multiple sets of rules targeting a single issue, so that different private actors compete for rule adopters. Interestingly, there is considerable overlap among rules, suggesting that private authority can serve as a means to embed rules—both public and private—and expand the scope of users. These stories are very different, but both demonstrate the multiple loci of authority in contemporary global environmental politics.

A Causal Theory of Private Authority

With a revised conceptualization of private authority, which accounts for the broad spectrum of ways in which private actors serve as rule makers and acknowledges the key role of public authority, I now turn to a causal theory. The theory, previewed here, has two main components. First, it explains when we should expect to see private authority emerge in world politics. Second, when it does emerge, it offers an explanation for the form of private authority—that is, whether it is delegated or entrepreneurial. While other works simply address the question of emergence, this book advances our collective understanding of private authority by also explaining the difference in form.

The Emergence of Private Authority

To explain the emergence of private authority, I use a model of supply and demand,[44] though in a metaphorical sense rather than as an economic concept. I argue that a demand for private authority will arise if there are actors who will benefit from such rules. These benefits can come in multiple forms. Like international institutions, institutionalized

[43] Cashore 2002; Cashore, Auld, and Newsom 2004.
[44] Mattli and Woods 2009b; Büthe 2010a.

forms of private authority can reduce uncertainty and the incentives for defection and can increase flows of information.[45] According to this logic, private authority emerges because actors in world politics—both states and nonstate actors—anticipate that they will benefit from adopting the rules and practices promulgated by private actors.

Specifically, private authority can offer four benefits to those choosing to adopt it. First, it can reduce transaction costs. Much of the logic of delegation is rooted in minimizing transaction costs; the costs of supervising an agent well versed in the issue at hand is often easier than taking the time to learn the task oneself. In terms of economic theory, it is cheaper to buy the knowledge or know-how than to make it.[46] States often adopt this logic when delegating to private actors.

Second, private authority can help enhance the credibility of commitments. Two actors are more likely to believe that the other will abide by the rules if they agree to have a third party monitor their behavior. As such, we see private actors monitoring treaty implementation, as demonstrated by the endangered species example. But they are also monitoring firms' behavior, as illustrated by the many civil regulations that require third-party verification.

Third, private authority can potentially confer first-mover advantage to early adopters. Rule takers may adopt private standards because they believe that they will not only benefit from doing so but also gain advantages relative to their competition. Essentially, if private authority seeks to solve a coordination problem, then early action can be beneficial.[47] This logic clearly motivated users of the Greenhouse Gas Protocol, who thought that managing their emissions would be a first step in preparing for future regulation under the Kyoto Protocol. This would not only allow them to insulate against future costs of regulation but also put them in a better position than their less forward-looking counterparts.

Fourth and finally, private authority can benefit its users by helping to improve their reputation. It is no secret that many multinational companies adopt various forms of entrepreneurial authority with the hopes of greening their reputation. Conroy notes that "'branding' is the name of the global corporate game in the 21st century."[48] Adopting privately created sustainability rules is often a way for firms to demonstrate their environmental commitments (though, of course, whether these achieve the desired effects is another story altogether).

There must also be a supply of private authority—actors capable of creating rules and securing consent. In this study, the supply of private

[45] Keohane 1982; Keohane 1984.
[46] Alchian and Demsetz 1972.
[47] Mattli and Büthe 2003.
[48] Conroy 2007, 1.

authority is derived, at its core, from expert knowledge.[49] It is a key reason that other actors choose to defer to private authority. In its common usage, to be "an authority" on something is to be able evaluate the veracity of information.[50] There are, of course, many sources of expertise in the world, not all of them necessarily private actors. Thus, private expertise is a necessary but not sufficient condition for private authority; it creates only the *possibility* of emergence. However, if private actors with expertise are able to provide one (or more) of the benefits described when others cannot, then private authority may emerge. Recall that private authority does not exist in a vacuum; accordingly, there is another piece to the supply part of the equation.

Expertise is not the sole route to private authority. Actors with market power, as demonstrated by Walmart, are capable of creating rules and promoting their adoption. In addition, those with moral legitimacy, such as in the TRAFFIC example,[51] are also potential rule makers.

The emergence of private authority also depends on *other* potential sources of authority: states and other actors will defer to private expertise—thereby transforming it into private authority—if there is no ready equivalent public expertise. Thus, in principle, states might be more predisposed to delegate to international organizations, which they can control more readily through direct governance structures and the power of the purse.[52] However, if IOs do not have the requisite skills or experience, developing them may be a time-consuming process, making delegated private authority more attractive. In this sense, the theory of private authority presented here is a theory of institutional choice: understanding how actors in world politics choose among myriad institutional arrangements to address transnational problems.

The Form of Private Authority

According to the first half of my theory, then, private authority should emerge in instances when private actors have existing expertise and can provide benefits that other actors cannot.[53] However, if a complete conceptualization of private authority must include both delegated and entrepreneurial forms, as I argue above, it follows that a causal theory must also explain both types. Because private authority constitutes one among many possible institutional designs, these hypotheses all describe neces-

[49] This is consistent with Cutler, Haufler, and Porter 1999a and P. Haas 1990 but is more expansive in the types of actors.

[50] Raz 1990, 2.

[51] On sources of legitimacy, see Weber 1978, chap. 3.

[52] For a similar argument about hybrid organizations, see Koppell 2003.

[53] This is consistent with Büthe and Mattli 2011.

sary but not sufficient conditions to explain the form of private authority. In this sense, the hypotheses presented below are probabilistic rather than absolute.

The second half of the theory explains when we should see delegated or entrepreneurial forms of private authority. The type that emerges can be explained by two key factors: whether or not there is an existing focal institution (often an IO), and the degree to which powerful states have similar preferences about the specific policies to be implemented.

When powerful states are in agreement about a given policy and a strong focal institution exists, delegated authority may emerge. A strong focal institution, which serves as point of convergence for actors' expectations, can also be a locus of state control.[54] If states are in agreement on a course of action, and they have identified private actors that are able to provide the benefits that they seek, delegated authority will occur. This is because the focal institution can serve as a means to screen and monitor private agents, to ensure that they are carrying out states' bidding. A focal institution lessens the possibility of "agency slack"—situations in which agents pursue their own interests in lieu of (or in addition to) the tasks assigned by the principal.[55] Such logic was evident in states' decision to delegate key monitoring tasks to private actors in the Clean Development Mechanism of the Kyoto Protocol. Private actors had both the experience and expert knowledge about carbon measurement, which international organizations had not developed as fully. Recognizing the need for an impartial third-party monitor, states delegated key regulatory tasks to private firms—an institutional design feature still in place today.

By contrast, when powerful states cannot agree on a course of action, and there is no focal institution to oversee agents, entrepreneurial authority may emerge. This situation is commonly identified by scholars as instances of public governance failure. Because states are unable to cooperate, a window of opportunity opens for private actors, who seek to address the problem. The absence of a focal institution often means that there is no other organization with the requisite expertise to provide similar benefits. Thus, private actors are able to insert themselves into the policy process. If they can attract adherents, their expertise will be transformed into authority.

The reader may object here, and point out that my argument appears to contradict my earlier claim that private authority does not exist independently of public authority. One could reasonably suggest that an absence of equivalent public expertise suggests just the kind of either-or relationship that this book eschews. The important distinction here is what

[54] Schelling 1960, 53–80.
[55] Epstein and O'Halloran 1999.

constitutes "similar benefits" and for whom. Entrepreneurial authority may not substitute for public regulation, but it can provide benefits for other relevant actors.

An example involving the International Tropical Timber Agreement (ITTA) serves to illustrate that the question of who benefits is central to the theory. The tropical timber treaty aims "to promote the sustainable management of tropical timber producing forests."[56] It is a clear example of public authority resulting from international cooperation. However, the treaty has been criticized as being largely ineffective, owing in part to the intransigence and veto power of exporting nations that wish to preserve revenue streams from exports.[57] Moreover, although the agreement aims to "improve marketing and distribution of tropical timber and timber product exports from sustainably managed and legally harvested sources," it deliberately rejected any attempts at a labeling scheme to achieve this goal.[58] At the same time, tropical deforestation soared to new heights.

As the weak rules of the treaty were being implemented, NGOs stepped up their pressure on large retailers who were selling products containing tropical timber. Companies such as Home Depot in the United States and B&Q in the United Kingdom became targets of naming-and-shaming campaigns by large international NGOs such as the World Wildlife Fund and Friends of the Earth, which called for boycotts.[59] Clearly, the public rules put in place by the ITTA were not benefiting these companies. B&Q could not forestall unwanted NGO attention by pointing to international treaties. Conveniently, the NGO movement around tropical deforestation eventually coalesced into entrepreneurial authority—creating rules to help these firms reform their deforesting ways and adopt more sustainable practices. The reputational benefits to these firms accrued only through private authority, not through extant public rules. Thus, private actors were able to provide benefits that public authority could not.

In sum, a theory of private authority must explain not only when it emerges but also what form—delegated or entrepreneurial—it will take. I submit that private authority emerges when conditions of supply and demand are met. When private actors have existing expertise that can potentially be parlayed into rule-making authority, they provide the supply of private authority. When other actors in world politics recognize that

---

[56] International Tropical Timber Agreement 2006. TD/TIMBER.3/12,1 February 2006. Available from http://unctad.org/en/Docs/tdtimber3d12_en.pdf.

[57] Gale 1998.

[58] ITTA, Article 1(k).

[59] Bartley 2003.

they will benefit from private rules, they are generating a demand. The particular form of private authority will depend on the configuration of powerful states' preferences and the presence or absence of a focal institution that can monitor private agents.

ALTERNATIVE PERSPECTIVES

This book constructs quantifiable measures of delegated and entrepreneurial authority and then uses these measures to describe the evolution of private authority over time. With this new data, I develop a theory and test its plausibility through two case studies in chapters 4 and 5. Although this is not meant to be a definitive test of my theory, some consideration of alternative explanations of private authority is appropriate.

The theory of private authority developed in this book falls between a strictly realist explanation and a wholly sociological one.[60] The realist explanation for private authority argues that it is merely a reflection of great power preferences. According to this view, regulatory outcomes, and private actors' involvement in them, will vary with the degree of agreement among great powers.[61] When great powers collectively recognize the benefits of joint action and the costs of coordination are low, they will harmonize their standards. If NGOs or other nonstate actors can offer some beneficial service, then states may choose to delegate to them. In this realist view, private actors exercise authority only at the behest and under the control of states. The explanation is strictly material: private authority will emerge only when private actors can offer some material benefit to states.[62]

As is clear from the preceding discussion, the realist view, though not entirely incorrect (and more on that in chapter 2), is most certainly incomplete. It suffers from an overly narrow conceptualization of private authority—omitting the possibility of entrepreneurial authority. The realist theory sees states as the sole locus of authority and therefore restricts the explanation to a hierarchical relationship between state and private actor. This conception is faulty because it reproduces the state-centric logic that, by definition, cannot allow for multiple loci of authority. Though private actors may serve as agents, authority remains hierarchical. Any

---

[60] For another useful attempt to bridge this divide with respect to private authority, see Dingwerth and Pattberg 2009.

[61] Drezner 2007, chap. 3.

[62] This is consistent with theories of international delegation, discussed in greater detail in chapter 3.

other role for private actors is irrelevant to policy outcomes.[63] In other words, in the realist view, entrepreneurial authority is not a possibility.

The sociological explanation of private authority is captured in a broad set of works examining the impact of global civil society, transnational networks, and epistemic communities.[64] These works posit that private actors are autonomous agents, who can influence world politics through three main mechanisms: information, accountability, and discourse. Information is a key source of authority. Epistemic communities influence states' beliefs about environmental problems, their causes and effects, and the desired solutions.[65] NGOs can also provide information about states' behavior, identifying instances of noncompliance and sounding a "fire alarm" in cases of egregious action.[66]

Private actors also engage in accountability politics. As Keck and Sikkink note, transnational advocacy networks can apply pressure to national governments to effect change at the domestic level.[67] In addition, private actors can hold others accountable through "peer accountability," where similar organizations evaluate each other, or through "public reputational accountability," where diverse audiences consider the reputation of those with authority.[68] Finally, some scholars have argued that private actors are transforming the landscape of world politics either by operating beyond the state[69] or by "reconstituting the public domain" to include a host of nonstate actors engaged in "discourse, contestation and action concerning the production of public goods."[70] By changing the terms of the debate, private actors are serving as change agents, which ultimately shape political outcomes.

This sociological account of private authority falls short on two counts. First, much of the literature focuses on successful cases of the influence of nonstate actors. As a result, we know little about failed attempts at influence or the conditions that give rise to the successes.[71] While they do not include failed cases, the longitudinal data on delegated and entrepreneurial authority in chapters 2 and 3 provide a broader view of

---

[63] Drezner 2007, 5.

[64] Some of the more prominent examples in the environmental arena include E. Haas 1990; Wapner 1996; Keck and Sikkink 1998.

[65] P. Haas 1990; Litfin 1994.

[66] Lupia and McCubbins 1994; Raustiala 1997; Dai 2000.

[67] Keck and Sikkink 1998, 12.

[68] Jordan and Van Tuijl 2000; Grant and Keohane 2005, 37.

[69] Lipschutz 1992; Wapner 1996.

[70] Ruggie 2004, 504.

[71] A number of scholars have discussed problems of selection bias in the study of nonstate actors, including Drezner 2007; Vogel 2008. For examples of failed civil society influence, see Cortright and Pagnucco 1997; Carpenter 2007.

the extent of private authority and an important context for successful cases. But, most importantly, the sociological approach fails to engage the same question as the one examined here. Explanations tend to focus on the behavior of *states* and the ways that private authority may influence their behavior. Sociological approaches show the ways that private actors change understandings and norms, which in turn may (or may not) lead to changes in policy outcomes. By contrast, the theory presented here explains when private actors are able to exercise independent rule-making authority. Thus, the chain of influence in the sociological explanation is more diffuse than the theory presented here. Here, the chain of authority is much more direct: from rule maker (the private actor) to rule taker. Sociological approaches insert a causally prior factor, the influence of private actors on rule makers.

In short, alternative explanations in world politics are incomplete. The realist explanation largely restricts itself to the ways in which states enable private authority. Sociological explanations tend to focus on successful examples of private actors influencing the state through information, accountability, and changing discourse. The theory presented here aims to bridge the gap between the realist approaches that focus on authority via delegation and sociological approaches that focus on private actors as sources of influence on states, rather than as rule makers in their own right.

WHY ENVIRONMENT?

Although the book casts its theoretical net widely, the empirical focus is on environmental governance and specifically on climate change. Environmental issues provide a fruitful area of inquiry for several reasons.

The first reason for the focus on the environment, and climate change in particular, is its intrinsic importance. The much-acclaimed Stern Review on the economics of climate change frames the issue quite starkly: "Climate change threatens the basic elements of life for people around the world."[72] We cannot simply relegate climate change to the "environmental" box. Although many political scientists consider environmental issues to fall in the realm of "low" politics, Stern's report, and indeed a passing glance at any major newspaper, illustrates that this dichotomy is no longer apt. Energy security, nuclear safety, food safety and supply, disaster preparedness, infectious diseases—all of these issues (and many more) affect and are affected by climate change. They will impact all

[72] Stern 2007, vi.

sectors of society, and most corners of the globe.[73] As Newell and Paterson succinctly note, "climate change . . . [is] something that affects everything we do . . . which will change how we live in the future, [and] how we live today."[74] If states are struggling to take action on climate change, then it is critical to examine whether other actors are capable of helping to address this important problem, and the circumstances under which they might be successful.

The other reason for the focus on environment is guided by principles of research design: global environmental governance is growing by leaps and bounds. The multiplicity of actors and density of institutions afford opportunities to see this new conceptualization of private authority "in action" and is helpful for explaining the emergence of private authority. Because environmental governance is often viewed as particularly permeable to the influence of nonstate actors, we should expect to see private authority in both its forms. In short, if we are to understand the extent of private authority, as well as its causes, environmental issues provide fertile ground for exploration. Finally, given that the aforementioned characteristics make the environment a most likely case for observing private authority, its absence would be a strong indication that arguments about multiple loci of authority are overstated.[75] Of course, choosing a most likely case raises questions about the degree to which the theory is generalizable to other issue areas in world politics. I take up this important question in the final chapter.

PLAN AND METHODS OF THE BOOK

The book has two main parts: descriptive and causal. Chapter 1 describes the concept of private authority and presents the theory in greater detail. It provides an in-depth discussion of the concept of authority, the definition of private authority, and how it is operationalized throughout the book. It expands on the causal theory, which is briefly outlined above, and discusses expectations about when each form of private authority should emerge.

As discussed earlier, there is a tension in the literature on globalization and global governance between those who believe that states remain firmly in control of world politics and those who argue that other nonstate actors are increasingly important for carrying out basic governing

[73] Intergovernmental Panel on Climate Change 2007. Despite widespread effects, it is rapidly becoming clear that the poorest parts of the world will be most affected by climate change.
[74] Newell and Paterson 2010, 3.
[75] Eckstein 1975.

functions. To date, there are few extant quantitative studies of private authority. As such, the first-order task of this book is to construct quantifiable measures of delegated and entrepreneurial authority—and to do so in a way to avoid selection bias as much as possible. As a result, chapters 2 and 3 provide some of the first "large-N" data on private authority—two original datasets on delegated and entrepreneurial authority, respectively. The goal of these two quantitative chapters is not to test causal relationships but to define the universe of cases, provide reproducible data, describe variation, and draw inferences from that variation. In this sense, they constitute "exploratory missions," providing much needed longitudinal data on private authority, which combat some of the selection bias problems outlined above. They also provide a useful frame for the case studies and help avoid generalizing on the basis of the cases alone.[76]

Chapter 2 presents a dataset that examines a century of multilateral environmental agreements (MEAs) for acts of delegation to international organizations and to private actors. It shows that delegated authority in MEAs is indeed on the rise but not as a percentage of total governance activities. In other words, the ratio of policy functions delegated to private actors to the total number policy functions is *not* growing. What we see instead is an overall increase in the amount of governance by *both* public and private actors. The loci of authority are multiplying and the density of relationships among them is increasing. The data also show that states prefer to delegate specific policy functions: monitoring and implementation. This finding is consistent with arguments that principals delegate to enhance the credibility of commitments and reduce transaction costs.[77] I also find that private agents are rarely the sole actors responsible for these tasks, which are often concomitantly assigned to either IOs or states. This suggests a growing complexity of governance arrangements, where more actors are responsible for performing the same tasks.

Chapter 3 examines entrepreneurial authority from the 1950s to the present by looking at the creation of environmental civil regulations—privately created rules that certify the environmental attributes of various goods and services. The data show a precipitous increase in their number, again suggesting that authority is diffusing across multiple actors, rather than concentrating among states. Moreover, most private rules were created in the past two decades, suggesting that this diffusion is relatively recent. The data also show a considerable repetition of the content of those rules. That is, although there is a growing number of civil regulations, their content is not increasing at the same pace. This suggests that there is competition among various sources of entrepreneurial authority:

---

[76] Ragin 2004, 176.
[77] In the international relations literature, see, e.g., Pollack 2003; Tallberg 2006.

different private actors are jockeying for market share in fairly narrow issue areas. Chapter 3 also shows that most civil regulations are "hard standards" in that they require monitoring and verification by a third party. This finding suggests that private rule makers are concerned with the credibility, if not the efficacy, of the standards they create.

With a better understanding of the basic patterns of private authority, chapters 4 and 5 then seek to explain them. I examine one case of delegated authority and one case of entrepreneurial authority, both drawn from the climate change regime. Although these are positive cases in the sense that private authority successfully emerges (and more on that below), both show that the configuration of state preferences and the presence (or absence) of a focal institution caused the emergence of private authority in its predicted form.

Chapter 4 studies the decision of states to delegate key monitoring tasks to private actors in the Clean Development Mechanism (CDM) of the Kyoto Protocol. It shows that private actors were selected to serve as the "atmospheric police" of the CDM for three reasons. First, the private sector had relatively long-standing experience in the intricacies of measuring carbon offset projects. As such, they were widely viewed as an appropriate overseer in this newly created market. Second, powerful states agreed that this market mechanism should be part of the Protocol, and that a third-party verifier was needed to monitor the quality of offset projects. The CDM was viewed as politically palatable to most and, at a minimum, nonobjectionable to others. Third, there was a focal institution, the CDM Executive Board, which could screen and oversee agents.

Chapter 5 examines a case of entrepreneurial authority in the climate change regime: the Greenhouse Gas Protocol. The protocol is a set of accounting standards to measure and report greenhouse gas emissions created by individual firms. These standards were created by two NGOs and have subsequently become one of the most widely accepted accounting methodologies for measuring and reporting emissions. The chapter explains how these NGOs were able to insert themselves into the policy process while the United States and European Union were arguing about an appropriate role for emissions trading. Building off the regulatory uncertainty resulting from states' disagreement, the Greenhouse Gas Protocol promised both material and reputational benefits to its adopters. Moreover, it was able to amass the expertise required to create such a sophisticated set of tools, because they were not present in any existing focal institution.

Chapter 6 synthesizes the findings of the book and discusses the theoretical implications—namely, appropriate ways to evaluate the effects of private authority in world politics. Moreover, it suggests potential contributions of private authority to the climate change regime as it moves forward. It also presents future avenues for inquiry, situating this study within a much broader set of questions about institutional complexity and density and the effects of private authority over time.

CONCLUSION

This book has three rather expansive goals. First, it provides a new conceptualization of private authority, which allows us to disaggregate it into two distinct phenomena while still considering their collective impact on global environmental politics. Second, it presents data that shows how private authority has changed over time and its relationship to public authority. Third, it develops a causal model to explain the emergence and form of private authority. In short, this book aims to respond to two clear gaps in existing work by providing new and much-needed data and further refining extant theoretical accounts.

Of course, there are limits to what one study can do. The main contribution of this book is to develop empirically informed theoretical foundations for a theory of private authority that moves beyond existing explanations. This choice has come at some cost of intensive hypothesis testing. Because the case studies aim to test the viability of my model, they are "on the regression line." I do not include deviant cases, where the independent variables do not produce the expected outcome of the dependent variable. Although there is a clear and careful logic to my approach, it does not provide definitive proof for the theoretical model presented in chapter 1. In sum, the book engages primarily in theory building rather than theory testing.

Moreover, although I contrast my argument with alternative explanations, I acknowledge that some of their components are compatible with my own. The theoretical model is therefore empirically driven, eschewing a categorical separation between the various "-isms" in international relations theory.

In the following chapters, I show that private authority is now a well-established fixture in global environmental politics. A careful examination of the two different forms of private authority demonstrates that we need to think more expansively about how nonstate actors are involved in world politics. They are not simply lobbying at the margins of intergovernmental forums. The evolution of the climate change regime—from centralized multilateral agreements to a more diffuse set of nonhierarchical activities—demonstrates how the landscape of institutions to produce global public goods is changing. This book shows how private authority is contributing to this shift.

CHAPTER ONE

A Theory of Private Authority

> States are no longer the exclusive source of regulatory
> global authority.[1]

THERE IS BROAD CONSENSUS that private actors are more important in world politics today than in the recent past. They are no longer simply influencing rule makers (though that is important too); now they *are* rule makers. However, we still have very little systematic knowledge about when and why nonstate actors serve in this capacity. This book aims to remedy this gap on two fronts: by presenting a theory about when we should expect to see private authority, and by providing historical data about how it has changed over time in the area of global environmental governance. In this chapter, I present the theoretical portion of the argument, which explains when private authority emerges and why, and whether that authority is delegated or entrepreneurial.

The answers to these questions are of interest to scholars of private authority but also have applications to the study of international relations more broadly. First, understanding the emergence of private authority provides insight into *states'* ability to govern. These questions are not just about the governing abilities of private actors but are fundamentally about the role of the state. As I explain in further detail below, private authority does not occur in a vacuum; rather, authority is polycentric, diffusing across multiple levels and through a variety of actors. Second, a theory of private authority contributes to larger discussions about institutional design. The study of international relations has traditionally focused on international law and international organizations as the mechanisms through which global governance—the management of affairs beyond individual states—occurs.[2] However, the arguments and evidence presented here demonstrate the need to include private authority as part of the constellation of institutions when considering approaches to global governance. Finally, the theory provides new insights into the mechanisms through which global cooperation might occur.

I begin with a discussion of authority: what it is, and why people obey it. Since actors sometimes defer to authority when they believe it to be

[1] Vogel 2009, 154.

[2] Governance can be understood broadly as "the sum of the many ways individuals and institutions, public and private, manage their common affairs." Commission on Global Governance 1995, 2.

legitimate or somehow "rightful," this discussion necessarily involves a brief detour into understanding the relationship between authority and legitimacy. Because legitimacy is not always observable, it is more useful to examine authority through the lens of consent: when actors consent to be bound by rules, they create authority.

I then turn to the application of these concepts to private actors. I define private authority and describe its major characteristics, including why actors choose to consent to privately created rules. I argue that in contemporary politics expertise is a key engine for legitimacy and thus for consent, because it allows actors to provide benefits to others. I then disaggregate the concept into its two forms: delegated and entrepreneurial. This distinction is critical because the sources of authority vary with each type, as does the timing of consent. More importantly, these two types of private authority occur under different conditions, for different reasons.

Despite their differences, it is paramount to consider each of these modes of rule making jointly under the rubric of private authority. Unless we examine *both* types, we cannot understand the full scope of how private actors govern, nor can we adequately explain it. Thus, this chapter develops a refined conceptualization of private authority—explaining how these phenomena differ but arguing that they should be considered in tandem.

With the concept of private authority clarified, I develop expectations about when it emerges in world politics—and *what type* of authority will likely develop. The theory is based on the notion of supply and demand. The general supposition is that private authority emerges when there is both a demand for benefits by states or other actors, as well as a supply of existing private expertise. If there are private actors with expertise and knowledge, and if states or others believe that they will benefit from adopting private rules, then both supply and demand conditions are met, and private authority can develop. In a second step, the theory predicts when either entrepreneurial or delegated authority emerges.

Authority, Consent, and Legitimacy

In international relations, power is commonly defined as the ability to make someone do something that they would not do otherwise.[3] Authority is a type of power and can be understood as the right to command.[4] Unlike power, which may involve coercion, authority implies that consent is granted by those who are subject to it.[5] An armed thief has the power

---

[3] Dahl 1957. For a useful overview of discussions of power in international relations, see Baldwin 2002.

[4] Hobbes 1996, 112.

[5] Hobbes 1996. On consent, see also Raz 1990; Friedman 1990; Lake 2009.

to take your wallet but not the authority to do so, since, presumably, you do not consent to have your money taken. Authority is therefore *mutually constituted*; the source of authority makes rules, and the target of authority agrees to obey them.[6] Lake notes that "authority is not a claim made by the ruler, but a right granted by the ruled."[7]

But why do the ruled consent to the authority of rulers? In many instances in world politics, consent stems from the belief that the source of authority is legitimate and that its actions "are desirable, proper and appropriate within some socially constructed system."[8] Although consent can be secured through other mechanisms such as fear or coercion,[9] in contemporary world politics these mechanisms are unavailable to most and very costly to others. As the economic, social, and cultural ties between nations and societies grow, recourse to force becomes less feasible and less desirable.[10] More frequently, consent is based on a perception that the ruler "should" be ruling, which in turn stems from the belief that the source of authority is legitimate.

Consent is a key foundation of authority in world politics: legitimacy begets consent and thus helps distinguish power from authority. When we speak of authority, we are interested in consent-based perceptions of legitimacy—"some form of normative, uncoerced consent or recognition of authority on the part of the regulated or governed."[11] While it is sometimes difficult to observe perceptions of legitimacy, we can observe its consequences. For this reason, consent is a key element in understanding authority: when actors perceive others to be legitimate sources of authority, they grant their consent to the rule maker and change their behavior accordingly. We can therefore infer that they believe that source of authority is legitimate.

Defining Private Authority

Although the most recent phase of globalization has kindled debates about the role of private actors as governors, the notion of private authority is not new. *Lex mercatoria*, or law merchant, emerged in the eleventh century to regulate an increasingly open set of markets in Europe.[12]

---

[6] Wolff 1990. For an opposing view, see Lukes 2005.

[7] Lake 2009, 20.

[8] Suchman 1995, 574. See also Cashore 2002; Bernstein and Cashore 2007.

[9] Koppell 2010, 43. Hurd 1999 adds a third logic, that of self-interest: A can accept B's authority if it benefits A to do so.

[10] Keohane and Nye 1977. See also Nye's concept of soft power (1990).

[11] Hall and Biersteker 2002, 4–5. While this theoretical construction of authority as legitimate is ubiquitous, as Koppell points out, it is also problematic, since there are plenty of examples of illegitimate authority in contemporary world politics (2010, 43).

[12] Braithwaite and Drahos 2000, 53; Cutler 2003, chap. 4.

An amalgam of Greek maritime custom and Roman law, these rules and practices governed trade by sea and exchange on land. Created by merchants themselves, the law merchant provided a framework within which to conduct commercial trade. Fairs were a particularly important locus for trade, developing across Northern Europe; they served as a source for the expansion of the law merchant. A system for adjudicating these privately created laws also evolved, creating yet another source of private authority—private judges.[13]

The medieval era provides other examples of private authority. Craft guilds regulated professional qualifications. Merchant guilds sometimes supplied military defense.[14] *Commendas* were systems for spreading risk through limited liability for long-distance traders; organized by traders, they provided financing and insurance for the purchase and sale of commodities acquired in the far corners of the world.[15] Trading coalitions managed by the Maghribis in eleventh-century North Africa overcame reputation and commitment problems, allowing traders to use agents abroad to expand their geographic reach.[16] In sum, the late twentieth century is not the first instance of globalization nor is it the first time private actors have regulated significant parts of political and economic life.

All of these provide useful examples of private authority, which I define as **situations in which nonstate actors make rules or set standards that other relevant actors in world politics adopt.** Recall that, since authority implies consent, private actors who project authority have necessarily secured the consent—either implicitly or explicitly—from those who adopt their rules. This definition implies two groups: those who aspire to authority (whom I will refer to as "potential governors"), and those who obey it (whom I will refer to as "the governed").[17]

There are several important implications of this definition. First, the right to make rules is not restricted to states. Potential governors beyond the state may include nongovernmental organizations (NGOs), private firms, multinational corporations, associations, foundations, transnational advocacy networks, and other nonstate actors. International organizations are *excluded* from the category of nonstate actors, since they comprise state representatives who are responsible for taking or delegating decisions. Generally speaking, in this study the sources of private authority are firms and NGOs, operating both domestically and transnationally. Because the distinction between public and private is not always clear

---

[13] Milgrom, North, and Weingast 1990.
[14] Braithwaite and Drahos 2000, chap. 9.
[15] Ibid.
[16] Greif 1993.
[17] I borrow the term of "governors" as a generic expression of those with authority from Avant, Finnemore, and Sell 2010b.

cut,[18] I have tried to maintain analytic clarity and consistency through transparent coding rules.[19]

Second, in this definition the right to make rules is operationalized as rule-making power. It excludes normative pronouncements or operational activities; rather, behavior prescriptions are required. In the realm of climate governance, nonstate actors have undertaken "governance experiments" that include networking, planning, and direct action to address climate change.[20] According to the definition above, NGOs or firms that establish links among groups or, say, publish action plans are *not* considered forms of private authority because they are not creating new rules. Private authority is limited to instances in which nonstate actors create rules, standards, practices, or regulation that govern others' conduct.

Third, by definition, in order to exercise authority, potential governors persuade the governed to follow their rules. Lake reminds us that "authority is a right granted by the ruled."[21] Governors must legitimate their claims to authority so that the governed consent to and adopt the rules. It is important to note that authority need not be legally binding to gain adherents. If private actors are able to legitimate their claims to authority, others will voluntarily adopt the rules. Potential governors then acquire authority and become governors in fact. Conversely, if they cannot attract adherents, then there is no private authority. Thus defined, authority means that some change in behavior among the governed should be observable.

Fourth, the exercise of authority is not a one-off situation but rather an institutionalized activity.[22] This means that the governed change their behavior in a recurring and systematic way that persists over time.

Fifth, there is the matter of who chooses to defer to private authority: Which actors are "relevant to world politics"? The definition provided here is deliberately broad. Certainly, states may recognize private authority. As Hurd notes, "To the extent that a state accepts some international rule or body as legitimate, that rule or body becomes an 'authority.' "[23] However, states are not the only actors who can legitimate claims to authority. If other actors in world politics choose to adopt the rules, then the potential governor becomes a source of private authority.[24]

---

[18] Koppell 2003; Scott 2004; Andonova 2010.

[19] These are described in greater detail in chapters 2 and 3.

[20] Hoffmann 2011.

[21] Lake 2009, 20.

[22] Hasenclever, Mayer, and Rittberger 1997, 15; Cutler, Haufler, and Porter 1999b, 334.

[23] Hurd 1999, 381.

[24] This broad conception of relevant audiences leaves open the possibility of competing sources of private authority, a topic I explore in chapters 3 and 5.

Certification organizations, like the Forest Stewardship Council or the Fair Trade Federation are examples of what might constitute the "relevant actors in world politics" that the definition invokes. These organizations have exercised authority via the market, persuading small businesses and multinational corporations alike to submit to rigorous production and monitoring standards in order to earn their "seal of approval."[25] In some cases, these standards have eventually been adopted by states.[26] Other forms of private authority, those not based on market logic, have also proliferated. Technical standard setting, particularly in the fields of finance and manufacturing, is dominated by private regulators.[27] Standard-setting bodies such as the International Accounting Standards Board, the International Organization for Standardization (ISO), and the International Electrotechnical Commission (IEC) have a sweeping impact on how the global economy is managed and how products are made. These examples show that private authority need not be restricted to state adoption of private rules.[28] Any group that accepts privately created rules or standards without being coerced creates a source of private authority.

Why Consent? The Role of Expertise

As noted in the previous section, consent links beliefs of legitimacy to the exercise of authority. It is the key observable element in the creation of authority. In this study, I focus on one specific reason for consent: expertise. An expert is someone "who can vouch for the reliability of particular information."[29] This person is viewed as a legitimate source of authority because of what she knows. Hence, we refer to an expert as "an authority"—clearly equating knowledge with legitimate power.[30]

Expertise can confer legitimacy when an actor has specific knowledge or technical experience. Thus, a scientist with an understanding of the atmospheric chemistry that depletes the ozone layer is a legitimate authority based on her expert training and knowledge. Similarly, an NGO with

---

[25] Private standards governing the environmental or social qualities of goods are referred to as "non-state market driven" governance. See Cashore 2002; Cashore, Auld, and Newsom 2004.

[26] Bartley 2007.

[27] Mattli and Büthe 2003; Mattli and Büthe 2005; Büthe and Mattli 2011.

[28] In some cases, states and IOs have recognized private standards. For instance, the International Organization for Standardization and the International Electrotechnical Commission standards are now formally recognized by the WTO's Technical Barriers to Trade Agreement. States must comply with these privately created standards unless there is a compelling reason to deviate from them.

[29] Raz 1990, 2.

[30] Friedman 1990.

an established record of successful development projects also possesses expert legitimacy, based on its technical capabilities and field experience.

To be clear, expertise is not, by any means, the only source of legitimacy for private authority.[31] However, it is a common requirement for rule-making authority, and it correlates highly with the ability to provide benefits to the would-be governed. As we will see in the following chapter, states frequently choose to delegate technical issues to private actors, because their expertise can facilitate quick and relatively low-cost decision making. Similarly, NGOs and firms must be well versed in their issue area if they are to create technical and procedural standards about sustainable products and activities, as in the case of entrepreneurial authority. An organization cannot, for example, decide what constitutes organic crop cultivation without an in-depth understanding of agriculture, fertilizers, and the effects of different chemicals both on crop growth and on human health and well-being.

Often private actors couple expertise with other justifications for exercising authority. One prominent justification is market pressure. Thus, Walmart's sustainability index is adopted by its suppliers because they want to maintain access to Walmart's global market. Timber producers that adopt private standards such as those created by the Forest Stewardship Council or the Sustainable Forest Initiative do so in part to appeal to a subset of the market concerned with ethical consumption. In these examples, expertise is required to create technical standards, but market-based pressures help promote their adoption.[32]

A second justification is moral legitimacy. In contemporary politics, NGOs often base their authority in being "do-gooders"—saving the whales, promoting human rights, and other largely unobjectionable causes. People consent to their authority because it is "the right thing to do." In these cases, private actors are granted authority not because of what they know but because of what they do. While I acknowledge that these logics may be invoked, the focus of this study is on expertise as a means to secure consent.

In short, states are not the only actors capable of projecting authority in world politics today. Private authority exists if the governed perceive the governors to be legitimate and consent to governors' rules as a

[31] However, if one is to believe arguments about ecological modernization or the risk society, expertise is an increasingly important source of legitimacy. See, e.g., Beck 1992; Mol, Buttel, and Spaargaren 2000. In contemporary world politics, private authority is also often based on moral legitimacy; people consent to the authority of NGOs, for example, because of their commitment to "doing good."

[32] Cashore 2002. Walmart has complemented its existing expertise and experience on supply chain management with consultations with sustainability experts to develop its standards.

result of that belief.[33] It manifests itself through changes in behavior—the adoption of the governor's rules. Thus, an actor may view another as a legitimate source of authority, but if it does not change its behavior on the basis of this belief, then, for the purposes of this study, no private authority exists.

Two Types of Private Authority

A key argument of this book is that the term "private authority" does not adequately capture the variation in its forms or the reasons for which it arises. To remedy these shortcomings, I disaggregate the concept into two different forms: delegated private authority and entrepreneurial private authority. (For brevity, I omit the word "private," referring to each as either delegated or entrepreneurial authority.) The distinction between delegated and entrepreneurial authority can most usefully be understood by considering the origin of authority.

The primary means of distinguishing between modes of authority is related to its provenance. If the private actor is making rules on behalf of the state—either directly or indirectly, as instructed by an IO—then delegated authority occurs. Some apparatus of the state is transferring authority, as in a traditional principal-agent relationship. If the source of authority does not originate with the state, then private authority is entrepreneurial. The former is *de jure* authority, whereas the latter is *de facto*.

Delegated authority is equivalent to a traditional principal-agent relationship, where the agent's authority stems from explicit transfer of authority from state to private actor according to agreed-upon terms that are revocable. As Pitkin states, "When we call a man someone's agent, we are saying that he is the tool or instrument by which the other acts."[34] Thus, those subject to delegated authority choose to consent because they recognize the legitimacy of the ultimate source of authority—the state. Because this study deals only with international rule making, the principal is always a group of states, acting collectively. Delegated private authority can also arise through a transfer of authority from an IO to a private actor.[35]

Note that in this relationship, the principal endows the agent with authority but is then also subject to that authority. In other words,

---

[33] There are also illegitimate forms of private authority, such as traffickers, mafias, and mercenaries. See Williams 2002; Muthien and Taylor 2002; Avant 2005.

[34] Pitkin 1967, 125.

[35] Delegation from IOs to nonstate actors is referred to as "re-delegation" by Bradley and Kelley 2008.

governments delegate but then adopt the rules and practices promulgated by the agents they have selected. In this sense, the agent—a private actor—becomes the governor, and the states are the governed.[36]

The extent to which the agent conforms to the preferences and instructions of the principal is a perennial source of concern for the principal, and for those who study delegation. Agents can fail to perform the tasks they are given or can instead pursue other priorities, according to their own preferences. Principals' ability to detect such deviations and control agents' actions will vary. If agents are selected for their ability to reduce transaction costs, on the basis of their expertise, as chapter 2 shows is often the case, then it may be difficult for principals to evaluate the extent to which private agents are acting autonomously, contrary to their mandate.[37] Concerns about the ability to control agents are a key factor in explaining whether delegated or entrepreneurial authority will occur, as I explain below.

Entrepreneurial authority, unlike delegated authority, does not confer *de jure* rights to act on behalf of the governed. Instead, authority accrues through a process that culminates in the governed deferring to the governors. Private actors must devise potential ways to govern and then peddle their ideas to those who might comprise the governed. If these potential governors can legitimate their claims to authority, the governed will choose to adopt them. However, if they fail to persuade adherents, there will be no private authority. As noted above, the number, type, and size of audiences that defer will determine the success of the entrepreneurial authority.[38] If few defer, the private actor will enjoy limited authority.

For example, the International Federation of Organic Agriculture Movements (IFOAM) was the first transnational organization to certify organic foods.[39] It has since faced competition from other labeling schemes, such as Fairtrade International and government organic labels. The result of this competition means that fewer producers seek IFOAM certification, thus reducing the number of potential adherents. In sum, there is a range of the extent of entrepreneurial authority; entrepreneurs may succeed in getting only a few actors or groups to defer, or the uptake of their rules and practices may be much more widespread. The success of entrepreneurial authority will also depend on whether the most important actors choose to adopt private rules.

[36] Jacobsson 2006.

[37] Hawkins et al. 2006b, 14.

[38] There are examples where *de facto* private authority becomes *de jure:* states officially recognize privately created standards. In these cases, the source of authority changes over time and private authority "hardens." See Abbott and Snidal 2000; Kirton and Trebilcock 2004.

[39] Auld 2008.

Often, the timing of consent can also help distinguish between delegated and entrepreneurial authority. In general, the consent of the governed is granted *ex ante* in cases of delegated authority, while it tends to be *ex post* in cases of entrepreneurial authority.

The concept of entrepreneurial authority overlaps with more familiar notions of "self-regulation," so a brief discussion of the relationship between the two is warranted.[40] Private authority occurs when nonstate actors make rules or set standards that *other* relevant actors in world politics adopt. This definition implies that there is at least some distinction between who makes the rules and who adopts them. Thus, a corporation that creates its own sustainability code of conduct, which is applied only to itself, is not considered private authority in this study. In this instance, the rule maker and the rule adopter are one and the same. This is what Gereffi and colleagues refer to as "first-party" certification, "whereby a single firm develops its own rules and reports on compliance."[41]

My definition of entrepreneurial authority excludes "first-party" standards; however, industry-wide standards are included as forms of entrepreneurial authority. In these instances, a few actors within an industry create a set of standards, which are in turn adopted by a broader set of actors. For example, the Responsible Care Program was created by the Canadian Chemical Producers Association in response to public relations fallout associated with the 1984 Bhopal disaster.[42] It established ten principles to improve the environmental safety and public accountability of chemical manufacturers. Over time, Responsible Care has expanded and now estimates that its membership accounts for more than 70 percent of global chemicals production.[43] Here, members within the industry devised standards of behavior that they "self-adopted." However, in addition other industry firms *also* incorporated these rules into their own practices. While some members of Responsible Care are at once rule makers and rule adopters, there are other participants that had little or no say in the creation of the rules and adopted them anyway. For this reason, industry-wide standards are considered a form of entrepreneurial authority. Although there is some overlap between governor and governed, they are not entirely the same set of actors.

In sum, private authority can be understood as the ability of nonstate actors to make rules or set standards that other relevant actors in world politics adopt. The key elements are that the claimant to authority is a private actor that promulgates rules or standards; that the actor relies on expert legitimacy to justify its claim; and that it is able to induce

[40] On self-regulation, see Haufler 2001; Porter and Ronit 2006.
[41] Gereffi, Garcia-Johnson, and Sasser 2001, 57.
[42] Garcia-Johnson 2000.
[43] http://www.icca-chem.org/en/Home/Responsible-care/What-we-do/.

behavioral changes in some relevant audience in world politics. There are two types of private authority—delegated and entrepreneurial—based on whether authority is *de facto* or *de jure*. In some instances, though not all, entrepreneurial authority can be understood as a form of industry-wide self-regulation. In the following sections, I present a theory of private authority, outlining the conditions under which we should expect to see delegated and entrepreneurial authority emerge.

A THEORY OF PRIVATE AUTHORITY

Private authority is but one potential institutional response to global co-operation problems—such as the need to mitigate global climate change, prevent the spread of avian flu, or reduce nuclear proliferation. Thus, a theory of private authority, is in essence one about the institutions that actors select to address cooperation problems. Successful resolution of such problems requires the mutual adjustment of actors' behavior.[44] Traditional theories of international cooperation focus on how *states* change their behavior, often through international institutions, to achieve mutually desirable outcomes. Private authority is another possible approach to addressing cooperation problems. Unlike traditional theories of institutional design,[45] the theory presented here does not restrict itself to problems defined and experienced by states. Many have asked: When do states cooperate, and how to they design institutions to facilitate cooperation? I begin from the same premise—that the demand for authority at the global level is generated by cooperation problems, which require the mutual adjustment of the behavior of some set of actors.[46] Yet in my version, these actors may be states or private actors, or some mixture of the two.

By broadening the set of relevant actors, the subsequent questions also expand. Given a need for cooperation, I first ask whether actors will use an institution, as opposed to some ad hoc form of cooperation. If they do, will it be public (i.e., traditional forms of interstate cooperation) or private? Clearly, the choice between public and private institutions exists for states but not for nonstate actors, which are not in the position to create public rules to address cooperation problems. Their choice is to create rules themselves or ask states to do so.

Finally, if private authority occurs, will it be delegated or entrepreneurial in form? Whereas other models of institutional choice focus exclusively

[44] Keohane 1984.
[45] See, e.g., Abbott et al. 2000; Koremenos, Lipson, and Snidal 2001; Rosendorff and Milner 2001.
[46] Keohane 1984, 51–54.

on the actions of states, the emergence of private authority is contingent upon the action (or inaction) of *both* states and private actors. Thus, neither can unilaterally ensure this selection of institutional form. Private authority will not necessarily emerge simply because states choose not to cooperate through multilateral institutions. Nor will entrepreneurial authority emerge simply because states choose not to delegate.

Structural and Agent-Based Explanations

Before presenting the theory, I review some of the relevant work to date. Explanations of the emergence of private authority can be grouped roughly into two categories of explanations—structural and actor based. Structural explanations focus on growing globalization and a general turn toward neoliberalism. Globalization—the increasing flow of people, goods, and ideas across borders—has increased the need for cross-border cooperation to address the effects of these transnational flows. Private actors have also been empowered by this fundamental structural shift. Strange argues that the postwar growth of markets has engineered a profound reorganization of power in the world: "Where states were once the masters of markets, now it is the markets which . . . are the masters over the governments of states."[47] Strange frames the argument in particularly stark terms; in its more moderate form, the rise of private authority does not necessarily come at the expense of state power.[48] Others see globalization as a catalyst for more global regulation,[49] some of which includes private authority.[50]

Theories of private authority also point to a general turn toward neoliberalism and a trend toward deregulation as a structural factor to explain private authority. Graz and Nölke invoke "a particular phase of modern capitalism" loosely equated with neoliberalism, as a condition that has allowed private authority to emerge.[51] Cashore and colleagues point to governments' increased used of market-based mechanisms as part of the reason for which "non-state market driven" governance has emerged.[52] Bartley argues that certification schemes, which evaluate the environmental and social impacts of consumer goods, are not merely market-based

[47] Strange 1996, 4.
[48] Falkner 2003; Ruggie 2004; Büthe 2010a.
[49] Braithwaite and Drahos 2000; Jordana and Levi-Faur 2004; Djelic and Sahlin-Andersson 2006; Mattli and Woods 2009a; Levi-Faur 2012.
[50] On the links between globalization and private authority see, e.g., Knill and Lehmkuhl 2002; Kirton and Trebilcock 2004; Fuchs 2007; Abbott and Snidal 2009; Vogel 2009; Mayer and Gereffi 2010; Fransen 2012a.
[51] Graz and Nölke 2008a.
[52] Cashore, Auld, and Newsom 2004, 9–10.

solutions to collective action problems but rather are the product of political contestation among a variety of actors within a neoliberal context.[53] Bernstein documents the "compromise of liberal environmentalism," which supports private authority as a key approach to managing environmental problems.[54] Both structural factors—globalization and the neoliberal turn—are important for understanding the general scope conditions that enable private authority.

A second set of explanations focuses on the characteristics of actors. Some describe the source of private actors' authority. Hall and Biersteker argue that private actors exercise market authority, moral authority, or illicit authority.[55] Avant and colleagues argue that actors may defer to global governors, including private actors, because of their institutional, delegated, expert, principled, or capacity-based authority.[56] I draw on some of these elements in my own theory—specifically, on the role of expertise and delegation. These categories are useful for understanding why private actors might serve as rule makers but do not explicitly outline when this might be the case.

A prevalent view is that private authority emerges as a response to actors' "demand for order and rules."[57] Firms may simply seek order in the absence of other rules, particularly if they occupy a dominant position in the industry.[58] Or they may demand private rules as a way to preempt the risk of domestic or international regulation or threats of activist pressure or to boost their reputation.[59] NGOs and advocacy networks may also demand private rules to regulate firms. Indeed, pressure tactics from NGOs contributed to the creation of private rules to govern forestry and labor practices.[60] Governments may also demand private authority as a way to reduce transaction costs, enhance credible commitments, or lock in policy preferences.[61] Some works also point to a supply of rule makers as part of the explanation of the emergence of private authority, a point to which I return below.[62]

The theory presented here on draws from these works in three important ways. First, I acknowledge, as many have, the critical role of

---

[53] Bartley 2003; Bartley 2007.

[54] Bernstein 2002.

[55] Hall and Biersteker 2002.

[56] Avant, Finnemore, and Sell 2010a, 11–14.

[57] Cutler, Haufler, and Porter 1999a, 8.

[58] Spar 1999; Fuchs and Kalfagianni 2010; Mayer and Gereffi 2010.

[59] Garcia-Johnson 2000; Haufler 2001; Prakash and Potoski 2006.

[60] O'Rourke 2003; Spar and LaMure 2003; Sasser et al. 2006; Bartley 2007; Conroy 2007, chap. 4–5; Locke, Fei, and Brause 2007; Merk 2008; Nadvi 2008.

[61] Hawkins et al. 2006b; Bradley and Kelley 2008 and the associated articles in the *Law and Contemporary Problems* symposium.

[62] Mattli and Woods 2009a; Büthe 2010b; Büthe 2010a.

expertise in explaining the emergence of private authority. Second, I also share the view that private authority is a function of the supply of and the demand for rules. Third, I incorporate extant explanations of demand into my own model. I frame this in terms of a demand for benefits by the would-be governed, which allows for a broad scope of potential demanders.

The theory here also advances the work to date in two ways. First, and most importantly, unlike most work that seeks to explain either private authority writ large or one specific type, such as self-regulation or environmental certification, I seek to develop a theory that can explain the variation in forms of private authority. The disaggregation of private authority into delegated and entrepreneurial forms aims to simultaneously broaden and specify the concept. This expanded conceptual framework provides the basis of a more refined theory—one that explains not only whether private authority will emerge but what form it will take.

Second, I explicitly acknowledge the role of the state by building it into both the conceptualization of private authority and the causal explanation.[63] As described above, there is an ongoing debate about what private authority means for the role of the state. The theory presented here seeks to move beyond a dichotomous characterization of authority as zero-sum to a more nuanced explanation that specifies *how* the state is involved in private authority. Unlike most other works, I include governments as one of the possible demanders of private authority. Thus, while some have argued that private authority emerges where governments cannot or will not regulate, I show that if the concept is specified correctly, this can only be part of the explanation for private authority. Moreover, states are also a key factor in explaining the variation in the form of private authority.

A Theory of Supply and Demand

My basic contention is that private authority emerges because actors in world politics—states, private actors, and institutions comprising both types of actors—anticipate that they will benefit from deferring to private authority. In other words, the effect, private authority, can be explained by its anticipated benefits.[64] In both delegated and entrepreneurial authority, one set of actors benefits from the rules promulgated by another. In the case of entrepreneurial authority, private actors exploit windows of opportunity to try to establish themselves as benefit providers to potential rule adopters.[65]

[63] Büthe 2010b, 11, also notes that government demand is largely overlooked.

[64] Keohane 1984, 80.

[65] This phenomenon is well documented in the social movements literature. See, e.g., Tarrow 1998; Meyer and Minkoff 2004.

I frame the argument about the emergence of private authority in terms of supply and demand. I use these concepts as a metaphor for understanding the need for these governance arrangements as well as their sources, rather than as a microeconomic model.[66] In general, private authority will emerge when there is a demand for benefits by states or nonstate actors, and there is a supply of existing private expertise. The supply of private authority is determined by whether private actors have preexisting expertise in the matter at hand. Expertise is needed not only because it is a key source of legitimacy, as described in the previous section, but also because it correlates with the ability of private actors to provide benefits. Both supply and demand are necessary but not sufficient conditions for the emergence of private authority.

Büthe makes a similar set of arguments to explain how private actors attain regulatory authority. However, he focuses on the actors themselves as demanders and suppliers of private rules rather than on the attributes attached to those actors. Demanders include civil society, firms, and governments. Similar to my argument, suppliers are often technical experts constituted in various types of collective bodies, who create rules because doing so is somehow beneficial for them.[67]

I seek to move beyond Büthe's and others' work by developing a complete theory that also explains what *type* of private authority will emerge. Given that the supply and demand conditions for the emergence of private authority are in place, the form of private authority that emerges can be explained by whether or not there is an existing focal institution, and the degree to which powerful states have similar preferences about the specific policies to be implemented. Figure 1.1 illustrates the general causal model. In the following section, I describe the theory in two steps. The first presents when we should expect private authority to emerge; the second depicts the conditions that produce either delegated or entrepreneurial authority.

The Emergence of Private Authority

The emergence of private authority is a function of the demand for and the supply of private authority. The demand for private authority can be understood as a demand for anticipated benefits, which help states and nonstate actors solve cooperation problems. To be clear, these are not benefits that inhere in private actors; because private authority is just one of many possible institutional designs, potentially any actor in

---

[66] Keohane 1982, 326–27. Büthe 2010b also speaks of supply and demand of private regulation.

[67] Büthe 2010a, 2–11.

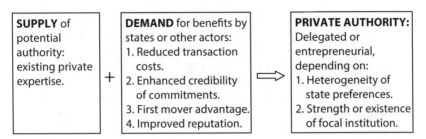

Figure 1.1. A causal model of private authority.

international politics could provide them. The task is to clarify the conditions under which private actors may be in a position to provide benefits that other actors, particularly IOs, cannot. Moreover, these benefits need not accrue solely to states. If private actors provide benefits to *other* private actors, including firms or NGOs, then private authority may emerge. The supply of private authority can be understood as a supply of private actors with preexisting expertise, which allows them to furnish the benefits described below.

The Demand for Private Authority

There are four different benefits that private authority can potentially provide: reduced transaction costs, enhanced credibility of commitments, first-mover advantage, and improved reputation.

The reduction of transaction costs is a first potential benefit, where these costs include the resources expended to obtain information; establish rights; and create, monitor, and enforce contracts.[68] Private authority can reduce transaction costs in different ways. As suggested by principal-agent theories of delegation, leveraging expert knowledge can make it more cost-effective to "buy" knowledge than to "make" it.[69] "Making" the relevant expertise may be both time-consuming and costly, suggesting the advantages to buying it from those who have already made such investments.[70] In other words, when transaction costs involve information, one way to reduce them is to delegate to those actors with ready access to the relevant information—namely, experts. Indeed, gains from specialization are almost a precondition for delegation, and those gains are likely to be largest when "the task to be performed is frequent, repetitive and *requires specific expertise*."[71]

[68] Coase 1960.
[69] Alchian and Demsetz 1972.
[70] Mattli and Büthe 2005, 229.
[71] Hawkins et al. 2006b, 14, emphasis added.

Another way in which private authority can reduce transaction costs is by helping to solve coordination problems. Coordination problems are exemplified by the challenge of standard setting. All actors would be better off if they agreed to a common standard, because they would not have to expend resources to adjust their behavior to conform to a variety of different requirements. Thus, by setting standards, private actors can reduce transaction costs by promoting one set of rules (though, of course, convergence is by no means guaranteed). Finally, private authority that replaces public regulation reduces transaction costs by obviating the need for government action. As such, Falkner argues that industry self-regulation may be both easier and cheaper than public authority, especially when there is no demand for public rules.[72]

If private actors are providing the benefit of reduced transaction costs, we should see them governing in areas that require expertise: namely, complex environmental issues that require active management. If authority is delegated, then this will be evident in the kinds of treaties in which private actors serve as agents. Active management treaties are inherently more complex than "abstaining" treaties, because they require proactive management of a problem, rather than simply refraining from action. In addition, private actors are likely to take on policy functions that make the best use of their comparative advantage—in the details of implementation and the knowledge required to monitor and to manage a given problem—thus lowering transaction costs for states. If authority is entrepreneurial, we should see private actors setting standards in complex issue areas that require technical knowledge.

A second potential benefit of private authority is increased credibility of commitments. When states face a collaboration problem, mutual adjustment of behavior produces the best outcome for all parties, but the incentive to free-ride on others' efforts is high. Enlisting third parties to monitor compliance or to enforce agreements can increase actors' confidence that other participants will honor their commitments instead of cheating.[73] Although third-party monitors may not always be the rule makers, they are charged with interpreting the rules and thus have rule-making authority. In cases where cooperating actors, such as states, choose an agent to be impartial and independent, the relationship between delegator and delegatee is not one of principal and agent but rather of trusteeship. When states delegate to a trustee, they bind themselves to the decision of another actor, as in the case of an international court.[74]

If private actors are improving the credibility of commitments, then

[72] Falkner 2003, 77.
[73] Martin 1992.
[74] Grant and Keohane 2005; Alter 2008.

they should perform tasks such as adjudication.[75] Adjudication by a third party means that states cannot simply interpret the rules in a way that is favorable to then when there are conflicts or uncertainties. More generally, private actors may collect and disseminate information to reduce information asymmetry and thus the likelihood of free-riding.

A third benefit of private authority is first-mover advantage. When actors face a coordination problem, early adopters may enjoy an advantage: moving first may allow them to set expectations for the outcome. To continue with the standards example, the actor who sets the standard then creates an expectation of conformity to that standard, thereby potentially avoiding the need to change practices in the future. First movers not only reap the benefit of setting the rule-making agenda, but they also avoid the costs of switching to new rules in the future, because they choose those rules that are most advantageous to them.[76] In this type of problem, the governed choose to adopt private rules because they see that they will benefit from doing so in the future. For instance, if firms anticipate new regulation or foresee a change in the business environment, adopting private rules may allow them to get "ahead of the curve"—implementing new practices before regulations are applied. This early action might earn them the ability to shape future rules. Chapter 5 shows that first-mover advantage was an important factor in explaining the collaboration of an environmental NGO with a business NGO to create standards for measuring greenhouse gas emissions.

If private actors are providing others with the potential material benefits associated with being a first mover, we may observe an imminent threat of regulation or the emergence of a new market. Arguably, firms constantly face the threat of new regulation; I seek to narrow this possibility by including only those threats that could plausibly materialize in the near future. Thus, if there is already a discussion by policy makers of the need for new rules, or if partial rules or pilot programs have already been enacted, the threat of regulation may be imminent, and first-mover advantage is a plausible benefit furnished by private actors.

Another observable implication of first-mover advantage is the possibility of a new market. When the Montreal Protocol began the phase-out of chloroflourocarbons (CFCs), the chemical compound responsible for ozone depletion, a new market emerged for "ozone-friendly" products. DuPont, the world's largest producer of the CFCs, viewed the Montreal Protocol as the catalyst for a new market in CFC substitutes—which it could supply. Indeed, Oye and Maxwell argue that the possibility of this new market was one of the reasons that DuPont agreed to support

[75] Koremenos 2008. A full discussion and definitions of these policy functions is available in chapter 3.
[76] Mattli and Büthe 2003, 4.

international regulation.[77] Another example is the ban on driftnets in fishing, which then created demand for other effective but more environmentally friendly fishing technologies.

The final and fourth potential benefit of private authority is intangible: burnishing one's reputation. Voluntary environmental standards provide a "club good," so that members benefit from the association with an environmentally responsible brand.[78] Members can thus create a public identity as greener or more socially responsible than the competition, which may even result in greater profits.

A variant of the reputation rationale is that actors may adopt private rules in order to avoid shaming or sanction.[79] Thus, when a group of NGOs threatened to boycott Home Depot unless it used products certified by the Forest Stewardship Council (FSC), Home Depot chose to make the change to avoid the negative publicity.[80] The NGO coalition made a credible threat: use products governed by standards that we approve of (as opposed to less stringent industry standards) or suffer the negative publicity and economic consequences. Thus, one "benefit" to Home Depot was the avoidance of further reputational and possibly economic damage as a result of the NGO campaign. Additionally, it received positive press by adopting purchasing practices based on NGO-approved standards, further enhancing its reputation through NGO support.

There are three possible indicators of private actors providing benefits in the form of an improved reputation or the avoidance of shaming. First, private firms should seek to avoid shaming only when there is a campaign or the threat of a campaign by an advocacy group in a given industry. Second, we may see a previously unorganized constituency come together and begin making demands or creating its own form of authority.[81] Third, adopters of private rules may have recently been associated with an environmental disaster, spurring the need for "damage control."

The Supply of Private Authority

For private authority to emerge, there must also exist a potential supply, in the form of preexisting private expertise: all four of the benefits described above require that the private actor possess expert knowledge at the time benefits are demanded.[82] In order to lower transaction costs, principals

---

[77] Oye and Maxwell 1994.

[78] Prakash and Potoski 2006; Conroy 2007.

[79] Haufler 2001; Spar and LaMure 2003.

[80] Bartley 2003; Cashore, Auld, and Newsom 2004, 105.

[81] Moravcsik 1999.

[82] On the role of expertise in private authority, see Cutler, Haufler, and Porter 1999a; Jacobsson and Sahlin-Anderson 2006; Avant, Finnemore, and Sell 2010a.

choose to "buy" existing knowledge from agents. To signal credibility of commitments, actors bind themselves to a third party that can render expert opinions. To secure first-mover advantage, actors seek those with experience to promulgate a solution before competing proposals are presented. To improve reputational standing, actors avoid sanction by adopting the practices of those with expert, and often moral, legitimacy.

I begin from the assumption that private actors *want* to project authority. With preexisting expertise, they have the ability to create rules and the incentives to do so: private actors can craft rules that favor their interests. Particularly in cases of interfirm cooperation, private actors can make rules that potentially preempt or postpone public regulation[83] or compete with more onerous private rules.[84] Favorable rules can also lower the cost of compliance, since rules can be created in line with existing practices.[85] In its most extreme forms, when rule making is entirely controlled by those who are subject to the rules, regulatory capture ensues, favoring the narrow interests of the regulated.[86] In sum, preexisting private expertise is a necessary but not sufficient condition for private authority.[87]

The Costs and Benefits of Private Authority

In order to understand the degree of benefit, we must also examine the costs of adopting private authority. In general, the benefits will be highest when costs incurred by its adopters are lowest. We can think of the costs of private authority in terms of the loss of autonomy. In instances of delegation, the loss of autonomy is measured by sovereignty costs—that is, "the reduction in state autonomy associated with ceding authority to international institutions."[88] With respect to nonstate actors, the same idea applies. When actor A cedes authority to actor B, A's autonomy is restricted. Thus, when Home Depot agrees to buy only FSC-certified products, it has less autonomy in its production practices than before it decided to do so.

The loss of autonomy is relatively low in instances of entrepreneurial authority: actors can choose whether to adopt private rules. Moreover, since the governor must convince the would-be governed to adopt their proposed rules, they are generally not too stringent. If the rules are draconian—requiring dramatic and costly changes—then they will

[83] Haufler 2001; Porter and Ronit 2006.
[84] See, e.g., Cashore, Auld, and Newsom 2004; Meidinger 2006.
[85] Büthe 2010a.
[86] In the international context, see Mattli and Woods 2009b. More generally, see Stigler 1971; Wilson 1980.
[87] Büthe 2010a, 7; Büthe and Mattli 2011, 44–45.
[88] Bradley and Kelley 2008, 1. See also Abbott and Snidal 2001.

likely not be adopted (unless the benefits are of doing so are proportionally large). Because sources of entrepreneurial authority must strike a balance between promulgating effective rules and attracting adherents, savvy governors will avoid rules that require drastic behavioral change (at least at the outset).

In cases of delegated authority, states have their choice of agents. If states choose to delegate, usually the choice is between an international organization and a nonstate actor as agent. One important criterion in making this choice is expected sovereignty costs. As sovereignty costs decrease, the benefits of delegation rise. In general, the easier it is to hold an actor accountable, the higher the overall benefits are. In a principal-agent relationship, "accountability is ensured when agents have incentives to do what the principals want them to do."[89] This congruence of preferences can be realized through screening (to ensure that agents have preferences similar to the principal), monitoring of behavior, incentives, or threat of sanctions.[90] Thus, the best way to lower sovereignty costs is to increase the likelihood that agents will do what is asked of them rather than pursue their own preferences. Ideally, principal and agent share preferences; the agent thus becomes an "ally" rather than someone difficult to control, which requires intensive monitoring on the part of the principal.[91]

To the extent that preferences diverge, accountability is enhanced through oversight—monitoring, required reporting, sanctions, and incentives. Of course, agents always enjoy some degree of autonomy as a result of incomplete contracts and the information asymmetries associated with delegation.[92] However, accountability mechanisms are more easily created and implemented when agents are IOs rather than private actors. Since states govern and fund IOs, any actions they find objectionable can be addressed through sanctions and the power of the purse. The same is not necessarily true for private agents, who are not merely eminences of the state. They have other constituencies and audiences and most likely, other sources of income.[93]

From this logic, we can deduce that if an IO and private actor are able to deliver the same benefits, the state will prefer the IO, because it is more easily controlled. Sovereignty costs to states will be lower with an IO, and therefore the net benefits of delegation increase. Because we assume that

[89] Grant and Keohane 2005, 32.

[90] In a trustee relationship, accountability is more complex, since the principal has selected the trustee so that she is impartial and insulated from influence. It can be considered a "discretionary authority," which is held accountable by justifying its actions in accordance with its jurisdiction and purpose. In practice, the trustee and principal-agent relationships may coexist in a given act of delegation, but my theory focuses only on the latter.

[91] Bendor, Glazer, and Hammond 2001.

[92] Pollack 1997; Pollack 2003; Nielson and Tierney 2003; Hawkins et al. 2006a.

[93] Public bureaucracies also have multiple masters; however, their financial well-being and continued authority ultimately lies with states as the collective principal.

the governed are motivated to maximize their well-being, I hypothesize that the IO will be preferred. Put another way, states will delegate to private actors if they can provide benefits that IOs cannot.

This argument underscores the notion that private authority is but one among many institutional arrangements to address cooperation problems. Clearly, the benefits enumerated above do not inhere in private actors. Theoretically, any actor in world politics may provide them. I posit that in some cases private actors may be better equipped to provide benefits than states or IOs, in which case private authority emerges. The goal of the theory is to understand the conditions under which this is the case.

If there is no IO capable of providing the same benefits as a private actor, we should observe one or more of the following. First, there should *not* be IOs with the required expertise for the policy function being undertaken by a private actor. Although potential IO actors may have related knowledge, they should not have programs, past activities, or publications demonstrating their long-standing experience on the issue. Second, we may observe overlapping institutions with competing rules and domains.[94] In this instance, there may be several IOs active in the area, but there may be considerable competition among them, each with varying ability to deliver benefits. Third, we might find failed attempts by IOs at gaining authority. Fourth, government officials involved in the decision to delegate should express confidence in the expertise or track record of the private actor, or concern about the ability of existing IOs to take on the task at hand.

In sum, the theory of supply and demand set forth here argues that private authority will emerge when there is a supply of private expertise that can potentially provide benefits to others. These would-be adopters of the rules are self-interested actors; they grant their consent to private rule makers because of the anticipated benefits of doing so. These include reduced transaction costs, increased credibility of commitments, first-mover advantage, and improved reputation. In general, the less autonomy the adopters have to sacrifice, the greater the net gain in deferring to private authority. For this reason, states will generally choose public agents—international organizations—who are more readily controlled. They will choose private agents only when IOs cannot supply the equivalent benefits.

The Form of Private Authority

We now have an idea of when private authority should emerge, but the model is incomplete unless it can also explain the *form* of private authority. When should we expect delegated authority versus entrepreneurial

---

[94] Raustiala and Victor 2004; Busch 2007.

authority? The variation in form can be explained by two key factors: the preferences of powerful states and the existence of a focal institution. It is important to reiterate here that explaining the form of private authority is contingent upon its emergence. In other words, in terms of the causal model, predicting the form of private authority assumes that there is both a demand for benefits as well as a supply of preexisting expertise, as indicated in figure 1.1.

STATE PREFERENCES

One key to predicting the conditions under which delegated private authority will arise is to understand when we should or should not expect excessive agency slack. Slack can be broadly understood as instances in which the agent fails to carry out the duties with which it has been charged by the principal. As the possibility of slack increases, the benefits—and the likelihood—of delegation fall. Epstein and O'Halloran note that "principals . . . can rarely control agents perfectly, but they can design contracts in a way that reduces the incentives for slack."[95]

Delegation theory tells us that the more homogeneous the preferences of the collective principal, the fewer the opportunities for agency slack. When states agree on a policy, they can give clearer instructions to the agent about its responsibilities, and they can be more vigilant in ensuring that the agent carries them out. Put another way, homogeneous preferences increase the likelihood that states can employ the "ally principle" and select an agent whose preferences are closest to their own.[96] When states have heterogeneous preferences, they are more likely to give the agent ambiguous instructions. For instance, Nielson and Tierney show that the lending practices of the World Bank changed significantly once principals (i.e., states) agreed on the reforms to be implemented.[97] With a clear and consistent directive from states, World Bank staff knew what changes to make and recognized that there was increased likelihood of being held accountable for implementing those changes. Following this logic, I argue that as state preferences converge, so does the likelihood of delegated private authority. Hawkins and colleagues make a similar argument with respect to IOs.[98]

When states are relatively unified in their goals, they can focus on overseeing agents' efforts to achieve them. In addition, states with similar

[95] Epstein and O'Halloran 1999, 28.

[96] Bendor, Glazer, and Hammond 2001. For evidence to the contrary, see Green and Colgan 2013.

[97] Nielson and Tierney 2003.

[98] Hawkins et al. 2006b, 20–21. There is, however, some disagreement in the international relations literature on the relationship between preferences and delegation to IOs. For an opposing view, see Green and Colgan 2013; Koremenos 2008.

preferences are more likely to agree on an agent that will be closely aligned with the principal, thus reducing the likelihood of slack.[99] Of course, these agent characteristics depend on the composition and preferences of the collective principal: a large collective principal (such as one composed of all UN members), is likely to face collective action problems in controlling the agent. This leads to the conclusion that one cannot simply refer to "the preferences" of a collective principal; I discuss how to deal with this challenge below.

By contrast, when states cannot agree on policies or desired outcomes, they are less likely to delegate in the first place (because they are unable to come to a consensus on what the agent should do). Moreover, if delegation does occur, slack is more likely, because agents may be able to exploit differences in the views among the collective principal to pursue their own goals. This potential reduction in benefits may dissuade states from delegating in the first place.

This discussion illustrates that we cannot treat the collective principal as a unitary actor but rather must consider the constellation of preferences and the distribution of potential winners and losers that result from delegation. Indeed, Lyne et al. warn that delegation at the international level cannot be understood without a clear conception of who constitutes the principal.[100] The collective principal is also a "complex principal"—a reflection of its diverse views and preferences.

At a minimum, I posit that there must be consensus among the most powerful nations involved (which will vary by issue) that delegation will be advantageous for them. If powerful states are in agreement, they may be able to persuade others to support the delegation decision. State preferences range on a continuum from agreement to deadlock. Greater agreement among powerful states about the preferred course of action increases the likelihood of delegation.

Conversely, as preferences of powerful states become more heterogeneous, private authority is apt to take the entrepreneurial form. When states cannot agree on how to proceed, they are more open to weakly institutionalized arrangements, such as those exemplified by private authority. Not only is the flexibility of these arrangements desirable for states,[101] but experimentation with different policies may increase the possibility of finding a solution that is acceptable to all states in the future.[102] Thus, when states disagree about regulation, private actors shift discussions outside the intergovernmental realm, and opportunities for entrepreneurship emerge.

[99] Bradley and Kelley 2008, 31.
[100] Lyne, Nielson, and Tierney 2006.
[101] Andonova 2010.
[102] Auld and Green 2012; Green 2012.

In determining the degree of preference convergence, there is also the matter of which states are considered "powerful" with respect to a given issue. To be clear, the theory does not assert that *all* states must share the same preferences in order for preferences to be considered homogeneous—just that the most powerful states do. Who these powerful states are will vary by issue, depending on natural resource endowments and dependence, resources available for negotiation, and distribution of economic gains and losses, and, more generally, the intensity of interests. The economic interests of individual states are particularly important in determining national preferences.[103] The higher the economic stakes, the stronger the state's preferences will be.[104]

The degree of convergence of state preferences can be identified in several ways. When state preferences are homogeneous, decisions should be taken quickly; thus, we should see that new agreements are made in subsequent meetings of the parties to an MEA. Interviews with negotiators should affirm that states are largely in agreement. Finally, we should not see states engaging in attempts at forum shopping—raising similar issues or taking decisions in other policy-making arenas. When state preferences are heterogeneous, we should observe the opposite. There will likely be little movement or impasse in the intergovernmental realm. Decision making will be slow, inconclusive, or weakly legalized. Side payments to veto players are likely. Government officials should affirm the existence of polarized viewpoints. We may also observe attempts to forum shop, where governments pursue their desired policy in different fora to avoid conflict.

FOCAL INSTITUTIONS

The existence of a focal institution enhances the likelihood of *delegated* authority because it reduces opportunities for agency slack. A focal point can be understood as a natural point of convergence of actors' expectations. This convergence can occur without prior communication, or can be present in situations of explicit bargaining.[105] A focal point can be a place, such as Schelling's example of the information desk at Grand Central. I use it to refer to a specific institution.

If there is an extant focal institution around which states' expectations converge, then delegated private authority is more likely to emerge for two reasons. First, the focal institution mitigates the possibility of slack.

---

[103] Moravcsik 1998.

[104] This is consistent with Broz and Hawes's (2006) principal-agent analysis of the International Monetary Fund, where they find that the pecuniary financial interests of private actors within one powerful state—the United States—drive the government's position on contributions to the IMF.

[105] Schelling 1960, 53–80.

Slack can occur because of either shirking, where an agent simply does not make all efforts to achieve the desired outcome,[106] or slippage, where the agent pursues its own preferences in addition to or instead of those of the principal.[107] A previously established, vetted institution—usually an IO—provides a relatively easy and low-cost way to screen and monitor private agents. A focal institution is generally viewed as more neutral and credible than any individual state that constitutes part of the principal and therefore as a useful information generator.[108] Credible screening and monitoring can reduce (though, most agree, cannot eliminate) the opportunities for both types of slack and increase the potential benefit to states. Second, Schelling points out that a focal institution can facilitate agreement even when there are divergent preferences among states. He notes that focal points have an "intrinsic magnetism" that can promote agreement.[109] According to Schelling's logic, although delegation may be less likely to occur with heterogeneous preferences among states, the existence of a focal point may help diminish these differences, thereby increasing the likelihood of delegation.

Conversely, the lack of a focal institution or the existence of a weak one makes entrepreneurial authority more likely. This argument was made by Susan Strange, who contended forcefully that "at the head of the international political economy, there is a vacuum, a vacuum not adequately filled by inter-governmental institutions or by a hegemonic power exercising leadership in the common interest."[110] Strange raises a useful point for my model: where public authority is weak, private authority will have an opportunity to insert itself.

How can we evaluate the strength of a focal institution? First, since focal institutions are a way of reducing slack, there should also be strong screening or monitoring procedures for agents. Thus, we should be able to see clear selection criteria for agents, as well as requirements for regular reporting. By contrast, a weak (or nonexistent) focal institution will have few staff, a small or highly variable budget, or a weakly legalized mandate. The presence of overlapping institutions with competing rules or domains is also likely when there is no clear focal institution.

I acknowledge here that the two key factors that determine the form of private authority are likely correlated. Because focal institutions are generally IOs, which are created by states, they will always be, at least in part, a reflection of state preferences. However, I include the strength or existence of a focal institution as an explanatory variable because it

[106] Moe 1990.
[107] See, e.g., McCubbins, Noll, and Weingast 1987.
[108] Thompson 2006.
[109] Schelling 1960, 60.
[110] Strange 1996, 14.

is an important component in tracing the process through which the outcome—the form of private authority—is produced. Simply examining state preferences would not provide as fine-grained a picture of this causal process or how the variables interact.[111]

The theory does not provide conclusive predictions for the other combinations of the independent variables. Building on Lazarfeld's work, Ragin notes that "most 'type concepts' involve sets of attributes that make sense together."[112] Such is the case with the theory presented here; it is engaged in developing an empirically informed typology of private authority and an explanation of that typology. The theory sets forth the logic as to why the combinations of the independent variables produce the two different forms of private authority. The cases demonstrate the causal process through which they jointly produce the outcome—delegated or entrepreneurial authority. As a result, the combinations of independent variables are "interpretable configurations" rather than an attempt to explain all combinations of the variables.[113]

Conclusion

A theory of private authority has three key components: a completely specified definition of private authority that distinguishes between its different forms, a model of supply and demand that elaborates conditions under which it will emerge, and explanatory variables that predict what *type* of authority will emerge. Although delegated and entrepreneurial authority differ in significant ways, if we are to understand the full range of ways that private actors serve as rule makers, a theory must also consider them in tandem. The distinction between delegated and entrepreneurial authority hinges on the timing and source of consent. When private actors have *ex ante* permission to act on behalf of others, they exercise delegated authority. If there is no *ex ante* permission, the private actor must persuade others to adopt their rules. This distinction can also be understood as the difference between *de facto* and *de jure* authority and is critical if we are to understand the full range of ways that private actors serve as rule makers in world politics.

The emergence of private authority requires that there is both a demand for it as well as a supply. The supply is contingent on private actors possessing the expertise that allows them to furnish benefits to the rule demanders. Without expertise, private actors cannot provide such

---

[111] Ragin 2004.
[112] Ragin 2000, 77.
[113] Ibid., 72.

benefits to the governed and cannot legitimate their claims to authority. The demand for private authority stems from the existence of some type of cooperation problem. In such situations, private actors can potentially reduce transaction costs, enhance the credibility of commitments, provide first-mover advantage, or help adherents improve their reputation. Conditions of both demand and supply are necessary but not sufficient for private authority to emerge.

Given that these conditions are in place, the theory also predicts whether we will see delegated or entrepreneurial authority emerge. The form depends on the existence or strength of a focal institution, and the configuration of preferences of powerful state actors. As it stands, the theory dichotomizes these two variables (which are, of course, continuous in reality) to present ideal types. It predicts that a strong focal institution and shared preferences among powerful states will give rise to delegated authority. By contrast, when there is no focal institution (or a weak institution) and powerful states have heterogeneous preferences, entrepreneurial authority will emerge.

CHAPTER TWO

Agents of the State: A Century of Delegation in International Environmental Law

THIS CHAPTER IS THE FIRST of two exploratory missions.[1] If private authority is on the rise, as many have claimed, where and how is this growing phenomenon occurring? Theories of delegation suggest looking to the state as the likely engine of private authority. With more governing to do, states are enlisting others to help them through the delegation of authority. As such, this chapter examines a century of multilateral environmental treaties (MEAs), asking two basic questions: How often do states delegate to private actors, and for what tasks?

Surprisingly, we do not have very many answers to this question. Nor do we know much about patterns of delegation to private actors over time.[2] Theories of delegation abound, but historical data do not. Therefore, it is premature to formulate expectations about the amount or pattern of delegation to private agents. The task of this chapter is to provide much-needed information on the landscape of private delegated authority. On the basis of a systematic evaluation of a century of international environmental law making, I draw some preliminary conclusions about when and why states choose to delegate to private actors.

The findings contradict claims by some about the "retreat of the state."[3] The data show that, on the whole, delegation to private actors is a relatively rare occurrence. Although overall rates of delegation have increased markedly in the past twenty-five years, only a small percentage of the policy functions delegated have been assigned to private agents (rather than international organizations). Of the almost two thousand policy functions contained within the treaties examined, only 3.8 percent of them were delegated to private actors.

Another interesting picture emerges from the data: the total amount of governance is increasing. Not only is the number of treaties growing, but the number of actors responsible for a given policy function is also rising.

---

[1] This chapter is based on Green 2010a.

[2] There are a number of works that examine historical examples of private authority, but most of these are entrepreneurial rather than delegated authority. See, e.g., Greif 1993; Braithwaite and Drahos 2000; Cutler 2003; Greif 2006.

[3] Strange 1996.

Whereas states might have assigned monitoring to one actor in the past, now there are two or three. Moreover, the small role for private actors shrinks further when one measures the policy functions for which they are solely responsible. Less than one-tenth of 1 percent of all policy functions are the sole purview of a private agent. More frequently, states tap different actors to perform the same task. This finding shows that there are multiple loci of authority in world politics and that they continue to expand. The data presented here provide a compelling illustration of the growing "institutional density" of global governance.[4] Put simply, there are more issues with global reach, requiring more institutions and actors to manage them.

Fifteen years ago, Jessica Mathews described a "power shift" in world politics—from states to nonstate actors.[5] In fact, the data here suggest that a "power share" is a more accurate description of the changes underway. States are actively governing—indeed, they are making more rules, laws, and treaties than ever before.[6] At the same time, they are enlisting a diverse set of actors to aid them in this project. However, they do so in a strategic way, delegating those activities that are relatively lower in "sovereignty costs"—activities that result in the fewest restrictions on their autonomy. States are more likely to delegate implementation and monitoring than functions that could potentially have a greater impact on their autonomy, such as rule making and enforcement.

This exploratory mission also examines what happens *after* a given treaty enters into force. At this point, states continue to take legal decisions to further the implementation of the treaty's goals. Do they also continue to delegate to private actors? The data show that the answer is a resounding yes; in fact, they are more apt to delegate at the post-treaty stage. Delegation to private agents after entry into force increases to 8.4 percent of total policy functions. Neither of these figures, however, provides evidence that private actors are "taking over." Rather, the evidence for the power share is further reinforced. States regularly rely on private actors for a limited but consistent role as "helpers," contributing their expertise to complex environmental issues.

Why Delegate?

Delegation can be understood as "a conditional grant of authority from a *principal* to an *agent* that empowers the latter to act on behalf of the

---

[4] Raustiala 2012; Abbott, Green, and Keohane 2013. For similar arguments with different terminology, see Young 2002 and Raustiala and Victor 2004.

[5] Mathews 1997.

[6] Brown Weiss 1993 refers to this as a problem of "treaty congestion."

former."[7] Delegation occurs on a continuum, ranging from high to low levels of legalization.[8] At the highest levels of legalization, principals are strongly bound by the rules delegated to the agent; at lower levels, there is greater room for principals' political maneuvering. For example, when states delegate rule-making authority to an IO, the agent may be empowered to create binding enforceable regulations—an instance of highly legalized delegation, since principals will have a much more difficult time contesting the rules. However, if the IO is empowered only to give recommendations or issue normative statements, the impacts on the principal are much lower, and delegation much less legalized. Although the data presented here treat delegation as a dichotomous variable (either states delegate or they do not), in practice there is much more nuance and variation in each act of delegation.

Drawing from theories of delegation in economics and American politics, international relations scholars have a well-developed set of theories about why states choose to delegate to international organizations. Dominant explanations are based in the logic of transaction costs: delegation occurs when agents can lower the costs of cooperation.[9] There are various ways in which they can accomplish this goal. Perhaps most importantly, agents can help states surmount collective action problems by providing information about other states' behavior.[10] Information provision helps to overcome the classic free-rider problem: when there are multiple parties to an agreement, each is concerned about whether others will comply. By collecting and disseminating information about parties' activities, agents perform a valuable service to states, which no longer have to undertake this labor-intensive task themselves.

Agents can provide other important benefits to principals. First, they can enhance the credibility of states' commitments to each other.[11] Although it may be in states' collective interest to make a set of promises about long-term behavior, there are often incentives to renege in the short term. For example, under the Convention on Biological Diversity, states have agreed to a variety of measures to conserve biological diversity and ensure its sustainable use. However, short-term needs for raw materials or farm land provide powerful incentives to degrade or destroy

[7] Hawkins et al. 2006b, 7, emphasis in original. For a broader definition, see Bradley and Kelley 2008, who do not insist on conditionality.

[8] Abbott et al. 2000.

[9] For a cogent critique of the functionalist explanation of delegation, see Stone 2011, chap. 2.

[10] The classic statement on this is Keohane 1984. See also Koremenos, Lipson, and Snidal 2001.

[11] Majone 2001.

valuable ecosystems. Delegating to a third party can help address this time-inconsistency problem and signal the serious intentions of states to each other.[12] By providing information about others' behavior, agents can also signal to principals when defection has occurred.[13]

Second, delegation can also help facilitate collective decision making. Many multilateral environmental agreements have a large number of signatories, where each has its own priorities and goals. The Convention on Biological Diversity has 193 parties; the Convention on International Trade in Endangered Species has 175. Regional agreements may have fewer parties, but still must navigate among the preferences of tens of countries. Delegating to an IO to set or manage the agenda can help direct the negotiation process, which generally becomes more complicated by the presence of a greater number of actors. Instead of having each country pile on its pet issue, delegation to a third party, such as a subsidiary body or chairperson, can narrow the items up for debate. This idea is simply captured by Abbott and Snidal who note that "centralization enhance[s] . . . efficiency."[14] Delegation to enhance the efficiency of decision making is evident in the Montreal Protocol, which seeks to prevent further depletion of the ozone layer. The protocol's Technical and Economic Assessments Panel was charged with deciding what constituted "essential uses" of ozone-depleting substance—therefore not subject to the phase outs required by the treaty.[15] This facilitated decision making by restricting the number of actors involved in the process. Such delegation can prevent what Tallberg refers to as "agenda failure," where progress toward agreement is stymied by "shifting, overcrowded or underdeveloped agendas."[16] This process can be formal, with rules determining who may propose or vote on proposals[17] or more informal, by constructing focal points around which bargaining can occur.[18]

Third, delegation can help with the implementation of an agreement by making use of the comparative advantage of experts. Specialization is at the core of the logic of delegation; thus, states may delegate to an IO to leverage its expertise.[19] Experts may have either knowledge or know-how. Arguments about the power of epistemic communities are grounded in the logic of knowledge. Epistemic communities are "knowledge-based

---

[12] Martin 1992; Stone 2002.
[13] Reinhardt 2001.
[14] Abbott and Snidal 1998, 9.
[15] Parson 2003, chap. 8.
[16] Pollack 2003b; Tallberg 2006, 20.
[17] Tallberg 2006.
[18] Garrett and Weingast 1993.
[19] Hawkins et al. 2006b, 13.

groups of experts . . . with claims to authoritative understanding" of the problem at hand.[20] They have served a particularly important role in environmental regimes because of the importance of scientific information in decision making.

As the discussion below on post-treaty delegation illustrates, states often delegate technical matters to them precisely because of their specialized knowledge. Thus, the NGO TRAFFIC has been delegated a key role in monitoring states' compliance with the Convention on International Trade in Endangered Species because it has the best data on wildlife trade in the world. Similarly, the Scientific Committee on Antarctic Research (SCAR) is an international network of professional scientists that study Antarctic ecosystems, which is regularly asked to provide information and proposals on the best ways to achieve the various conservation and management goals set forth in the Antarctic Treaties. In sum, epistemic communities have played a key role in agreements ranging from the conservation of the Antarctic to management of the global climate.[21]

Finally, delegation can promote treaty implementation through the use of a third-party arbiter of disputes, which in turn promotes effective enforcement. An impartial agent can preserve the credibility of the agreement by ensuring that states abide by their commitments. Examples of IO agents involved in dispute resolution include international courts such as the International Court of Justice and the European Court of Justice, as well as those charged with interpretation of rules associated with a specific agreement or set of agreements, like the World Trade Organization Dispute Resolution Board. Appointing a third-party arbiter helps states "self-bind": states limit their own authority by requiring themselves to be subject to authority of a third party.[22] The degree to which delegation to third-party arbiters is binding depends in part on the extent to which their authority is insulated from principals—that is, states.[23] Acts of delegation that insulate agents signal the intentions of signatory states to comply with their commitment and help address the key issue of treaty enforcement.[24]

Despite the well-developed causal explanations of delegation, there is a lack of systematic study of international delegation.[25] As a result, "debates in international relations and law about how much delegation

[20] P. Haas 1990, xxiii.
[21] Haas 1989; Haas 1992; Litfin 1994; Joyner 1998; Raustiala 2001; Dimitrov 2003.
[22] Alter 2008.
[23] Keohane, Moravcsik, and Slaughter 2000.
[24] On the latter point, see Koremenos, Lipson, and Snidal 2001.
[25] But see Hawkins et al. 2006a, Bradley and Kelley 2008, and the rest of the *Law and Contemporary Problems* symposium.

there is and how much it matters, are, therefore, largely anecdotal."[26] Recent works have attempted to remedy this problem through collections of case studies. However, few large-N studies examine patterns of variation across institutions.[27]

There is even less study of the role of nonstate actors as agents in international relations.[28] Bradley and Kelley note that delegation to international bodies might include private bodies or public-private partnerships, but their study does not examine these actors in depth.[29] They also acknowledge that NGOs and other nonstate actors may serve as agents through "re-delegation," where the international body serving as the agent in turn delegates to another entity.[30] For example, the UN Environment Programme often turns to local NGOs to help with the implementation of programs and projects.[31] Yet Bradley and Kelley focus on identifying the mechanisms through which private actors become agents rather than on specific empirical contexts. The analysis of delegation at the post-treaty level, in the second half of this chapter, investigates redelegation, providing quantitative data on the phenomenon.

There are a few notable exceptions. Mattli and Büthe's body of work on accounting and product-related standards explicitly tackles the question of when and why states delegate to private agents. They offer a functional explanation as well as a political one.[32] Private actors may be attractive agents because of their expertise or because they provide a convenient target for blame shifting by principals. Cafaggi and Janczuk examine delegation to technical standard-setting bodies by the EU Commission as a response to concerns about transparency and accountability.[33]

Other works discuss delegation to private actors from a variety of perspectives. Koremenos's work provides useful data on patterns of delegation to private actors, noting that delegation to NGOs is most likely

---

[26] Bradley and Kelley 2008, 32.

[27] Koremenos 2007 and Koremenos 2008 appear to be the only other studies that examine delegation patterns across treaties, and even across issue areas. Green and Colgan 2013 examines patterns of delegation to IOs within the area of environment. See also Broz and Hawes 2006.

[28] In the international arena, delegation to private actors has been more carefully considered by lawyers, particularly those examining the emerging field of global administrative law, where delegation is a mode of ensuring accountability. See Kingsbury, Krisch, and Stewart 2005.

[29] Bradley and Kelley 2008, 8–9.

[30] Ibid., 17.

[31] Abbott and Snidal 2010 describe a softer form of this IO-NGO cooperation as "orchestration."

[32] Mattli and Büthe 2003; Mattli and Büthe 2005; Büthe and Mattli 2011.

[33] Cafaggi and Janczuk 2010.

in human rights agreements.[34] Research on private military companies examines the normative implications of delegating a key function of the state—the use of violence—to private agents.[35] Cooley and Ron's investigation of humanitarian NGOs shows how competition in a crowded field can lead to dysfunctional outcomes.[36] Drezner also examines the role of nonstate actors as agents responsible for the management of the Internet, arguing that delegation to private agents is the result of great-power preferences.[37]

On the whole, however, delegation theory in international relations tends to focus more on the demand side (principals) than the supply side (agents). As Lake and McCubbins note, understanding the role of non-state actors is the "next frontier" in delegation theory. Interestingly, they focus on the capacity of private actors to monitor IOs in their exercise of delegated authority rather than considering private actors as agents themselves.[38] This exploratory mission aims to help move toward that next frontier.

Data and Methods

I investigate patterns of delegation to private actors through a random sample of 152 multilateral environmental treaties, sampled from all extant multilateral treaties from 1857 to 2002.[39] The earliest treaty in the sample is the 1902 Convention for the Protection of Birds Useful to Agriculture, signed by various European and Northern European royalty. The most recent is a 2002 agreement signed by Mozambique, South Africa, and Swaziland promoting the protection and sustainable use of the Incomati and Maputo watercourses. The agreements cover a range of environmental issues including energy, freshwater resources, habitat, oceans, pollution, and species.[40] Figure 2.1 shows the number of agreements by subject area.[41]

Through the compilation and analysis of the data, I investigate two basic questions: What activities does the treaty undertake, and who is

[34] Koremenos 2007; Koremenos 2008.

[35] Avant 2005; Chesterman and Lehnardt 2007.

[36] Cooley and Ron 2002.

[37] Drezner 2004.

[38] Lake and McCubbins 2006, 341–368.

[39] This sample was originally compiled by Ron Mitchell, available from http://iea.uoregon.edu/page.php?query=list_codes. The sample was drawn from 497 multilateral agreements that had been signed by 2002; this excludes amendments, protocols, and other modifications to extant agreements.

[40] The definition for each of these issue areas is available from http://iea.uoregon.edu/page.php?query=static&file=definitions.htm.

[41] Because agreements can be included in multiple categories, N > 152.

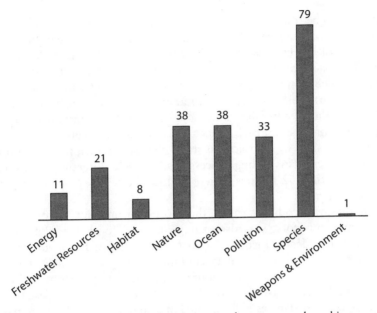

Figure 2.1. Sample of multilateral environmental agreements, by subject area.

responsible for them? To answer these questions, I coded each paragraph of each treaty for two dependent variables: policy functions named and the actors responsible for them.[42] Each paragraph could contain one or more of the following five functions: rule making, implementation, monitoring, enforcement, and adjudication.

Four possible actors are responsible for implementing these functions: states themselves (i.e., no delegation), a subset of states, an international organization, or a nonstate actor. Nonstate actors were identified using organizational websites and the Union of International Associations.[43] If all states that are party to the treaty are responsible for the policy function, then it is coded as no delegation, since each state is charged with implementing the function domestically. It is certainly possible that each state individually chooses to delegate to a private domestic agent. However, because this study is concerned with delegation at the *international* level, these domestic cases of delegation are excluded. By contrast, if the parties to the agreement agree collectively to delegate to one state or a subset of states, then this is coded as an act of delegation. For example,

---

[42] The data were coded using the Coding Analysis Toolkit, which is available from http://cat.ucsur.pitt.edu/.

[43] If I could not make a determination based on these sources, then the actor was coded as "ambiguous agent."

France could be responsible for collecting and disseminating all monitoring data for a given treaty. France is then considered a "state agent."

Because of the complexity of the agreements and of legal language, more than one actor may be responsible for a given policy function. For instance, some monitoring requirements may not be delegated; states may have to report their activities on an annual basis. But, an IO may then be responsible for compiling and disseminating this information, which helps states understand each other's behavior. In this example, monitoring is undertaken by two actors: states themselves (i.e., no delegation) and an IO agent. This coding process yielded 1,847 different policy functions across the 152 treaties, where multiple actors may be assigned to the same function.

In addition to coding treaties, the process of implementation *after* a treaty enters into force was also examined. These "post-treaty" decisions are taken in order to further the goals of the treaty. For example, the Cartagena Protocol on Biosafety contains vague provisions about how compliance will be evaluated, noting only that the parties will decide upon compliance measures at the first Conference of the Parties.[44] (The Conference of the Parties is the annual meeting of states which are party to the protocol, in which they assess the status of the agreement and take decisions about how to move forward.) Thus, in order to create actual compliance procedures and mechanisms, a subcommittee was created after the treaty entered into force. This post-treaty decision-making process—the Compliance Committee of the Cartagena Protocol—meets annually. During the course of its meetings, it has created mechanisms to promote capacity to implement the protocol effectively, established procedures for dealing with noncompliance, and created guidelines to promote domestic implementation of the treaty's provisions.[45]

The investigation of post-treaty decisions provides further insight into when and why states choose to delegate to private agents (among other actors). Environmental law making is increasingly complex and goes well beyond the simple act of drafting a treaty.[46] Many MEAs meet annually in a Conference of the Parties. Some have established subsidiary bodies that meet more frequently. The Kyoto Protocol now has two subsidiary bodies, a compliance committee, two bodies overseeing the market mechanisms, and a board that supervises the Adaptation Fund. There are also

[44] Cartagena Protocol on Biosafety, Article 34, available from http://bch.cbd.int/protocol/text/.

[45] The Compliance Committee was created by decision BS 1/7 of the first meeting of the parties; the text of the decision is available from http://bch.cbd.int/protocol/decisions/decision.shtml?decisionID=8289.

[46] The Earth Negotiations Bulletin, which reports on multilateral negotiations in a variety of environmental issue areas, is testimony to this complexity. See http://www.iisd.ca.

five bodies overseeing various aspects of the financing of the regime.[47] In turn, some of these bodies have their own subcommittees. The UNFCCC calendar is chock-a-block with meetings, the majority of which are taking decisions about the implementation of the convention and protocol. Many of these involve acts of delegation. Thus, the analysis of post-treaty decisions is a way to provide a fuller picture of how states carry out the law-making process and how private actors are involved in that process.

Examining these decisions is also motivated by the potential objection that states are unlikely to include delegation provisions in the treaty itself—a highly legalized form of cooperation that is difficult to reverse—when they could do so after the treaty enters into force. The data show that states are in fact more likely to delegate to private actors at the post-treaty stage—when decisions are more easily reversed. The random sample for post-treaty decisions includes 518 such decisions. The same categories for policy functions and possible actors were used.

Treaty Data: One Hundred Years of Delegation

Table 2.1 shows the distribution of policy functions at the treaty level, irrespective of delegation or actor. In general, the data show that states appear more interested in "doing" environmental protection and management than reporting or enforcing it. As such, the majority of the policy functions named in the 152 treaties deal with matters of implementation (in part, admittedly, because this category of activities is broadly defined). Implementation includes conducting specific projects, training, capacity building activities, and technology transfer. All discussion of budget, finances, and financial mechanisms is also considered implementation.[48]

The second most prevalent activity is rule making, which includes creating administrative rules, filling in gaps, or interpreting extant rules, as well as matters of procedure and voting.[49] The least common policy function is enforcement. Enforcement activities include initiating or conducting investigations about compliance, intervention in other states' behavior, imposing sanctions or retaliatory actions, and mandating corrective actions be taken in response to noncompliance. The relative paucity of enforcement functions is an interesting finding itself. Despite the desire to cooperate under conditions of anarchy, states are generally wary of including provisions that could adversely affect them in cases of noncompliance.

[47] See http://unfccc.int/bodies/items/6241.php.
[48] Since implementation outlines the activities that actors will undertake and deciding how those activities will be configured, it is consistent with my definition of private authority.
[49] Bradley and Kelley 2008, 14.

TABLE 2.1
Distribution of Policy Functions, Treaty Level

	N	%
Rule making	400	22%
Adjudication	119	6%
Implementation	1,010	55%
Monitoring	218	12%
Enforcement	100	5%
TOTAL	1,847	100%

WHEN DO STATES DELEGATE?

Figure 2.2 shows the growth in delegation to private actors at the treaty level over time, and provides another key finding: the use of private actors as agents accelerates in the 1990s. I also include data on delegation to international organizations, which demonstrates that delegation to private agents pales in comparison to states' use of IOs as agents. The overall N is small: only 70 policy functions are delegated to private agents over the course of the century. By contrast, 408 functions are delegated to IOs.

The early nineties, which featured the 1992 Rio Conference on Environment and Development and the creation of several landmark treaties, is commonly viewed as a turning point for modern environmental law. Correspondingly, it appears to be a turning point in the use of different kinds of actors to accommodate the growth of legal instruments. Although there is a marked uptick in the 1990s, there is no consistent pattern across the entire sample. States begin delegating to private actors in 1954 in the International Whaling Convention, and for the subsequent three decades, the number of policy functions delegated fluctuates somewhat randomly. The spike in 1968 is explained by one agreement, the Agreement on Administrative Arrangements for the Prek Thnot (Cambodia) Power and Irrigation Development Project. This agreement is a large-scale development project paid for by Western governments but implemented largely by a Cambodian corporation, which relies heavily on private engineering to provide expert advice on constructing and tendering contracts. Thus, this particular fluctuation appears to be an anomaly.

The steady increase in delegation to private actors begins in the 1990s and continues at a high rate in the first three years of the 2000s. Those that espouse the view that nonstate actors are becoming more prominent in world politics would most certainly point to these last twelve years of the sample, which contain 59 percent of all instances of delegation to private actors across the century. It is also noteworthy that almost half

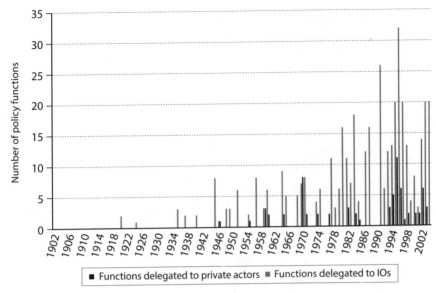

Figure 2.2. Number of policy functions delegated to private agents and international organizations, treaty level, 1902–2002.

of the functions delegated in these dozen years, or 47 percent of all the policy functions, are "agent only" instances of delegation—that is, functions where there is no state involvement at all (recall that each function can have more than one actor responsible for its execution).

However, the number of MEAs also doubled between the 1980s and 1990s.[50] Thus, there is no increase in the *proportion* of private delegated authority, only the overall amount. Table 2.2 shows delegation to private actors as a proportion of the total number of policy functions per decade. The proportion is small, never exceeding 8 percent, which it approaches between 1960 and 1969. This suggests that the observed growth is therefore a reflection of the growth of MEAs themselves. This finding speaks to the notion of a power share rather than a power shift: as governance arrangements become more numerous and more complex, states are increasingly enlisting multiple actors to help in the governance process. These data provide clear evidence of the move toward multiple loci of authority.

WHAT POLICY FUNCTIONS DO STATES DELEGATE?

Many scholars and politicians see the expansion of global governance as a worrisome trend. They are concerned that international institutions are "taking over," managing problems that were once considered the

[50] See Mitchell 2010.

TABLE 2.2
Percentage of Total Policy Functions Delegated
to Private Actors, Treaty Level

1902–9	0%
1909–19	0%
1920–29	0%
1930–39	0%
1940–49	1.9%
1950–59	5.4%
1960–69	7.9%
1970–79	1.7%
1980–89	1.5%
1990–99	4.8%
2000–2	4.6%

province of the state. The result is concern about "world government" or, in its milder version, the threats to national sovereignty posed by global bureaucracies.[51] The data here show that these concerns are overblown, to say the least.

Delegation, to *any* actor, is a relatively rare occurrence. Although a large proportion of treaties feature some form of delegation, the actual number of specific activities delegated is low. Of all treaties, 81 percent delegate to some agent—a state or group of states, an IO, or a private agent. But, when this figure is disaggregated to look at actual policy functions, the proportion falls markedly: less than one-third of all policy functions include some form of delegation.

In general, states guard their sovereignty carefully, and see delegation as a potential threat to their autonomy.[52] Delegation can divert states from their preferred policy outcome, either owing to compromise with other states or because the agent does not faithfully carry out the states' preferences. Delegation can also potentially raise the costs of noncompliance, because agents may be empowered to impose sanctions. Thus, states are likely to delegate in a way that minimizes sovereignty costs, which can be understood formally as "reductions in state autonomy through

[51] See, e.g., Rabkin 2005.
[52] The exception, Bradley and Kelley 2008, 26 note, is when delegation helps states better control the movement of goods and people across borders; enhanced control enhances sovereignty.

displacement of its decision making or control."[53] This logic hardly suggests strong evidence for a world government. Rather it suggests the opposite: as sovereignty costs rise, delegation will likely decrease.

Indeed, this hypothesis is borne out by the data. When they do delegate, states overwhelmingly prefer to delegate implementation activities, which impinge less on state autonomy than some of the other policy functions, such as rule making or enforcement. While implementation activities are no doubt important to the functioning of the treaty, they are not likely to have a profound impact on the autonomy of any individual state. For example, a capacity-building program may provide training for government bureaucrats on how to meet the requirements of some provision of a treaty. However, this is not likely to impinge significantly on the state's self-rule.

A brief assessment of previous research on delegation suggests that the five policy functions can be roughly sorted by degree of sovereignty costs. Two of the functions, rule making and adjudication, have relatively high sovereignty costs, since they have the potential to substantially change states' behavior. Rule making determines what states can and cannot do; adjudication determines whether states are in compliance with an agreement. Monitoring and enforcement fall in the medium range. There will be some variation in the degree of sovereignty cost depending on the specific provisions of the delegation. For instance, the delegation of enforcement could potentially have high sovereignty costs, but this will depend on the type of sanctions attached. Implementation by contrast, is the least intrusive and thus has the lowest sovereignty costs.[54] Figure 2.3 shows that states generally prefer to delegate those policy functions with lower sovereignty costs. Implementation is the second most frequently delegated, whereas rule making, which potentially has very high sovereignty costs, is the least frequently delegated. There is an unexplained outlier, adjudication, which is actually the most frequently delegated function, contrary to the hypothesis that the frequency of delegation falls as sovereignty costs rise. I examine this anomaly further below.

TO WHOM DO STATES DELEGATE?
In terms of the choice of agents, the first important finding is that states rarely allow agents to act on their own. That is, the number of policy functions where states have no role, and agents of any kind are solely responsible for carrying out the task, is extremely small. Only 12.3 percent of all policy functions are "agent only." In other words, states maintain

[53] Bradley and Kelley 2008, 27. The term originally comes from Abbott and Snidal 2000.
[54] This interpretation of the sovereignty costs associated with different functions is consistent with Bradley and Kelley 2008.

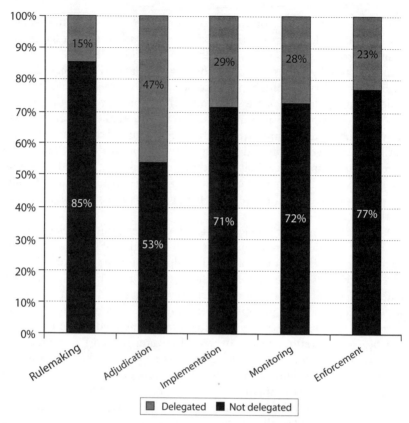

Figure 2.3. Rates of delegation by policy function, treaty level.

some degree of responsibility and control in 88 percent of all policy functions at the treaty level. This finding helps explain the prevalence with which adjudication functions are delegated. Although it is the most frequently delegated function, there are only fifteen instances in which adjudication is *only* delegated—that is, there is no state actor involved. States prefer to work out disagreements through negotiation, and only in the case of last resort will they consult with a third-party agent, often the International Court of Justice.

As Table 2.3 demonstrates, when states do choose to delegate, they greatly prefer IOs as agents. Because they have already invested in IOs, and can directly control their work as well as their budget, this preference appears to help reduce sovereignty costs. Moreover, they overwhelmingly prefer IOs for matters of implementation and very rarely for other functions. This lends some support for the transaction cost account of

TABLE 2.3
Total Number of Policy Functions Delegated to Each Actor, Treaty Level

State	State Agent	State Agent %	IO Agent	IO Agent %	Private Agent	Private Agent %
Rule making	18	21%	41	10%	6	9%
Adjudication	11	13%	39	10%	23	33%
Implementation	45	52%	259	64%	25	36%
Monitoring	8	9%	50	12%	11	16%
Enforcement	5	6%	15	4%	5	7%
TOTAL (per actor)	87	100%	404	100%	70	100%

Note: Percentages may exceed 100 due to rounding.

delegation: principals agree to trade some degree of control for information—in the form of IO expertise.[55]

Table 2.3 also shows the small role that private agents play. At the treaty level, only 3.8 percent of all policy functions were delegated to private actors. Recall that more than one actor can be responsible for the same policy function; as such, the 3.8 percent figure does not imply that these functions are delegated *exclusively* to private actors. When states do delegate to private actors, they tend to select those functions with low sovereignty costs, especially implementation. For this reason, two of the three high-sovereignty-cost functions—rule making and enforcement—are seldom delegated to private agents. The prevalence with which states delegated to private actors to adjudicate is the notable exception, because such ceding of control over this policy function could potentially impose considerable sovereignty costs. However, closer examination reveals that delegation of adjudication tasks follows the logic outlined above: private agents seldom act as the sole agent charged with a given task. Instead, private agents are just one of a number of actors, and are often named as the agent of last resort. In most instances, states agree that conflicts will be adjudicated by states themselves; delegation to the International Court of Justice, or a yet-unnamed third-party arbitrator is invoked only in instances when states cannot resolve the disagreement themselves.

Overall, private actors rarely serve as the sole agents at the treaty level (table 2.4). Of the 1,847 policy functions in the sample, only 19, or one-tenth of 1 percent, are delegated solely to private actors. They are indeed a very small part of the story. The majority of these "private agent only"

[55] For further investigation of patterns of delegation to IOs, see Green and Colgan 2013.

TABLE 2.4
Private Actors as *Sole* Agents, Treaty Level (N = 70)

	Policy Functions Delegated	Co-occurring with Another Actor	% of Private Actor as Sole Agent
Rule making	6	6	0%
Adjudication	23	16	30%
Implementation	25	17	32%
Monitoring	11	7	36%
Enforcement	5	5	0%
TOTAL	70	51	27%

functions are adjudication and implementation. In the former, states are likely looking for an impartial arbiter. In most of these cases, the arbiter is yet unknown; there is simply a provision for the creation of independent arbitration in case of unresolved disputes. Thus, the actual act of delegation may never occur. The comparatively large number of adjudication functions delegated to private actors can be explained by this two-tiered approach. In the latter function, states are looking for actors that possess the necessary specialized knowledge. For example, the Scientific Committee on Antarctic Research is one of the few nonstate actors referred to by name in the sample. It is charged with implementation, largely because it is one of the few bodies with the necessary scientific knowledge to evaluate the information that states provide about their behavior.[56]

SUMMARY

There are four main lessons to draw from the treaty-level data. The biggest finding is the nonfinding: private actors do not figure prominently in multilateral environmental treaties. Second, when states do delegate to private agents, it is frequently in tandem with other actors, often states themselves. This leads to a third important lesson: the way in which states are governing appears to be changing. There are more actors responsible for the same tasks. This finding suggests that the field of governance is expanding, which quite simply requires more "hands on deck." Fourth, although the amount of delegation to private actors is increasing, the proportion is not. There are simply more MEAs and thus more work to be done. Private actors are being enlisted in this project, but not at the expense of states or IOs. This is not a zero-sum pattern of governance but an ever-growing one.

[56] Clark 1994.

Post-Treaty Decisions: The Past Five Decades

If the ambit of environmental governance is expanding, growth in delegation at the post-treaty level should be evident—and indeed it is. The sample of post-treaty decisions spans roughly the past five decades—from 1946 to 2008.[57] The post-treaty data show that states delegate more frequently after a treaty has entered into force than during the design of the treaty. Over the sample, 8.4 percent of all policy functions are delegated to private agents; this compares to just 3.8 percent at the treaty level.[58] In other ways, post-treaty patterns of delegation resemble treaty-level patterns: most delegation happens in the recent past, and when states choose to delegate to private agents, the preferred function is implementation. As with the treaty level, states vastly prefer IOs as agents.

WHEN DO STATES DELEGATE?

As with the treaty-level data, it appears that delegation to private agents is largely a modern phenomenon: 67 percent of all functions delegated to them occur in the last twelve years of the sample (figure 2.4).

Though the majority of delegation occurs in the last dozen years of the sample, there are three spikes—in 1954, 1968, and 1981—that merit further examination. Interestingly, one treaty represents the majority of the delegation in these three years: the Asia-Pacific Fishery Commission (formerly the Indo-Pacific Fisheries Council). The commission relies on private agents for different purposes. In 1954, member states nominated workers in the fishery industry to serve on an ad hoc panel to advise the Technical Committee. They also asked that biologists be selected to draft requirements for protection of fish populations in dammed rivers. In 1968 the council planned for the creation of a working party of experts to assess fish stocks—again, expertise is clearly the motivation for delegation. Finally, in 1982, the commission requested that fishery experts conduct country visits in order to prepare draft management policies. All three instances are clearly cases of lowering transaction costs through consultation with experts. In fishery matters, states judged it cheaper to "buy" expertise from private agents than to have it "made" by governments or IOs.[59] The need for expertise is driving much of the delegation at the post-treaty level.

[57] The difference in time frame is due to the availability of data rather than the occurrence of delegation.

[58] Because the documents containing state decisions varied in their format, I used a stratified sample that required estimation of the total number of decisions taken by states in one of the strata. Although there are reasons to think that there may be some upward bias in the estimated rate of delegation in the post-treaty sample, if the real rates were identical, the upward bias would be more than 230 percent, which is highly unlikely.

[59] The "make or buy" decision is applied to firms by Alchian and Demsetz 1972.

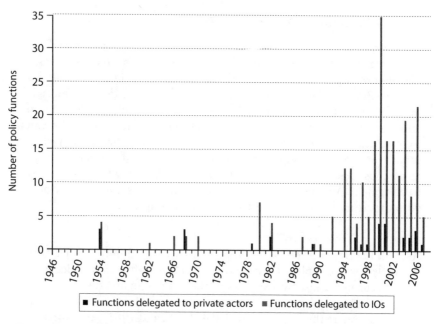

Figure 2.4. Number of policy functions delegated to private agents and international organizations, post-treaty level, 1946–2008.

WHAT POLICY FUNCTIONS DO STATES DELEGATE?

Table 2.5 shows the general distribution of policy functions. Note that adjudication is entirely absent from the sample; not a single post-treaty decision in the sample performs an adjudicatory function. This finding contrasts with the treaty-level data, where adjudication constituted 6.4 percent of all policy functions named. It seems that states tend to decide how conflicts would be resolved at the outset, so that future disputes would not require resolution on an ad hoc basis. Similarly, there are very few instances of enforcement in the post-treaty sample; they constitute a mere 2.3 percent of all policy functions. Again, this suggests that states prefer to decide on compliance issues before entering an agreement.

Despite the relative paucity of adjudication and enforcement functions, overall states appear to be much more comfortable delegating once the treaty has entered into force (figure 2.5). The overall rate of delegation across the four types of policy functions (because there are no instances of adjudication) is 56 percent. Monitoring and implementation are the most frequently delegated. Even though rule making and enforcement have relatively high sovereignty costs, they are delegated quite frequently. This suggests that the nature of delegation at the post-treaty level is somehow different and does not present the same threats to states' autonomy. The

TABLE 2.5
Distribution of Policy Functions, Post-Treaty Level

	N	%
Rule making	135	30.8%
Adjudication	0	0.0%
Implementation	222	50.7%
Monitoring	71	16.2%
Enforcement	10	2.3%
TOTAL	438	100.0%

discussion below indicates the technical nature of post-treaty delegation, and of rule making in particular, and provides support for this assertion. In sum, delegation is much less problematic in post-treaty decision making.

TO WHOM DO STATES DELEGATE?

As with the treaty-level data, the post-treaty data shows that states prefer to delegate to IOs (table 2.6). When private actors are named as agents, they are overwhelmingly selected for implementation tasks, as well as rule-making tasks. This latter finding is interesting and appears inconsistent with the treaty-level data, where states delegate rule making much less frequently. Given that rule making has relatively high sovereignty costs, we would not expect there to be much delegation of this function at all, much less to private actors. However, it turns out that private actors *never* serve as the sole agent in instances of rule making at the post-treaty stage; states or IOs are *always* named for these tasks as well. There is a similar trend at the treaty level, where private actors were often named as "adjudicators of last resort"; here, they serve as "rule makers of last resort."

Moreover, not all rule making is the same; some rules have greater implications for state autonomy than others. Thus, rules that set targets for greenhouse gas emissions have much higher sovereignty costs than those that set forth technical reporting requirements about emissions. Although technical questions can be very political—determining costs for winners and losers—they are often of a magnitude different from more basic rules about distribution. And, indeed, we find at the post-treaty level, that technical rule making abounds; 70 percent of all functions delegated to private agents are to solicit expert input. For example, in the 1954 meeting of the Indo-Pacific Fisheries Council, states delegate to biologists and engineers to draft dam-specific rules about fish ladders and other measures to preserve fish production. To be sure, rules to ensure the sustainability

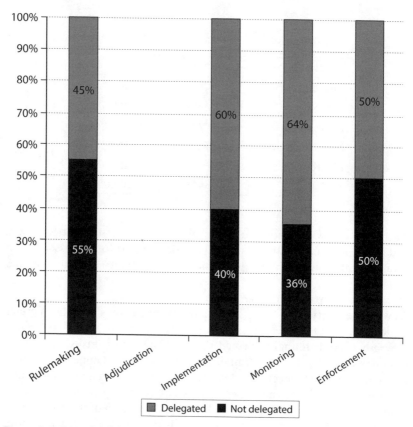

Figure 2.5. Rates of delegation by policy function, post-treaty level.

of a fishery are important but are on a political scale different from those that have wide-reaching and potentially costly domestic impacts.

Although private actors never serve as the sole agents in rule-making functions, they are selected as the sole agent for other tasks. Of all functions delegated to private agents, 13 percent are "agent only" (though note that this is only four functions). Three of the functions delegated solely to private actors are focused on implementation; one is focused on monitoring. Again, this confirms that when states choose private actors as agents, they prefer to delegate those functions with low sovereignty costs.

SUMMARY

Delegation in the post-treaty phase appears to be a somewhat different phenomenon. Delegation is much more common, and so is delegation to private agents. Given that these decisions are more easily reversed, and

TABLE 2.6
Total Number of Policy Functions Delegated to Each Actor, Post-Treaty Level

	State Agent	% of Total Functions Delegated to State Agents	IO Agent	% of Total Functions Delegated to IOs	Private Agent	% of Total Functions Delegated to Private Actors
Rule making	39	27%	56	23%	7	23%
Adjudication	0	0%	0	0%	0	0%
Implementation	72	50%	139	57%	20	65%
Monitoring	29	20%	45	18%	4	13%
Enforcement	4	3%	5	2%	0	0%
TOTAL	144	100%	245	100%	31	100%

Note: Percentages may exceed 100 due to rounding.

are narrower in scope, this finding is unsurprising: as sovereignty costs fall—which they do by definition with post-treaty decision making—the rate of delegation increases. Similar to the treaty data, we find that delegation to private actors happens most frequently in the recent past. However, so does the majority of decision making. Indeed, fully 85 percent of all policy functions in the sample occur after 1990. Again, this is evidence of an overall expansion of governing activities rather than a shift from public to private authority.

The Role of Expertise

The final step in this exploratory mission is to look more closely at the positive cases. In the instances where states do delegate to private actors, what is the subject matter of the treaties, and what, specifically, is requested of them? Three main trends stand out.

First, at the treaty level, the majority of the treaties that involve private actors—fully 60 percent—are related to species management. These include a variety of MEAs pertaining to biodiversity, water birds, fisheries, dolphins, seals, endangered species, timber, and tree species. These types of treaties are highly technical, involving complex scientific information as well as a significant number of reporting requirements. In short, these are just the type of MEAs that would benefit greatly from scientific expertise—to inform the rule-making process, to monitor progress, and to evaluate data. Diplomats are generally ill-equipped to decide on what level of fish catch is sustainable (though they certainly advise on what level is economically advantageous). They are similarly disadvantaged at evaluating the health of species or the success of certain measures on the basis of incoming scientific data. In some cases, they may enlist the aid of scientists at the domestic level, but in others, they turn to independent scientists or scientific bodies to help make sense of complex technical information.[60]

Second, and consistent with the first trend, states are frequently asking private actors for their expert opinions and codifying these requests in the body of the treaty. Thus, in the 1992 North Atlantic Marine Mammal Agreement, states agreed to create a scientific committee composed of independent experts. The 1996 Convention on Sea Turtles created a consultative committee, composed in part of nonstate actors, responsible for evaluating the efficiency of various conservation measures and proposing additional measures that might be taken.

Finally, the role of expertise is similarly important at the post-treaty level, where states frequently tap private agents for expert input and review. Parties to the Antarctic Treaty and its associated agreements frequently request that an independent scientific advisory body, the Scientific Committee on Antarctic Research, provide its expert opinion. In one post-treaty decision, SCAR is requested to help prepare plans to study the Southern Ocean. In a later decision, they request that SCAR undertake three specific studies related to hydrocarbons in the Antarctic environment and develop a new methodology for measuring them. Similar examples are evident in other MEAs. In the Convention on International Trade in Endangered Species, for example, states request that the International Union for Conservation of Nature, an international scientific body, review the status of certain species listed in the treaty. The Convention on Biological Diversity called on the Global Invasive Species Program, an NGO, to develop a global strategy to deal with invasive species. These examples all illustrate that there is one role in particular that accounts for much of the delegation to private agents, that of the scientific expert.

CONCLUSION

Theories of delegation abound; data do not. Thus, the data presented here has helped fill in the considerable number of blanks in the study of international delegation. The history of delegation in environmental law making reveals several important findings. First, and most importantly, private actors are a small part of international environmental law. States rarely delegate to them and do so in ways that limit their influence.

---

[60] This is consistent with Steffek 2010, who finds that the environmental policy field is more open to transnational actors because of a demand for expert knowledge.

Second, throughout the law-making process—during treaty negotiation and in post-treaty decision making—private actors fulfill a niche role as experts. For this reason, the majority of delegation to private agents occurs in treaties that involve technical and scientific issues, often related to the management of species. Experts from NGOs, the private sector, and the scientific community are called upon to provide their input and opinions, based on their preexisting expertise. Otherwise, states prefer to do the job themselves—especially when it comes to potentially sovereignty-constraining issues, such as making or enforcing rules. The second-best option for carrying out agreements is international organizations, which are more closely controlled by their principals than private agents.

The data also show that international environmental law is expanding, as are the numbers of actors responsible for its implementation. There is a surprising amount of redundancy in carrying out each of the policy functions: often there are multiple actors responsible for the same task. If the number of MEAs continues to grow, and the "redundancy approach" continues, then we should expect a growing role for private agents. To be sure, this does not mean that there will be *less* public authority; there is no evidence to support that contention. But it does mean that private actors will continue to play a small but predictable part. To the extent that environmental issues become more scientifically complex, then we should expect some proportional increase in the role of private actors.

The main finding of this chapter is that delegated private authority is hardly rampant. If anything, private actors are more frequently enlisted as "helpers," contributing largely to the implementation of treaties because of their expertise. Yet this finding raises a further question. If private actors are growing more important in global governance, as many claim, where is this phenomenon occurring? If the loci of authority are multiplying and diffusing, and the nature of state authority is changing, then there should be evidence of a growth in private authority somewhere. Clearly, this growth is not occurring through delegated authority. Thus, we turn to an investigation of entrepreneurial authority—our second exploratory mission—to better understand the ways in which private actors are serving as rule makers in global environmental politics.

CHAPTER THREE

Governors of the Market: The Evolution of Entrepreneurial Authority

DELEGATED PRIVATE AUTHORITY plays a relatively consistent but minor role in global environmental politics. As I have demonstrated, private agents are most often useful for their expertise in technical matters and are delegated other tasks with little impact on state autonomy. However, they are rarely charged with potentially weightier tasks such as enforcement or rule making, and they are seldom the sole agents charged with a given task.

Yet, if private actors are increasingly important in the landscape of global governance as many have claimed, where and how are they projecting authority? The answer to this question lies in the concept of entrepreneurial authority—situations in which private actors create rules or set standards *without the explicit delegation* of authority by states. The data presented in this chapter show that entrepreneurial authority is on the rise, which not only helps answer the question outlined above but, in so doing, confirms the importance of distinguishing between different types of private authority.

This chapter is the second of two exploratory missions of this book, which aims to understand the "big picture" of private authority over the past century. The data presented here are among the first to examine aggregate patterns of entrepreneurial authority in the area of environmental policy. The aim of the analysis is to provide a basic picture—a snapshot in time—of the creation of private rules and standards and their basic attributes. These new data provide a critical first step in understanding both the scope and effects of private authority in global governance.

Entrepreneurial authority can take many forms. The data presented in this chapter focus on one specific type, referred to by some as "civil regulations" and others as certification schemes. It includes "codes, regulations, and standards that are not enforced by any state and that address the . . . environmental impacts of global firms and markets, especially in developing countries."[1] Thus, one can purchase products that are "carbon neutral," "organic," or "sustainable," according to standards created by

[1] Vogel 2008, 262.

nonstate actors. Conformity with these standards is usually conveyed by a label or seal of approval. But entrepreneurial authority is more than just certification schemes. It also includes codes of conduct or best practices that guide behavior. The International Chamber of Commerce's Business Charter for Sustainable Development sets forth sixteen principles for environmental management that have been adopted by more than twenty-three hundred companies globally.[2] This can be viewed as an instance of entrepreneurial authority; the ICC is a private actor that dictates standards for behavior and practice that have been adopted by others. One of the goals of this chapter is to outline precisely what types of activities fall under this label.

The data include all known forms of transnational civil regulations relating to the environment from 1954 to 2009. They reveal several important trends that further our understanding of the role of private authority in world politics. First, entrepreneurial authority is growing precipitously—particularly in the past decade. More private actors are making rules, and more firms, organizations, and individuals are adopting them. This provides additional evidence that the loci of authority are expanding. Second, the data provide preliminary evidence for the theory presented in chapter 1: entrepreneurial authority appears to be emerging in areas that require technical expertise and that have relatively weak international focal institutions governing them. Third, most civil regulations require third-party certification. This finding demonstrates that creators of civil regulations are concerned about compliance; these are indeed real governance tools. Moreover, the growth of third-party certification is creating a demand for certifiers. These certifiers are, in effect, regulators: they determine who is following the rules and who is not. The trend toward third-party certification has therefore created an additional layer of private authority. More rule makers means more rules, and more adjudicators of those rules. In short, private authority is creating the demand for more of the same. Fourth, the growing number of amended civil regulations—those which adopt some part of existing private rules—demonstrates the complex relationships among different sources of entrepreneurial authority. When newly created civil regulations draw on existing ones, certain rules may emerge as "standard practice" among a variety of related certification schemes. Thus, there is a possibility for convergence among a diverse set of civil regulations, creating robust and widely accepted private rules.

I begin by examining what we already know about entrepreneurial authority, including the extensive set of labels that have arisen to describe it, and extant explanations for why it has emerged. The data then help to fill

---

[2] http://www.iisd.org/business/tools/principles_icc.aspx.

in the numerous gaps in our collective knowledge. Finally, using the case of carbon standards, I examine the implications of the growing *density* of entrepreneurial authority—when multiple rules overlap and compete in a given issue area. A detailed examination of one sector, carbon standards, underscores the point that often we cannot consider private rules separately but must examine them within the broader context of competition and cooperation, both among private rules and between public and private forms of authority.

What Do We Know about Entrepreneurial Authority?

There are significant gaps in our knowledge of entrepreneurial authority. We know relatively little about its extent, the degree to which it has changed over time, or the variation across issue areas in world politics. In the environmental arena, we know a lot about a few cases—like forestry, and increasingly, climate change—but very little about most. By and large, we have few quantitative data.

This is not to suggest that private authority is a black hole. In this section, I review what we *do* know about entrepreneurial authority and use this as the basis for the exploration of the data in the rest of the chapter. The work to date can be roughly divided into three main areas: what, how, and why. The "what" examines the definitional issues: entrepreneurial authority has many names, corresponding to different subtypes. I begin by sorting through the many labels to clarify what types of activities are subsumed under the guise of entrepreneurial authority. The "how" explains the mechanics of entrepreneurial authority—how these private actors gain and maintain rule-making authority. Many of these discussions focus on the legitimacy of private actors as global governors. The "why" offers explanations for the occurrence of entrepreneurial authority. Some of these causal arguments have been discussed in chapter 1, but I revisit the key explanations here.

Definitions: What Activities Constitute Entrepreneurial Authority?

Entrepreneurial authority is a form of regulation, which can be understood as "the organization and control of economic, political and social activities by means of making, implementing, monitoring and enforcing rules."[3] Certification schemes, also referred to as "nonstate market driven" governance, are perhaps the most common form of

---

[3] Mattli and Woods 2009a, 1.

entrepreneurial authority.[4] These governance systems obtain authority through the logic of the market and rely on evaluations by external audiences; the role of governments is limited to permitting the occurrence of these nonstate, market-driven rules. Discussions of the governance of global value chains by firms and NGOs describe the same phenomenon: "the shifting governance structures [that arise] in sectors producing for global markets."[5] In the environmental arena, certification schemes verify the environmental and social attributes of a diverse array of commodities including fisheries, forestry, coffee, foodstuffs, cocoa, tea, cosmetics, among many others.[6] There are similar arrangements in the area of labor and apparel.[7]

But entrepreneurial authority is more than just certification schemes. Additional rule-making activities fall under the rubric of entrepreneurial authority.[8] Information-based standards, for example, set forth informational requirements for participating actors, who must gather and report the requisite information.[9] In some cases, private standard setters simply assemble the framework for information gathering; in others, they actually collect and report the information. The Global Reporting Initiative has created a comprehensive sustainability reporting framework that "enables all organizations to measure and report their economic, environmental, social and governance performance – the four key areas of sustainability."[10] Although GRI aggregates available data from users, its main goal is not to collect and disseminate this information; it simply provides the tools for participating actors to do so themselves.[11] The Carbon Disclosure Project, by contrast, emphasizes the dissemination of reported information, sending out annual surveys to firms in order to compile public reports about firms' activities and emissions.

Environmental management systems are yet another form of entrepreneurial authority. These focus on how individual firms and other organizations manage environmental issues internally, through decisions such

---

[4] Cashore 2002; Cashore, Auld, and Newsom 2004; Bernstein and Cashore 2007.

[5] Gereffi, Humphrey, and Sturgeon 2005, 79. See also Nadvi 2008.

[6] In forestry, see, e.g., Cashore, Auld, and Newsom 2004; Gulbrandsen 2004; Meidinger 2006; in fisheries, see e.g., Constance and Bonanno 2000.

[7] O'Rourke 2003; Barrientos and Smith 2007; Bartley 2007; Locke, Fei, and Brause 2007.

[8] These categories are drawn selectively from Auld, Bernstein, and Cashore 2008.

[9] Gupta 2010 refers to this as "governance by disclosure." Examples drawn from private authority include Dingwerth and Eichinger 2010; Haufler 2010.

[10] https://www.globalreporting.org/information/about-gri/what-is-GRI/Pages/default.aspx.

[11] Reports from participating organizations have been available through GRI's "Sustainability Disclosure Database" since November 2011. Available from http://database.global-reporting.org/.

as energy consumption, efficiency, and procurement.[12] The International Organization for Standardization (ISO) 14001 standard is an example of an environmental management standard created by a private body.[13] It requires that participating firms devise their own environmental goals and then implement a management system to achieve those goals. Conformity with the standard can be evaluated either by the firm itself or by a third-party. ISO 14001 is not prescriptive about specific behaviors; nonetheless, it promulgates a set of rules and practices for implementing management systems.

A final common type of entrepreneurial authority is the industry code. The chemical industry created the Responsible Care program in response to the Bhopal disaster in which chemicals leaking from the Union Carbide pesticide plant in Bhopal killed thousands of Indian citizens. The industry responded by creating ten principles to be adopted by chemical producers to improve safety and enhance transparency. These principles were initially promulgated by the Canadian Chemical Producers Association but have since spread to be broadly adopted among producers globally.[14] This voluntary framework provides a set of standards that govern the behavior of participating firms.

These categories provide some sense of what types of activities constitute entrepreneurial authority. They all share three key characteristics: there is no delegation of authority by the state, private actors are engaged in rule-making or standard-setting activities, and these actors must attract adherents who adopt the standards.

Other labels are also used to describe entrepreneurial authority, including voluntary clubs,[15] self-regulation,[16] and regulatory standard-setting institutions,[17] to name just a few. Often, the empirical overlap among these different theoretical categories is considerable. As is explained more fully below, I exclude "first-party" codes of conduct, in which the rule maker and rule adopter are one and the same. Vogel speaks more broadly of "civil regulation" that "employ[s] private, non-state or market-based regulatory frameworks to govern multinational firms and global supply networks."[18] I use Vogel's term "civil regulation" to describe the diverse types of private authority examined in this chapter and use it interchangeably with the terms "entrepreneurial authority" and "private standards."

[12] Wood 2005.

[13] Clapp 1998; Potoski and Prakash 2005; Prakash and Potoski 2006; Delmas and Montiel 2008.

[14] Garcia-Johnson 2000; King and Lenox 2000.

[15] Prakash and Potoski 2006.

[16] Haufler 2001; Porter and Ronit 2006; King and Toffel 2009.

[17] Abbott and Snidal 2009.

[18] Vogel 2009, 153.

Mechanics: How Does Entrepreneurial Authority Work?

With so many diverse forms of entrepreneurial authority, there are a range of approaches to undertsanding how it operates. First, some works examine how private actors acquire rule-making authority. These are distinct from explanations of the emergence of private authority that focus on system-level attributes, such as the nature of globalization. Rather, these works emphasize the strategies and attributes of individual rule makers. Cashore argues that successful private rule makers cultivate legitimacy from external audiences who consent to private rules "based on material benefits . . . moral suasion . . . or because it has become an accepted and understandable practice."[19] Later work expands this explanation to include a gradual process whereby private rule makers build widespread support and, if successful, cultivate a transition to norm-driven behavior, which culminates in political legitimacy.[20] In their work on global production, Abbott and Snidal trace the evolution and implementation of civil regulation through the five stages of the regulatory process: agenda setting, negotiation, implementation, monitoring, and enforcement. They argue that variation in the competencies of different actors at different stages of the process will change the relative bargaining power of each group and, ultimately, the final institutional arrangement.[21]

Second, because virtually anyone can become a source of entrepreneurial authority, scholars have been particularly preoccupied with the effects of competing civil regulations. This discussion began in the forestry sector, where an NGO-based certification scheme was quickly followed by competition from an industry-promulgated scheme.[22] Fransen explicitly asks why the proliferation of civil regulations does not always produce convergence among them. He argues that political differences among interest groups produces value conflicts, which result in harmful fragmentation.[23] Green suggests a more implicit approach to convergence, whereby carbon offset standards choose to recognize others in the field, thereby producing some degree of harmonization.[24] Sabel and colleagues offer a reputational model for the upward harmonization of standards, which allows leaders to publicize their accomplishments and push laggards toward better behavior.[25]

Third, although it is a fundamental question for both scholars and practitioners, we know surprisingly little about whether entrepreneurial

---

[19] Cashore 2002, 511.
[20] Bernstein and Cashore 2007.
[21] Abbott and Snidal 2009.
[22] Cashore, Auld, and Newsom 2004. See also Gulbrandsen 2005; Meidinger 2006.
[23] Fransen 2011.
[24] Green 2013.
[25] Sabel, O'Rourke, and Fung 2000.

authority affects real-world outcomes.[26] Although there is fairly good data on the uptake of entrepreneurial authority,[27] there is much less work on its impact on social and environmental outcomes.[28] Does fair trade agriculture improve the lives of poor farmers? Does sustainably harvested fish improve the long-term prospects for fisheries? In general, "there is little systematic evidence about how most civil regulations have actually affected corporate practices and the extent to which they have ameliorated the oft-cited shortcomings of state regulation and interstate treaties."[29] To be fair, numerous measurement challenges are associated with evaluating the effects of civil regulations.[30] Nonetheless, many extant studies focus on management systems, information reporting, or other process-oriented goals rather than real-world results. There is now an emerging research network run by the ISEAL Alliance that seeks to fill this gap, focusing on the real-world effects of certification schemes,[31] but its work is preliminary.

Explanations: Why Does Entrepreneurial Authority Occur?

One explanation for the creation of civil regulations stems from macro-level changes in the global economy that result in governments' diminished ability to regulate industry and the global supply chain.[32] Another view is that private actors have the expertise that governments lack and are generally better-equipped to serve as regulators.[33] Thus, civil regulation is seen as a way to fill in the regulatory gaps created by the globalization of the economy. Ruggie describes this phenomenon more abstractly, as a "reconstitution of the public domain" in which the interstate realm is becoming embedded in a broader transnational arena, which includes many types of nonstate actors.[34] Others take a more cynical view, seeing entrepreneurial authority as a way to manage risk or preempt govern-

[26] Bartley 2010.

[27] See, e.g., Auld, Gulbrandsen, and McDermott 2008; Green 2010b; Hamilton et al. 2009; Hamilton et al. 2010.

[28] For a useful review of extant sources of information, see Blowfield 2007.

[29] Vogel 2008, 267. Blowfield 2007 poses the same question with respect to the effects of corporate social responsibility on social justice.

[30] Lenox and Nash 2003; Khanna and Brouhle 2009.

[31] See Esbenshade 2004; Barrientos and Smith 2007; Locke, Fei, and Brause 2007.

[32] Knill and Lehmkuhl 2002; Gulbrandsen 2004; Pattberg 2005; Pattberg 2007; Auld, Bernstein, and Cashore 2008; Dingwerth and Pattberg 2009. I make a similar argument in chapter 1, that heterogeneous preferences among key states (which would result in a lack of regulation) are a key explanator of entrepreneurial authority.

[33] Büthe and Mattli 2011.

[34] Ruggie 2004, 499.

mental regulation.[35] A variant of this explanation is that civil regulation emerges when civil society threatens boycotts and naming and shaming campaigns; in these instances, agreement between business and civil society on ways to lessen environmental impact is a second-best solution.[36] Or, as Bartley argues, civil regulation is the result of political contestation, in which states, NGOs, and market actors struggle for supremacy in the creation of market institutions.[37] A more optimistic view is that codes of conduct and other types of standards are a way to promote learning and best practices in a given industry.[38]

What We Do Not Know about Entrepreneurial Authority

The study of entrepreneurial authority goes well beyond political science; diverse bodies of research in public administration, management, sociology, and environmental studies provide some of the basic what, how, and why of entrepreneurial authority. There remain, however, some sizable questions. As noted above, we know relatively little about whether and how civil regulations have actually affected environmental quality. Moreover, there is a dearth of large-N and comparative research. Most studies tend to focus on a single standard or certification scheme; among these, forestry is the overwhelming favored object of study. Vogel notes that "more research has been published on the [Forest Stewardship Council] and forestry codes than on all other codes combined."[39] Some works expand beyond one standard to look more broadly at the sector. Even fewer efforts compare private standards across issue areas.[40] The result of this bias is limited knowledge about the universe of cases, and a lack of knowledge about many understudied standards.

Finally, there are only a few studies on why and how competing civil regulations result in convergence or fragmentation of entrepreneurial authority.[41] When multiple civil regulations exist in a given sector, when should we expect them to converge upon one agreed upon set of practices, and how might such convergence occur? This chapter addresses these important questions by examining the content of each set of civil

---

[35] Garcia-Johnson 2000; Haufler 2001.

[36] Conroy 2007; King 2007.

[37] Bartley 2007.

[38] This is the basis of the Global Compact, which is described by John Ruggie, its creator, as "a learning forum." See Ruggie 2002 and Kell and Levin 2003. Haufler 2001, 27, notes that self-regulation is a way of coming to consensus about the relative costs and benefits of voluntary initiatives.

[39] Vogel 2008, 275.

[40] Notable exceptions include Bartley 2003; Bartley 2007; Auld 2008.

[41] See Cashore, Auld, and Newsom 2004; Auld et al. 2009; Fransen 2011; Green 2013a.

regulations, and the extent to which it draws on other existing schemes. The mechanisms of convergence are probed in greater depth in the final section, which looks specifically at civil regulations in the area of carbon accounting and offsets.

The data and analysis presented here address all of these gaps and make four important contributions. First, since most research on civil regulation focuses on a single certification scheme or those within a single issue area, one key goal of this dataset is to contribute to our collective understanding about what constitutes the universe of cases. Second, though there is a considerable body of literature arguing that civil regulation and private authority more broadly are on the rise, there are few, if any, large datasets to substantiate this claim.[42] The data presented here are able to provide richer empirical detail, and therefore theoretical nuance, to this discussion. Third, the data are broken down into individual sectors to examine patterns of variation in entrepreneurial authority across environmental issues. This approach provides a broader picture of the kinds of environmental issues addressed through civil regulation. Fourth, it provides preliminary insights into patterns of interaction among certification schemes within a specific issue area.

The Data

The dataset offers a comprehensive picture of transnational environmental civil regulation as a way to conduct basic descriptive inference about this political and regulatory phenomenon. The primary challenge of compiling the data is determining the universe of cases. Few works in the scholarly literature have attempted a complete catalog of entrepreneurial authority.[43] Thus, the first step requires locating both scholarly and policy works that discuss civil regulation at any level beyond an individual case.

The departure point was the extensive list of certification schemes available at Ecolabel Index, which aims to gather information about all ecolabels (i.e., environmental certification schemes) on one common platform.[44] In turn, they compiled their database through extensive web research as well as submissions and suggestions by environmental certification schemes and other interested parties.[45] I triangulated the data

[42] Vogel 2008.

[43] The best recent effort is Abbott and Snidal 2009, though their data are broader than just entrepreneurial authority.

[44] See http://www.ecolabelindex.com/about/ for information about their goals and practices.

[45] Anastasia O'Rourke, personal communication, 15 April 2010. As of 17 September 2009, there were 161 different certification schemes listed on Ecolabel Index.

from Ecolabel Index by comparing it with multiple additional sources in the academic and policy literatures. With this extensive list, websites and organizational documents were reviewed to ascertain whether each scheme met the transnational criterion described below. In cases where there was ambiguity about the transnational criterion or other information, a brief email survey was sent. Of the approximately fifty email surveys sent, only three organizations failed to respond. These nonresponses were omitted from the dataset. In some cases, the email surveys yielded additional sources of information on various civil regulations or sectors, which were also examined for additional labeling schemes; any "missing" private rules that met the transnational criteria were subsequently added to the dataset. In sum, a broad set of data sources was used to ensure that the dataset is as complete as possible. Moreover, the quality and breadth of the data was improved through an iterative process of finding new information, checking for potential omissions, and making adjustments as appropriate.

This process yields information on what appears to be all existing transnational civil regulation related to the environment.[46] The dataset lists 119 private codes, regulations, or standards that include some environmental criteria.[47] I exclude civil regulations that focus exclusively on labor practices, social justice, or human rights.[48]

The civil regulations included in the dataset are limited in two important ways. First, only *transnational* civil regulations are included. Civil regulations are considered transnational if they function in at least two countries. The "two-country" criterion can be met in two ways. It can mean that the civil regulation is used in multiple countries. An example would be Fairtrade International, which has certified products sold by retailers around the world. Alternatively, the two-country criterion can mean that certification and verification activities take place in two countries. For example, a civil regulation such as a certification scheme may be used for marketing purposes in Canada but may require inspections and reporting in Malaysia. If the regulation requires activities in both the producer and the consumer nation, then the two-country criterion is met.[49]

[46] The list of standards is an amalgam of certification and labeling schemes presented in Usui 2007; Bartley 2007; Conroy 2007; Kollmuss, Zink, and Polycarp 2008; Abbott and Snidal 2009; Starobin 2009.

[47] This determination was made by examining the website, mission statement, annual report, and other organizational materials.

[48] However, if they have multiple goals that include specific environmental criteria or, more generally, sustainability or sustainable development, then these civil regulations are included in the universe of cases.

[49] The only exception here is national organic labels, which may draw products from other countries but are sold exclusively in one nation. These were excluded simply because of the number of them.

The logic behind this criterion is to capture the global reach of the value chain; without the movement of goods across borders, such interventions would not be possible.[50]

Second, voluntary rules created or run by governments are excluded, as are those created by a firm solely for its own products. In other words, standards created and administered by governments such as the U.S. Department of Agriculture Organic standard or Taiwan's Green Mark are not included in the dataset because they are not private forms of authority. However, if civil regulations draw on some portion of public rules (for example, those created by an international organization), while still generating their own substantive provisions, then this is considered an "amended" private standard.[51]

In other cases, firms have their own green labels, sometimes referred to as "first-party certification."[52] For example, Philips has a line of products called Philips Green Logo, which states that certain products among those they manufacture are "better" for the environment, according to some criteria. These are essentially forms of self-regulation: the actor is not adopting someone else's rules but rather creating its own. These rules are therefore excluded. For similar reasons, I exclude corporate codes of conduct focused on individual corporations.[53]

By and large, the civil regulations examined here are rules governing the production of consumer products. These are frequently goods that bear logos—such as "dolphin-safe" tuna or "fair trade" coffee. However, not all of the regulations presented here conform to this model. Some fall under the categories of information-based standards, environmental management schemes, or industry codes, as described above.

The dataset includes only civil regulations still in use. It does not include regulations that have "died" or merged with other labeling schemes, simply because, without going into the details of each case, there is no ready evidence to show that either of these phenomena has occurred. The data presented here provide a snapshot of civil regulations that are currently active; they do not show the dynamics of change that led to the picture that we see here. Unfortunately, there is no quick remedy for this problem, save to acknowledge it, and note that it likely results in an underestimation of the total number of private standards.[54]

The dataset includes three pieces of information for each private

[50] Gereffi, Humphrey, and Sturgeon 2005.

[51] In some instances, these standards might be consistent with "orchestration," whereby IOs mobilize private actors to help achieve regulatory goals, as long as private actors are promulgating rules to achieve these goals. See Abbott and Snidal 2010.

[52] Gereffi, Garcia-Johnson, and Sasser 2001, 51.

[53] More information about corporate codes of conduct can be found at OECD 1999; Kolk et al. 1999; Kolk and van Tulder 2002.

[54] King, Keohane, and Verba 1994, 133.

standard that meets the transnational criterion (many did not). First, what year was the standard first applied?[55] This approach is used to ensure that all of the schemes listed are in fact operational—that is, that some actor has adopted the rules. Collecting data on the date of creation also provides some insights as to whether the rate of creation of certification schemes is increasing over time. Second, each standard is coded as either "hard" or "soft," in which I draw on Abbott and Snidal's identification of hard law as "legally binding obligations that are precise (or can be made precise through adjudication or the issuance of detailed regulations) and that delegate authority for interpreting and implementing the law."[56] Hard civil regulations can be thought of in a similar way: they may be legally binding, or sanctions may follow from noncompliance. The main difference is that they are voluntary. In other respects, however, they conform to Abbott and Snidal's definition: hard civil regulations are precise, and they delegate authority to a third party to interpret the rules. I operationalize this concept by looking at third-party verification. A hard civil regulation requires third-party verification; in other words, a user of the standard cannot simply declare itself to be in compliance. A soft civil regulation has no such requirement. Tracking whether civil regulations are hard or soft provides information about the overall levels of legalization both within and across sectors.

Finally, each civil regulation is coded as either *de novo* or amended. As the name suggests, *de novo* regulations are entirely new; they are not based on existing regulations. By contrast, in some cases civil regulations are based on existing rules; these are "amended" rules. In other cases, a given certification scheme will draw on an existing one and then add to it, so the net effect is a mix of old and new rules. One example of this phenomenon is Bird Friendly coffee. Bird Friendly coffee has its own criteria for what constitutes shade grown (and therefore bird friendly) coffee beans. However, it also stipulates that the beans be certified organic but relies on an existing methodology for organics criteria. As such, it is coded as an "amended" private standard, using both new and extant standards. Extant labels may be private or public: Bird Friendly coffee, for instance, uses the U. S. Department of Agriculture Organic label. In an ironic twist of self-perpetuation, there are now standards about setting standards.[57] For example, the ISEAL alliance has developed codes

---

[55] If there is more than one standard within a given certification scheme, the date of adoption of the earliest standard is used. For example, in some cases, a given organization has many standards simply because it covers many species; despite the multiple standards, this is counted as one certification scheme.

[56] Abbott and Snidal 2000, 421.

[57] For example, ISEAL's Code of Good Practice, available from http://www.isealalliance .org/our-work/codes-of-good-practice/standard-setting-code or ISO 17021, Part 2, available fromhttp://www.iso.org/iso/catalogue_detail?csnumber=59884.

of good practice to help other actors develop private sustainability standards. Any private standard that uses a standard-setting standard is also coded as "amended."

Although most amended civil regulations are a combination of new and old, there are some that are simply a repackaging of existing ones. The Certified CarbonFree labeling scheme certifies that a given product has a net carbon footprint of zero. That is, all emissions generated in the manufacture of the product are offset through carbon offset projects. However, Certified CarbonFree has not created its own rules for measuring emissions but rather uses existing accepted private standards. As a result, I also code this scheme as "amended," since it does not contain any new rules.

The distinction between *de novo* and amended civil regulation is critical for understanding the spread and depth of entrepreneurial authority. When *de novo* civil regulations proliferate in a given sector, fragmentation is likely: there are multiple regulations with different measures and rules.[58] As the number of *de novo* civil regulations proliferates, the information-signaling value of any given regulation is diminished, because the information that the consumer must obtain about each one increases. Thus, what one private standard considers sustainable forestry might be entirely different from the criteria established by another; indeed, this has occurred in the forestry sector, where two of the largest civil regulations have very different rules. One, created by an NGO, is considered to be much more stringent than the other, which was created by a consortium of timber companies. However, the untrained consumer may have difficulty distinguishing between the two.

Conversely, if a large proportion of civil regulations in a given sector is amended, there is some repetition in the content of the standards. Because each set of civil regulations may draw on different existing rules, many amended rules do not necessarily signify convergence among them. However, at a minimum, it suggests less fragmentation than when there is a large proportion of *de novo* civil regulations.

Simply measuring the number of amended civil regulations indicates only the *possibility* of convergence among standards, not the extent to which it has occurred. In order to understand whether convergence on a particular certification scheme (or schemes) is occurring, one must look closely at the content of each set of rules or the interaction among different sources of entrepreneurial authority.

---

[58] One possible exception to this would be if there is a high level of mutual recognition among different *de novo* certification schemes. However, given fundamental differences in their rules, mutual recognition would likely be more difficult and costly than with amended schemes that share some content.

EMPIRICAL FINDINGS

The dataset contains 119 civil regulations that adhere to the criteria outlined above. The earliest one, Spiel Gut (Good Toy), was founded in 1954 to evaluate the educational and environmental attributes of toys. The subjects of these private standards, described in table 3.2, cover a variety of issues from fisheries to tourism. With the exception of Spiel Gut, most of the earliest civil regulations are focused on organics. Only five were established before 1980; 90 percent of standards in the dataset were created between 1990 and 2009. The most recently created were established in 2009.[59] The data demonstrate four key trends. First, entrepreneurial authority is a relatively new phenomenon that is growing quickly. Second, hard rules, which require third-party verification, are the norm. Third, the proportion of amended standards is growing. Finally, the substantive focus of the standards, on technical issues, is broadly consistent with the theory presented in chapter 1.

Growing Entrepreneurial Authority

The distribution of founding dates in figure 3.1 shows the precipitous increase in civil regulation. This finding is consistent with many conjectures but has yet to be shown in such a comprehensive way. It is also evidence for the "compromise of liberal environmentalism," which predicates environmental protection on the maintenance of liberal economic order.[60] Entrepreneurial authority is by definition, voluntary and thus introduces none of the constraints of domestic regulation or international law. In other words, it promotes environmental protection without the perceived costs of regulation.

Hard Rules Dominate

Interestingly, most civil regulations are hard, requiring some sort of third-party verification. Only 17 percent are soft civil regulations. The prevalence of hard standards, particularly in the recent past, is a significant finding: it demonstrates that these rules are being used as real governance tools. They go beyond mere second-party certification, where the firm itself judges whether it is in compliance. Rather, a hard standard means that any actor that wishes to reap the reputational or monetary benefits of using entrepreneurial authority has to invest some time and effort to do so. The actor must defer to the rules and pay someone to certify

---

[59] The last year for which data were collected was 2009.
[60] Bernstein 2001.

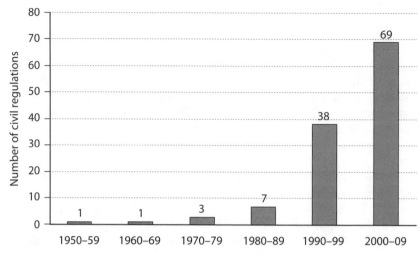

Figure 3.1. Creation of environmental civil regulations, 1950–2009.

compliance with them. Although it may seem rather obvious, there is an important design implication of third-party certification: hard rules are a necessary (though not sufficient) for enforcement.

The prevalence of hard rules also underscores the importance of repu-tational benefits as a potential explanation of the emergence of private authority. If actors choose to defer to entrepreneurial authority because of the expected benefits, then it follows that they would prefer an institu-tional design that would best deliver those benefits. Hard rules introduce the possibility of separating out noncompliers—who would water down the benefits of the standard. In other words, if the rules have no way of distinguishing leaders from laggards, then less information is signaled by adoption of the standard, and the reputational benefits are diminished.

Independent verification of compliance allows for the possibility of sanction. Such a sanction may be administered by the standard-setting organization or by a third party. In most civil regulation, the approach to noncompliance is more managerial than premised on "deep cooperation," focusing on better management of constraints to improve compliance rather than painful sanctions.[61] In general, to the extent that enforcement mechanisms exist, they are to promote communication between the pri-vate regulator and the regulated to discern how to correct inconsisten-cies.[62] The only strong sanction the regulator has is to expel the regulated;

[61] On the managerial approach to compliance, see Chayes and Chayes 1993. On the no-tion of deep cooperation and its associated sanctions, see Downs, Rocke, and Barsoom 1996.

[62] Enforcement mechanisms can also include domestic administrative and judicial mech-anisms; see Cafaggi 2012.

monetary or legal sanctions are very rare.[63] Stronger sanctions tend to come from *outside* of the rule structures created by the standard, such as when an NGO conducts a naming and shaming campaign of standard users who are not in compliance. In this sense, monitoring allows for the possibility of sanction, though the two may not be explicitly linked in the rules themselves. Nonetheless, monitoring is at the very least an indication that these private rule-making systems are concerned with protecting the credibility of their standard.

It is difficult to discern a definitive trend over time. Given the small number of civil regulations created in the first four decades of the dataset, any inference about verification practices from these few schemes will not be robust. However, it is interesting to note that in the past two decades of the sample, the percentage of hard standards ranged from 89 percent (1990–99) to 81 percent (2000–2009). This finding provides a preliminary indication that, as civil regulation has proliferated, third-party verification has become the norm.

Reinventing the Rules: The Growth of Amended Standards

Recall that the data also distinguishes between *de novo* and amended regulations. The former category includes those private standards which have created entirely new sets of rules. By contrast, amended regulations appropriate some aspects of existing civil regulation in the creation of their own standards. This information aims to capture the extent to which entrepreneurial authority is fragmenting—creating ever greater numbers of unrelated schemes—or converging, by reproducing the content of some rules through appropriation or recognition.

Of all civil regulations, 47 percent draw on some existing form of civil regulation; that is, they are amended standards. For example, the Marine Stewardship Council promulgates rules on the activities that constitute sustainable fishing. However, their rules draw on the aforementioned IS-EAL's Code of Good Practice, which details how the standard-setting process should be approached, as well as the Food and Agriculture Organization's Code of Conduct for Responsible Fisheries. Thus, the MSC civil regulations are coded as amended.

The fact that 53 percent of civil regulations are created *de novo* suggests, at first glance, that the world of entrepreneurial authority is not infinitely expanding; in fact, there is a considerable amount of overlap in the content of these privately created rules. To gain greater insight into the meaning of these figures, table 3.1 shows the breakdown of *de novo* versus amended civil regulation over time. Unsurprisingly, in the first

---

[63] Email communication, Greg Busler, Chicago Climate Exchange, 11 January 2010.

TABLE 3.1
Ratio of *De Novo* Civil Regulations over Time

Founding Dates	Total N	Number of De Novo Standards	% of De Novo per Decade
1950-59	1	1	100%
1960-69	1	1	100%
1970-79	3	3	100%
1980-89	7	5	71%
1990-99	38	28	74%
2000-9	69	25	36%
Total	119	63	53%*

*53% is the total proportion of de novo standards across all six decades.

three decades of the sample, all labeling schemes are *de novo*. Because these regulations were pioneers in the field, they had fewer (if any) existing criteria on which to base their own rules.[64] However, in the last three decades of the sample, the number of *de novo* standards falls steadily. More than half the civil regulations in the dataset were created between 2000 and 2008; of those, about 60 percent were based in part on existing rules. In other words, although the *number* of private standards has grown over time, their *substance* is increasingly reproducing itself.

Substantive Focus on Technical Issues

The issues areas covered by the civil regulations in the dataset are shown in table 3.2. Each private standard was assigned one or more issue areas, depending on the content of the rules. The categories were developed after collecting all of the data.[65] They were created inductively, to see whether the rules cluster in particular areas, and whether there are any observable patterns within or across issue areas. The standards can be classified into one or more of sixteen categories. In some cases, a standard will have multiple goals and therefore can be fit into more than one category. In this case, multiple codes were assigned—up to four per individual civil regulation (though most have only one). This classification

[64] This is not to say that there was no civil regulation before 1954, when Spiel Gut was created, just none that meets the criteria of my sample. The ISO has been issuing international standards since 1947. National governments have been doing the same for much longer. On the history of standardization, see Loya and Boli 1999.

[65] The coding instrument lists what activities fall into each category; it is available from the author upon request.

TABLE 3.2
Distribution of Civil Regulations by Sector

Sector	N	% of Total Schemes (total N = 119)	% of Hard Schemes (within sector)	% of De Novo Schemes (within sector)	Years between First Scheme and 2009
Consumer products	16	13%	81%	50%	55
Fisheries	8	7%	100%	63%	42
Organics	10	8%	100%	80%	42
Coffee	9	8%	100%	56%	37
Corporate social responsibility	5	4%	0%	80%	32
Industrial production	6	5%	67%	50%	23
Energy efficiency / renewables	8	7%	100%	75%	21
Agriculture / livestock products	7	6%	100%	57%	21
Buildings / building materials	10	8%	100%	70%	19
Indoor environmental quality	8	7%	88%	50%	19
Textiles	8	7%	100%	88%	17
Plants and flowers	6	5%	100%	50%	17
Tourism	6	5%	67%	67%	16
Forestry / forest products	5	4%	100%	80%	16
Carbon	24	21%	88%	17%	11
Other*	7	6%	57%	57%	na

*Comparing variation within the "other" category is not instructive and thus is omitted.

also permitted measurement of the "age" of each sector, which calculates the number of years that have elapsed between the year the first scheme was created and 2009, the last year included in the dataset. Table 3.2 shows the categories and the frequencies for each; they are listed from oldest to youngest sector. "Other" is used as a catchall for schemes ranging from environmental education to environmentally friendly beaches to professional certification.

The data provide some preliminary evidence in support of the theory of private authority. Civil regulations have emerged in sectors where private expertise can help provide functional benefits. Some sectors require significant technical knowledge and thus could potentially help reduce transaction costs or promote coordination. Indoor air quality standards designate safe emissions levels for volatile organic compounds from furniture, building materials, paints, and adhesives, requiring detailed knowledge not only of the chemical characteristics of these products but also of extant domestic regulation.[66] Other sectors, such as building

[66] http://www.scscertified.com/docs/SCS-EC10.2-2007.pdf.

materials, forestry, carbon, and industrial production, are similarly complex in their technical requirements. In general, the focus of these rules is the management of environmental risks rather than their elimination by abstaining from environmentally damaging behaviors. Managing risks requires expertise, as it is much more complex than avoiding them, which is a simpler regulatory endeavor.

Moreover, although an in-depth investigation of the status of international law in each sector is beyond the scope of this chapter, a quick scan of the sectors shows that some have weak or absent focal institutions. International law on forestry is weak, and the network of regional organizations governing fisheries is highly diffuse.[67] There are few international institutions regulating the environmental impacts of tourism,[68] plants and flowers, and (beyond basic safety requirements) consumer products such as household goods, cosmetics, or alternative medicines. In many areas, such as corporate social responsibility or renewable energy, only soft law exists at the international level, indicating weak focal institutions. Further research on variation in public authority across these issue areas would bring greater focus to these patterns, but a brief review provides preliminary additional support for the hypotheses about the form of private authority.

Several other interesting patterns emerge from table 3.2. First, the age of the sector does not appear to have a strong relationship with the number of civil regulations therein. The three oldest sectors—consumer products, fisheries, and organics—vary considerably in the number of civil regulations. Overall, the mean number of civil regulations per sector is 9, with a standard deviation of 4.9. Fisheries hovers around the mean at 8, while the consumer products sector is approximately 1.5 standard deviations above the mean. By contrast, the carbon sector, which is the youngest at only eleven years, has the largest number of certification schemes (24). This is a full 3 standard deviations above the mean. These highly varied findings suggest that, at best, the number of civil regulations is not simply a function of time. Indeed, the r-squared for the relationship between age and number of civil regulations is a virtually nonexistent 0.02.

Second, the relationship between age and the proportion of *de novo* standards is also ambiguous. That is, they do not indicate that we should expect civil regulations to fragment or converge over time. Because the data do not specify whether a given amended standard adopts rules within the sector, we cannot ascertain whether convergence has *actually* occurred. Rather, we can only surmise whether there is a possibility of convergence, as evidenced by a relatively high proportion of amended

---

[67] Humphreys 1996; Cochrane and Doulman 2005.

[68] There is soft law related to tourism in the Antarctic. See ATCM XXXIV 2011, Resolution 3. Accessed at http://www.ats.aq/devAS/info_measures_listitem.aspx?lang=e&id=496.

standards. In the "average" sector, 62 percent of civil regulations are created *de novo* (with a standard deviation of 17 percent). The major outliers are carbon and textiles. The former has a very low level of *de novo* standards and thus the potential for a considerable amount of convergence. The latter, textiles, has a very high level of *de novo* standards, suggesting more fragmentation.

Third, table 3.2 demonstrates that more than half the categories are entirely comprised of hard standards and that almost all other categories have a majority of the same. Because the norm is clearly to have third-party verified civil regulations, departures from this norm suggest weak rules, which may not induce changes in behavior. The general critique of entrepreneurial authority is its weakness, since it is ultimately not backed by the authority of the state. This finding provides something of a rejoinder to this critique, demonstrating that there is a mechanism for distinguishing between (relatively) strong and weak private rules.

The large number of hard schemes also suggests a corresponding need for actors to serve as third-party verifiers. These verifiers are themselves an additional source of private authority, because they decide which actors are in compliance with a given set of private standards and which are not.[69] In this sense we can think of third-party verification as creating an exponential increase in the depth and significance of private authority.

Finally, it is striking that corporate social responsibility (CSR) is the only category to be composed entirely of soft schemes, standing in stark contrast to the others. One possible interpretation lies in the inherent differences between CSR and other sectors. Whereas all of the other sectors create civil regulations primarily to certify consumer goods, CSR applies to a much broader ambit of practices. In the case of most of the civil regulations, the power lies with the consumer; she decides what basket of goods to consume, on the basis of information about their quality, including environmental attributes. The same logic does not hold in the case of CSR schemes. Executives in a corporation are only marginally trying to convince consumers to buy their products. Rather, they are aiming more generally to improve the value of the brand.[70] Products are tangible, but brands are not. It follows then, that consumers do not have the same power of the purse as they do with other goods. The different configuration of interests offers a preliminary account of why there are no hard labeling schemes in CSR: consumers do not require the same quality assurance.

In sum, the sample provides preliminary support for the theory of private authority. It also shows that the number of civil regulations is growing rapidly. Moreover, there is reason to believe if there is some bias

---

[69] I expand on this point in chapter 4. See also Starobin and Weinthal 2010.
[70] Conroy 2007.

present that it *underestimates* the total number of standards that have been created (and subsequently become inactive).[71] At the same time, the substance of these civil regulations is increasingly being reproduced, particularly in the past decade. Yet there are no overarching patterns to this reproduction of standards and a great deal of variation across sectors. Thus, in some cases—like carbon accounting—there is a possibility for a large amount of convergence, because the proportion of *de novo* labeling schemes is very small. In others, like textiles, energy, and CSR, most schemes promulgate rules *de novo*, suggesting a large amount of fragmentation. Time does not appear to be a factor in either the number of civil regulations in an issue area or the proportion of amended schemes.

THE DYNAMICS OF DENSITY: DOES PROLIFERATION PRODUCE CONVERGENCE?

The rapid growth of civil regulations could result in a patchwork of competing rules or a coherent set of harmonized rules.[72] This issue is critical for two reasons. First, we cannot begin to understand and evaluate the impacts of entrepreneurial authority (recall the dearth of knowledge about their real-world impacts) unless we examine the interactions among them. Second, it provides insights into issues of complexity in global governance more broadly.[73] Certainly, civil regulations do not just interact with each other, but they also exist within the context of international law and organizations. Exploring dynamics of convergence or fragmentation contributes to a better understanding of interactions among private institutions and between public and private ones, and it moves toward developing some answers to the key regulatory question: Under what conditions should we expect convergence or fragmentation of civil regulations?

Two examples will help illustrate the implications of these questions. Competition among civil regulations could produce a race to the bottom or, conversely, a mechanism for "ratcheting up" the stringency of rules, potentially producing better environmental outcomes.[74] If a large

---

[71] Of course, if there were tens of standards created in the earlier part of the sample that subsequently died out, the net growth in the number of standards would be smaller. However, I believe this to be highly unlikely: there is no record in any of the literature of such a phenomenon occurring.

[72] Most work to date focuses on fragmentation with respect to *public* authority. See, e.g., Biermann et al. 2009; Zelli 2011.

[73] The literature on regime complexes addresses this question directly. See, e.g., Raustiala and Victor 2004; Alter and Meunier 2009 and other articles in the special issue and Keohane and Victor 2011.

[74] Sabel, O'Rourke, and Fung 2000; Cashore et al. 2007; Overdevest 2010.

multinational firm chooses to adopt weak rules, greenwashing ensues, and there is little to no change in behavior. However, adoption of comparatively stronger rules could potentially change firm behavior substantially. Multiplying such a choice across entire sectors could have profound impacts on environmental outcomes. Second, interactions between civil regulations and public authority, discussed in further detail below, can potentially induce widespread use of private rules. For example, as part of the World Trade Organization, the Technical Barriers to Trade (TBT) Agreement provides general guidelines for standardization while ensuring that such standards do not obstruct free trade. Although it does not explicitly prescribe a certain set of regulatory standards, the TBT recognizes the ISO—a private regulatory body—as a basis for international standards in the implementation of the agreement.[75]

This section examines the dynamics of fragmentation and convergence in the issue area of carbon measurement and offsetting in greater detail.[76] I identify three mechanisms through which convergence can occur: adoption of some civil regulations by others, as evidenced by the example of the GHG Protocol discussed in detail in chapter 5; deliberate attempts to coordinate among different standards by agreeing upon a set of best practices and reporting requirements among various carbon certification schemes; and the presence of public standards, created through the Kyoto Protocol.

Carbon is the largest sector in terms of the amount of entrepreneurial authority: twenty-four of the civil regulations in the dataset have some component relating to carbon measurement or offsetting. These standards can be classified broadly into two main types. The first type of civil regulation is measurement standards, which prescribe ways to calculate emissions. In some cases, these are linked to reporting procedures as well, though not always. Thus, the Carbon Disclosure Project is a set of civil regulations that collects and discloses information on corporations' emissions. In order to present this information in a readily digestible way, it has developed reporting standards that allow for ready comparison across reporting organizations.[77] These measurement standards are simply about calculating emissions; they are not related to any regulatory requirements for emissions reductions.

The second type of civil regulation in the carbon sector is related to offsetting. States, firms, and individuals can choose to offset their carbon emissions by paying for activities that reduce carbon emissions elsewhere

[75] Büthe and Mattli 2011, 137.
[76] See also Green 2013a.
[77] Increasingly, the Carbon Disclosure Project uses standards created by the Greenhouse Gas Protocol—yet another example of one of the three convergence mechanisms. See Green 2013b.

in the world. Some of these offsetting activities occur under the auspices of the Kyoto Protocol, via the Clean Development Mechanism. Others, however, are purely voluntary—undertaken, as one scholar puts it, for "public image considerations, reduction of guilt, a sense of moral obligation, or all three."[78] The demand for voluntary reductions has given rise to a spate of civil regulations to meet (and capitalize) on that demand.

The carbon sector presents the conditions for convergence: there are a large number of standards, with a relatively small number of *de novo* standards. Hence, a large proportion of civil regulations in the carbon sector draws on existing regulations. The earlier examples demonstrate that these existing regulations need not be restricted to the area of carbon. For instance, the Planet Positive certification "combines best practice from a number of international methodologies," including those related to life-cycle analysis and building standards."[79] Thus, to understand the degree to which there is recognition among different carbon certification schemes, it is necessary to look beyond the number of amended standards to the specific standards they draw upon.

The first way that convergence occurs is through the adoption of extant standards. The Greenhouse Gas Protocol, examined in detail in chapter 5, provides an example of this phenomenon. The protocol provides rules for firms who wish to measure their greenhouse gas emissions. An early entrant in the field of GHG measurement, it has been widely accepted as the gold standard for firm-level emissions. Virtually all firm-level standards created since reference the Greenhouse Gas Protocol in some way. Thus, the Climate Registry, which encourages voluntary reporting in the United States, Mexico, and Canada, based both the accounting principles and reporting mechanics of its own standard on the GHG Protocol.[80] A variety of other carbon accounting standards, including the standard created by the International Organization for Standardization, also rely on the GHG Protocol in a similar fashion. In this sense, there is some convergence occurring among standards: although they may have different foci or applications, they share a common foundation—the GHG Protocol. There is shared content among the multiple standards.

A stronger version of adoption is full recognition or intercompatibility, which also promotes convergence. Thus, the CCB standard for offsets specifies requirements for biodiversity related to carbon offset projects. It can be used in combination with a variety of other offset standards, including the publicly created Clean Development Mechanism. The CCB is

[78] Hunt 2009, 67.

[79] Henry Simonds, Planet Positive, email communication, 15 October 2010; Sarah Gillet, Planet Positive, email communication 19 October 2010.

[80] The Climate Registry, 2008. Accessed at http://www.climateregistry.org/resources /docs/protocols/grp/GRP_3.1_January2009.pdf.

therefore compatible with any other offset standard. The notion of compatibility becomes particularly significant when considering the interrelationships between civil regulations and public regulations (i.e., those promulgated by states).

A second avenue for convergence is through explicit coordination among standards. This is distinct from the adoption of extant civil regulations, because coordination happens *after* the regulation has been created. The International Carbon and Offset Alliance (ICROA) is attempting to promote some degree of harmonization among offset standards by creating rigorous standards and best practices in the voluntary carbon market. Founded in 2008, it draws on extant carbon standards, including the Greenhouse Gas Protocol. Members of ICROA—a variety of nonstate actors involved in the voluntary carbon market—are required to adopt practices used by these approved standards. Moreover, ICROA members are only permitted to purchase offsets generated by a small number of standards: the Gold Standard, the Voluntary Carbon Standard, and the Climate Action Reserve, as well as public standards, including the Clean Development Mechanism, and government-approved schemes.[81] Thus, the partial appropriation of certain civil regulations and the wholesale recognition of others is promoting convergence through a conscious, deliberate strategy of coordination: of the many private carbon standards, only a few are recognized by this effort at harmonization.[82] In other issue areas, new "meta-standard" organizations are emerging, with the explicit goal of creating one overarching set of standards to govern the multiple related ones.[83]

A final pathway toward convergence occurs through public authority, which may, indirectly, encourage such convergence. The voluntary carbon market exists in parallel to the emissions market created by the Kyoto Protocol. The protocol allows countries to meet their reduction requirements through the use of offsets, which are created, bought, and sold via the Clean Development Mechanism. The CDM, therefore, has its own set of rules about what types of offsets are permissible and how they should be measured. Civil regulations created under the voluntary market, though separate from public rules, are very cognizant of them. As a result, there is a high degree of recognition of public rules by private ones. Indeed, fully 77 percent of privately created offset standards recognize

[81] See http://icroa.org/30/carbon-credit-accounting-and-verification-standards.

[82] Sophy Greenhalgh, ICROA. Interview by author, 27 April 2012.

[83] Fransen 2012b. A particularly successful effort at meta-standards is evident in the ISEAL alliance, which created the Code of Good Practice for Setting Social and Environmental Standards. A set of rules and procedures for creating new standards, the code is widely accepted as best practice for the creation of legitimate and robust standards, and has become the accepted practice for private actors creating civil regulations of their own.

rules created under the CDM.[84] This finding indicates convergence in two ways. First, civil regulations in the area of carbon offsets appear to be reinforcing public rules. They are serving as a means to appropriate and further embed rules and practices promulgated by the CDM.[85] Second, this suggests an indirect tie among many civil regulations; they are joined by their common recognition of public rules.

Conclusion

The data presented here furnish new insights into the existence and growth of entrepreneurial authority in the environmental arena, overcoming much of the selection bias that pervades other studies. Several important conclusions can be drawn from the analysis.

First, the data confirm that entrepreneurial authority is growing: there is a precipitous growth in the number of standards over the past two decades. Second, most of these are hard standards. This demonstrates that the creators of civil regulation are concerned with compliance: most private rules require third-party verification. At a minimum, this requirement shows that rule makers are concerned with preserving the perceived legitimacy of their rules. A more optimistic interpretation is that they want to encourage compliance through monitoring and the threat of sanction. It is important to note that third-party verification creates an additional layer of private authority: those responsible for verifying. This suggests that the growth in hard standards will continue to spur exponential growth in entrepreneurial authority. Third, the technical nature of the standards and the relative weakness of associated focal institutions provide preliminary support for the theory. Fourth, the increasing proportion of amended certification schemes over time increases the likelihood of convergence within sectors. As newly created civil regulations draw on existing ones, rules and standards become embedded as "standard practice."

The growth in the number of civil regulations and in the proportion of amended ones raises questions about fragmentation of entrepreneurial authority: Should we expect an ever-expanding universe of civil regulations? The analysis suggests that the answer is emphatically no. Despite an overall growth in the number of civil regulations, the sectoral evidence does not indicate that regulations within issue area increase steadily over time. Indeed, there is no correlation between the "age" of a sector (i.e., the number of years it has had functioning civil regulations) and the number

[84] Green 2013a.
[85] For further elaboration on this mechanism, see Auld and Green 2012.

of civil regulations. No sector appears to be on a path of unabated expansion. Indeed, even the carbon sector, which has seen an explosion of civil regulations in the recent past, has witnessed a decline in the emergence of new standards in the past three years.[86] If the number of civil regulations continues to grow, then we should expect expansion into new issue areas in addition to some increase within existing ones.

Moreover, the chapter suggests mechanisms through which convergence among standards might occur, thus reducing the total number of civil regulations. There may be a gradual process through which one or more standards rises to the top and is increasingly adopted by others. Recognizing the adverse effects of fragmentation, private actors may deliberately seek to coordinate among themselves. Alternatively, public authority may serve as a focal point, encouraging compatibility between privately created civil regulations and public rules. These processes for harmonization and convergence can potentially curtail the unabated growth of entrepreneurial authority.

The data presented here demonstrate a complex landscape of private authority and provide a broader understanding of what is meant by "multiple loci of authority." Not only does private authority coexist with public authority, as demonstrated in the previous chapter, but different forms of private authority interact with each other. Multiple civil regulations in a given issue area translate into competition among sources of entrepreneurial private authority. There is, of course, possibility for convergence among these competing sources, but such an outcome is by no means given.

[86] Capoor and Ambrosi 2008; Capoor and Ambrosi 2009; Hamilton et al. 2009; Kossoy and Ambrosi 2010.

CHAPTER FOUR

Atmospheric Police: Delegated Authority in the Clean Development Mechanism

THUS FAR, THIS BOOK has examined the broad contours of private authority, providing a theoretical explanation for its different forms and much
needed historical context. I now turn to a more focused causal analysis,
explaining why private authority emerges in each of its forms in the context of the climate change regime. This chapter shows that the delegation of key monitoring tasks to private agents in the Clean Development
Mechanism (CDM) of the Kyoto Protocol is consistent with the theory
presented in chapter 1. Delegated authority emerged because both the
supply and demand conditions were met. Private actors had been working on carbon measurement issues since the mid-1990s, thus ensuring a
ready supply of private expertise. In designing the CDM, states sought
various benefits—including reduced transaction costs and reduced likelihood of gaming or cheating—which private actors were better positioned
to provide than any other agent they considered. Finally, I show that
delegation was facilitated by the consensus among key states about the
role and design of the CDM within the protocol and by a strong focal
institution able to oversee agents.

The Kyoto Protocol, which requires developed countries to reduce
their emissions by, on average, 5 percent below 1990 levels between
2008 and 2012, has not been a resounding success. By most accounts,
these reductions are largely symbolic; they are not sufficient to prevent
rapid increases in atmospheric concentrations of greenhouse gases nor
to forestall precipitous increases in mean global temperatures.[1] Moreover, compliance with these modest targets is mixed. Most will meet their
targets, though in many cases, this is largely due to the global economic
slowdown of the last five years (economic growth is robustly correlated
to increased CO_2 emissions). A few countries, such as Austria, Italy, and
Luxembourg will exceed their allotted emissions unless they take further action, such as buying more credits, to achieve compliance.[2] Canada

---

[1] Intergovernmental Panel on Climate Change 2007.
[2] European Environment Agency 2011.

recently announced its intention to withdraw from the Kyoto Protocol, in part because it would have exceeded its target by an estimated 17 percent.[3] And the United States, one of the world's largest emitters, never ratified the agreement. Finally, the protocol expired at the end of 2012, and states are still debating what type of agreement should follow, when it should take effect, and which countries should reduce.

Despite questionable progress in the intergovernmental process, the CDM, one of three market mechanisms created by the protocol, has been remarkably robust. (There have been nontrivial critiques, which I consider below.) The CDM creates an international market for greenhouse gas offsets; it allows developed countries to meet some of their reduction requirements by funding projects that reduce GHG emissions in the developing world. Most nations have enthusiastically participated, and as a result, the market for these activities is currently valued at approximately US$171 billion.[4]

When states designed the CDM between 1999 and 2001, they agreed to delegate the very important roles of monitoring and verification of offset projects to private firms. These firms, called "Designated Operational Entities," are the atmospheric police of the CDM. They decide what is counted, bought, and sold as an emissions offset. They are responsible for maintaining the environmental integrity of this policy instrument.

This chapter tells the story of the institutional design of the CDM: why states chose the structure that they did, and why they delegated key aspects of monitoring to private actors. Private firms were among the first to develop measurement methodologies for carbon offsets, even before the Kyoto Protocol was signed. Their early prominence in the nascent carbon offset market was an attractive quality to states involved in designing the CDM. After Kyoto was signed, time was of the essence; states wanted to get the new market mechanisms up and running as quickly as possible. Choosing a monitor with experience seemed an easy way to expedite the process. Moreover, delegation to private actors avoided the political pitfalls of using a public agent, which would have involved lengthy negotiations.

But, the delegation of authority to private actors in the CDM is not simply a story of early movers. As designers of the institution, states had a pivotal role. In particular, the major polluters of the developed world, along with the largest negotiating bloc of developing countries, were in agreement on the role of a bilateral carbon offset mechanism and

---

[3] UNFCCC 2012, table 2. This figure does not include the use of carbon sinks.

[4] This includes allowance and offset markets, but excludes post-Kyoto transactions (i.e., after 2012). Kossoy and Guigon 2012, 10.

subsequently the need for third-party monitoring of carbon offset projects to reduce the risk of gaming and other opportunistic behavior. The agreement on these two issues was a key factor in delegation to private actors. Moreover, the presence of the executive board—the body charged with overseeing the CDM—helped assuage concerns about the use of private actors as monitors. The board is composed of states and has the final say in all matters related to the CDM. As the focal institution for the CDM, it is responsible for screening and monitoring potential agents. These oversight powers alleviated concerns about private actors overstepping their authority or failing to carry out the tasks delegated to them. Reduced likelihood of agency slack increased the benefits to governments, making delegated private authority both possible and palatable.

The Role of Private Actors in the CDM

The CDM is premised on the logic that global emissions reductions can be most efficiently achieved in the developing world, where the marginal cost of doing so is lowest. Thus, the CDM allows developed countries to meet part of their emissions reductions targets by financing carbon offset projects in the developing world. (Recall that the Kyoto Protocol requires developed countries to reduce their greenhouse gas emissions, but developing countries have no such requirement.) Carbon offset projects can include all types of activities, from reforestation to methane capture. Each project must estimate its "additionality," demonstrating that emissions are lower than they would have been in the absence of the project. Financial additionality ensures that funding for CDM projects is not simply the reorientation of existing development funds. The project cycle—in which additionality is estimated, the project is implemented, and the credits awarded—is extremely complex.[5] For the purposes of the arguments made here, the important point is that private firms are key participants in the process at several junctures, in which they monitor and verify a given project's activities.

The CDM is overseen by an executive board, which is composed of parties to the Kyoto Protocol. Among its other responsibilities, the board manages the project approval process, reviewing each project at both its beginning and end. To facilitate this review, it relies on third parties to monitor each project. These third parties are private actors that serve two functions. They review proposed projects to ensure that they conform to rules and methodologies established by the board (a process called validation). At the end of a project, these third-party monitors conduct an

[5] For a full explanation of the structure of the CDM, see Streck 2004; Green 2008.

evaluation to verify that the promised emissions reductions have in fact taken place (a process called verification). For a given project, two monitors will be hired by the project developer: one to validate the project at the outset, and one to verify at the end.[6] At the time of writing, forty-one monitors have been accredited by the board.[7] Many are large quality assurance firms or standards bodies. A few are NGOs. Despite the growing number of third-party monitors, a few dominate the market. Just three firms are responsible for almost one-half of all projects validated and 40 percent of all projects verified. One firm, Det Norske Veritas, has about one-fifth of total market share.[8]

The rules governing the CDM do not specify *who* can become a monitor, only the competencies that they must possess.[9] That is, any actor that meets the criteria established by parties to the protocol can be accredited. Two separate bodies under the executive board, composed of both diplomats and experts, are responsible for undertaking this review and making recommendations to the board about accreditation.[10] Once accredited, the monitor must submit annual reports to the board for review. The monitor is also subject to spot-checks as well as regular on-site surveillance. It may have its accreditation suspended or revoked after observations during these on-site reviews or if the board repeatedly finds fault with its validation or verification reports.

There are three main reasons that the delegated arrangement to third-party monitors merits further investigation. First, because they decide what "counts" as an emissions reduction, these private firms are, in effect, the guardians of the environmental integrity of the CDM. If they succeed in enforcing the rules, then credits granted represent real measurable reductions in GHG emissions.[11] However, if they validate or verify projects that have not produced the promised reductions, then the credits are without value, which in turn distorts price of emissions reductions on the CDM market. In sum, private actors are tasked with ensuring that each project is designed to deliver additional emissions reductions and that it successfully achieves that goal. They are the atmospheric police of the CDM. As agents, monitors are subject to oversight by the

[6] For a critique of the accountability of DOEs in the CDM, see Green 2008, Lund 2010. For a more sanguine view, see Lederer 2011.

[7] As of 28 September 2012; for an updated list see http://cdm.unfccc.int/DOE/list/index.html.

[8] Figures as of 10 October 2012, available from UNEP-Risoe at http://cdmpipeline.org/does-aies.htm.

[9] UNFCCC 2002c.

[10] A full explanation of the accreditation process is available from http://cdm.unfccc.int/Reference/Procedures/accr_proc01.pdf.

[11] Many have argued that the rules themselves are flawed, allowing states to receive credits for dubious reductions. See especially Wara 2008 and Wara and Victor 2008.

executive board; however, the sheer number of projects precludes an in-depth examination of all of their validation and verification activities.[12] Despite the inability to review every project, Lund has shown that there is a general trend of increase in both the number of projects reviewed and rejected by the board over the life of the CDM.[13] This increase in rejection rates provides evidence of problems with the quality of monitors' work.

Second, although the future of the climate regime is uncertain, the CDM continues to grow. It has already generated more than 1 billion credits, with each credit equivalent to one metric ton of carbon dioxide. The post-2012 market is currently valued at almost US$2 billion.[14] Despite changes in the content of intergovernmental agreements, it is unlikely that the carbon offset project will disappear. Indeed, negotiations around forestry and climate change (known as "REDD"—or reduced emissions from deforestation and forest degradation), suggest that the role of offsetting is only growing: the REDD market quintupled in size between 2009 and 2010.[15] In short, private actors are likely to continue to serve as verifiers and will thus be important for the future of any global climate regime.

Third, the most compelling reason for understanding private authority in the CDM stems from its role in broader efforts to combat climate change. The institutional landscape for climate is exploding.[16] National and global activities include domestic and private emissions trading schemes and voluntary registries to measure and report emissions. As chapter 3 describes, carbon offset standards are also appearing outside the Kyoto Protocol; a parallel voluntary carbon market is booming. Many of these standards replicate the design of the CDM: verification of projects is delegated to an independent private third party. Thus, this model of delegating authority to private verifiers is replicating itself.[17] More broadly, carbon offsets can be understood as the commodification of climate risk, where third-party monitoring and verification are crucial.[18] It is therefore important to understand the conditions under which this instance of private delegated authority arose in the CDM.

---

[12] A study of the executive board's oversight practices found that 19 percent of all projects submitted between December 2004 and June 2007 required additional review. See Green 2008.

[13] Lund 2010, 283.

[14] Kossoy and Guigon 2012.

[15] Linacre, Kossoy, and Ambrosi 2011, 54.

[16] See Bernstein et al. 2010; Michonski and Levi 2010; Keohane and Victor 2011; Hoffmann 2011; Abbott 2012; Bulkeley et al. 2012.

[17] Green 2013a.

[18] Lohmann 2009.

LEARNING TO MEASURE: THE ORIGINS OF THE CDM

A look back to early experiments in carbon offset projects helps establish the long-standing role of a handful of private firms in efforts to measure and verify emissions reductions. These early movers developed expertise that constitutes the supply of private authority. To understand the provenance of this supply, we begin with the "ancient history" of the CDM— almost two decades ago.

The first seed of the CDM was planted in 1995, when parties to the framework convention agreed that they could undertake "activities implemented jointly" (AIJ) to achieve emissions reductions. This allowed developed countries to carry out emissions reductions activities together, or to partner with developing countries.[19] This decision gave rise to demonstration projects that experimented with ways to offset carbon emissions. Many early projects focused on forestry.[20] Because AIJ was largely an exploratory effort, none of the reductions made would be counted toward future targets. Thus, monitoring and verification of project activities were not pressing issues; learning how to measure offsets was the priority. Accordingly, the reporting requirements for AIJ projects were minimal, and did not include any independent verification.

Demonstration projects also began to emerge under the auspices of other institutions—including the Global Environment Facility, the World Business Council on Sustainable Development, the Face Foundation, and the International Automobile Association.[21] A report commissioned by the U.S. Environmental Protection Agency in 1997 cites seven different protocols for measuring carbon offset projects; three of these were created by private firms or NGOs.[22] Of these, two contain provisions for monitoring, and both are by private actors. The same year, Winrock International published *A Guide to Monitoring Carbon Storage in Forestry and Agroforestry Projects*. As the guide notes, "If carbon becomes an internationally-traded commodity, as it appears likely, then monitoring the amount of carbon fixed by projects will become a critical component of any trading system."[23] It therefore developed methods for monitoring and verifying carbon sequestered in forest plantations, managed natural forests, and agroforestry.

[19] UNFCCC 1995; see also Articles 3.3. and 4.2(b) of the UN Framework Convention on Climate Change.

[20] A complete list of approved AIJ projects is available from http://unfccc.int/kyoto_mechanisms/aij/activities_implemented_jointly/items/2094.php.

[21] For a full discussion of these efforts and others, see Moura-Costa and Stuart 1998.

[22] Vine and Sathaye 1997.

[23] MacDicken 1997, 3.

In addition, in 1997 Société Générale de Surveillance (SGS) introduced the first independent third-party "Carbon Offset Verification Service" for forestry-related offset projects. The methodology combined elements from existing national rules (for AIJ projects), as well as its own experience as a large inspection, monitoring, and testing organization.[24] SGS issued the first independent certification report of the Private Forests Project in Costa Rica, which was able to sell "certified tradable offsets" because of third-party verification.[25] By 1999, SGS had already verified eleven projects in Africa, establishing itself as one of the foremost experts in verification.[26] At the same time, the creators and implementers of the SGS methodology published several papers arguing for the need for independent verification of offset projects, and the appropriateness of impartial third-party experts (such as SGS, unsurprisingly) to fulfill that function.[27] In sum, SGS's early activities not only created expertise within the private sector but also demonstrated the feasibility of having private actors serve as verifiers of offset projects.

The signing of the Kyoto Protocol in 1997 formalized Activities Implemented Jointly (now called "Joint Implementation"), created the Clean Development Mechanism, and, in so doing, changed the political stakes of offset projects. Because they could now be counted toward a country's overall reduction requirements under the Kyoto Protocol, monitoring and verification of offsets became essential. Although parties were able to agree on the basic tenets of a Clean Development Mechanism, they did not elaborate any accompanying rules or regulatory structures. As such, it was only *after* the signing of the protocol that the debate about the structure and design of the CDM began.

Despite the delay in designing the new institution, it was clear that monitoring and verification procedures were necessary; the protocol specified, "Emission reductions resulting from each project activity shall be certified by operational entities."[28] It further charged the parties with developing procedures to ensure "transparency, efficiency and accountability through independent auditing and verification of project activities."[29] Moreover, time was of the essence. Because the protocol allowed for banking of early credits, any state that accrued certified offset credits before Kyoto

[24] Moura-Costa et al. 2000.

[25] Uniform Reporting Format, Activities Implemented Jointly under the pilot phase. Costa Rica-Norway. June 2000. Accessed at http://unfccc.int/kyoto_mechanisms/aij/activities_implemented_jointly/items/1892.php.

[26] Moura-Costa et al. 2000, 40.

[27] Moura-Costa and Stuart 1998, 36; Yamin 1998.

[28] Kyoto Protocol, Article 12, para 5.

[29] Kyoto Protocol, Article 12, para 7.

entered into force could use them toward reaching its reduction target. There was an urgent need to create the structures that would get the CDM up and running.

THE DECISION TO DELEGATE

Discussions about the design of the CDM began immediately after the signing of the protocol. Several proposals varied considerably in their scope and design. However, agreement on the final institutional design occurred relatively quickly. Developing countries were quite supportive, because the CDM brought the possibility of extensive investment. And developed countries did not object.[30] The discussion, characterized by one scholar as a period of "acceptance and cautious engagement," quickly turned to the details of the new institution.[31]

There were two key design issues to consider. Should monitoring and verification be delegated to a third party, and if so, who was the most appropriate agent? It soon became clear that delegation was the best way get the CDM up and running quickly, to reduce the time and resources required to assemble the necessary expertise, and to minimize the chance of opportunistic behavior. After consideration of a number of possible monitors, the benefits of capitalizing on private actors' expertise were apparent.

The Benefits of Delegation

There was general consensus from the outset that the transaction costs of a project-based mechanism could be prohibitive.[32] In one early discussion of the CDM's design, several Latin American countries noted: "Excessive transactions costs have been identified as a primary cause of failure of previous project-based emissions offsets programs . . . Several studies have identified numerous and burdensome transaction costs as major obstacles to use of the CDM and access to the potential benefits."[33] Delegation was quickly considered as one way to reduce these costs. Delegation

[30] Yamin 2005, 7, notes that the JUSCANNZ bloc was more interested in developing emissions trading than project-based mechanisms such as the CDM, but they did not openly object.

[31] Ibid.

[32] The following discussion is based on multiple interviews. I attribute specific statements as appropriate; otherwise, the statements reflect recurring themes and comments throughout the interviews. See also UNFCCC 1998a.

[33] UNFCCC 2000a, 2.

to a third party promised several benefits: to reduce the *ex ante* transaction costs of reaching an agreement about the institution's design, to avoid the costs associated with developing expertise, to minimize the possibility of cheating by buyers and sellers, to reduce corruption and conflict of interest by regulators, and to ensure the general smooth functioning of the review process. I explain each in turn.

Because getting the CDM up and running in a timely fashion was a large concern, states wanted to shrink negotiation time. Delegating monitoring and verification tasks to a third party would shift the responsibility of figuring out implementation elsewhere and therefore save time at the negotiation stage. One delegate involved with the negotiations noted that by keeping monitoring tasks "in-house," delegates would also have to agree on budgetary issues, which were generally contentious and time-consuming. Moreover, such negotiations would have to be repeated on a regular basis.[34] By outsourcing monitoring and verification, negotiators' task was quicker and simpler: to specify the terms of the delegated authority. Instead of deciding how to create and implement rules for monitoring and verification, they only had to figure out how to oversee the monitors.

Delegation also offered a quick fix to the "make or buy" problem. There was a clear need for expertise; evaluating carbon offset projects requires specialized and technical knowledge. Although a few members of the executive board had experience with these technical issues, in general it lacked the depth and breadth of expertise needed for monitoring projects. Were the board to be involved in these activities, it would need to develop this technical capacity. Alternatively, and perhaps more expediently, it could search elsewhere for this knowledge. "Buying" expertise through delegation would be quicker and less resource-intensive than developing it in house.

States realized that the CDM created an incentive for cheating: both the buyer (the developed country) and seller (the developing country) of emissions reductions would want to inflate the number of credits generated by a given project. Developed nations could then earn more credits toward compliance, and developing nations could collect project funding without producing the promised emissions reductions. A third-party monitor with independent powers of review was viewed as a way to minimize cheating and the likelihood of "empty credits" being issued.

In considering the CDM's design, states were also concerned about the possibility of corruption and conflicts of interest facing the regulators.

---

[34] Farhana Yamin, former negotiator, Alliance of Small Island States. Interview by author, 8 October 2008.

Members of the board are required to sign a document declaring that they have no financial interests in the projects they oversee. Nonetheless, the board has leeway in deciding which projects are approved without review, and which are rejected. An impartial third party to inform this process would mitigate opportunities for the board to approve or reject projects for political or financial reasons.

The same logic held for a more general conflict of interest. Because the board is responsible for helping move projects through the project cycle (i.e., general project support), there would be a potential conflict of interest if it was also to be tasked with monitoring. One interviewee noted that it was quickly viewed as necessary to separate the actors responsible for project support from those responsible for compliance.[35] A third-party review would enhance the impartiality of monitoring and verification and reduce the possibility of opportunistic behavior by the board. Indeed, in an informal workshop among states about design issues surrounding the governance of the CDM, there was emphasis on "the need to ensure total professional independence of third parties undertaking validation."[36] Certainly, any regulator, public or private, could potentially be bribed. However, the consensus among those involved with the negotiations was that corruption within the bureaucracy was more likely than if private firms were involved.

Finally, negotiators anticipated that the volume of projects would be large; thus, there was a need for an efficient way to validate and verify them. Without sufficient capacity, there would be a wait to get each project approved. In other words, there was concern that the entities in charge of monitoring and verification be sufficient in number to avoid the possibility of a bottleneck.[37] One interviewee referred to this as the "one window" problem: if each project had to queue at one window—the UNFCCC Secretariat, a different international organization, or some other entity—the line would soon be endless, and possibilities for corruption could arise.[38]

In sum, there were five main perceived benefits to delegating monitoring and verification activities to a third party: reduced negotiation time, utilization of existing expertise, reduced possibility of cheating and issuance of bogus credits, reduced likelihood of corruption or conflicts of interest by the verifiers, and efficient processing of projects.

[35] Dan Reifsnyder, Deputy Assistant Secretary for Environment and Sustainable Development, U.S. Department of State. Interview by author, 7 May 2009.

[36] Earth Negotiations Bulletin 1999.

[37] Ironically, it is the executive board that has been accused of slowing the approval process down, since every project must be reviewed twice—at the beginning and the end.

[38] Reifsnyder, Interview; Annie Petsonk, International Counsel, Environmental Defense Fund. Interview by author, 11 September 2008.

Considering Possible Agents

Once it became clear that a third party was needed to undertake the validation and verification of projects, states faced a choice about whom to use. They could enlist the aid of national governments, IOs, private actors, or some combination of the three. Among the possible IO agents, interviews with policy makers involved suggest that there were three main contenders: the UNFCCC Secretariat, the International Organization for Standardization (ISO), or the Global Environment Facility.[39] Private actors were also considered. The following discussion considers the relative strengths of each potential agent, based on the potential benefits outlined above. Table 4.1 provides a summary of their relative desirability. Strong evidence in support of providing each benefit is scored as 1; strong evidence against the benefit as 0. If the evidence is mixed or ambiguous, then it is scored at 0.5. Additional strengths and weaknesses beyond the five criteria outlined above are scored at 0.5.

NATIONAL GOVERNMENTS

Many multilateral agreements delegate various aspects of implementation to member governments. It was therefore logical to consider the possibility that the host country (i.e., the country in which the project is geographically located) would be responsible for monitoring and verifying projects taking place within its borders.

Delegating monitoring and verification of projects to host country governments had two attractive features. First, because governments generally prefer to preserve their sovereignty and maintain as much control as possible over treaties, the option of delegating to their own government was politically attractive to all. This was especially true of developing nations, which tended to oppose the involvement of IOs in the climate change regime.[40] Second, the general consensus on this issue would certainly speed up negotiations.

In terms of the other transaction costs, however, there appeared to be little advantage in delegating to national governments. Most developing countries had little to no experience in the technical details of evaluating carbon offset projects. A great deal of time and expense would be required to build capacity in this regard. Until sufficient capacity was developed, this would certainly slow the functioning of the whole institution. Moreover, many analysts were worried about the conflict of

---

[39] One interviewee from the UNFCCC Secretariat noted that the Intergovernmental Panel on Climate Change had also been briefly considered as a candidate for developing monitoring and verification methodologies. However, since she was the only person to mention this, I infer that this discussion was brief and that the possibility was quickly dismissed.

[40] Najam 2005.

TABLE 4.1
Strengths and Weaknesses of Potential Agents

	National Governments	World Bank / Global Environment Facility	UNFCCC Secretariat	ISO	Private Actors
Shorten negotiating time	1	0	0	1	1
Utilize existing expert knowledge	0	0.5	1	0	1
Reduce opportunities for cheating	0	0	0.5	1	1
Reduce corruption and conflicts of interest	0	1	1	1	1
Ensure an efficient project process	0	0	0	0.5	1
Other strengths (scored at +0.5)	Preserve sovereignty (+0.5)				
Other weaknesses (scored at -0.5)			Potential conflict with its administrative / project support role (-0.5)	Independent organization with competing principals (-0.5)	
Total score	1.5	1.5	2	3	5

interest: host countries had a vested interest in getting projects approved for the maximum amount of credits possible. This would keep investors happy and, hopefully, attract future projects. With this as a motivating factor, national reviewers would have an incentive to be dishonest or to accept bribes to ensure a favorable outcome. A 1998 study by the UN Environment Programme about possible designs of the CDM notes, "It is difficult . . . to see how the impartiality and integrity underpinning verification could be maintained if verification were carried out by a network of national institutions."[41] One Costa Rican negotiator, who was very involved in discussions about the CDM, put it more bluntly: "Government was never going to be independent."[42] In sum, issues related to capacity and corruption illustrated that transaction costs would not be notably reduced by delegating monitoring and verification tasks to national governments.

THE WORLD BANK AND THE GLOBAL ENVIRONMENT FACILITY

The Global Environment Facility (GEF) is an IO that was established in 1991 to facilitate the funding and implementation of efforts to promote sustainable development and environmental protection, primarily in the developing world. It serves as the financial mechanism for the UNFCCC and thus has been involved with funding developing country efforts of adaptation and mitigation. The details of its institutional history and structure are complex. For the purposes of this analysis, the important point is that the GEF is managed in part by the World Bank, which oversees the GEF Trust fund and performs administrative functions. As such, I consider these two institutions in tandem.

Like the ISO, the GEF was also viewed as a likely candidate to be tasked with monitoring and verification of offset projects. Article 21 of the UNFCCC names the GEF as the financial mechanism, responsible for disbursing funds to facilitate the transfer of technology and, more generally, achieving the goals of the UNFCCC. In 2000 it was also named as the financial mechanism for the Special Climate Change Fund and the Least Developed Country Fund to help developing countries cope with climate change.[43] As a result of this work, the GEF had accrued considerable experience with project-based activities. Although some of these projects were substantively related to mitigation activities that might occur under the CDM, the GEF focused on quantifying additional costs rather than emissions reductions.

Independent of the GEF, the World Bank was developing climate offset projects through the Prototype Carbon Fund, established in 1999. Its aim

[41] Yamin 1998, 77. See also Stewart et al. 2000, 71.
[42] Franz Tattenbach, former delegate and executive board member, Costa Rica. Interview by author, 11 January 2010.
[43] UNFCCC 2002a; UNFCCC 2002b.

is to funnel private funds into emissions reductions projects. Thus, at the time of the discussions surrounding the CDM's design, the World Bank was developing knowledge and experience about carbon offset projects, though it did not have a long-standing track record in the field. In other words, it was accruing expertise but did not already possess it. Because the GEF had some experience with carbon offset projects, and the World Bank was quickly developing expertise on accounting and measurement methodologies, I code "utilizing expert knowledge" at .5 in table 4.1.

The GEF was an unattractive choice for three reasons. First, because it was an IO, negotiating the terms of the relationship between the Conference of the Parties (the supreme body of the climate change regime) and the GEF would be time-consuming. The legal relationship between the two IOs would have to be sorted out and would likely result in a power struggle. Resolving these conflicting preferences would require considerable negotiation, which was incompatible with a prompt start to the CDM. Second, negotiators did not have sufficient confidence that the GEF would be an impartial evaluator of projects. Because of its work on the Prototype Carbon Fund, the World Bank (and by extension, the GEF) was viewed as very pro-market. Indeed, according to its website, "the Prototype Carbon Fund was created as a response to the need to understand and test the procedures for creating a market in project-based emissions reductions . . . The PCF has placed a pioneering role in developing the market for greenhouse gas emissions reductions."[44] One interviewee noted that "the [World] Bank clearly had a dog in the fight."[45] Given this perceived bias, it was not clear that the GEF would reduce the tendency toward credit inflation by the buyer and seller. Third and finally, if the GEF were the only entity verifying projects, the usual concerns about bottlenecks and delays applied. Indeed, one negotiator said that the thought of any UN agency overseeing monitoring would be a "logistical nightmare."[46]

THE UNFCCC SECRETARIAT

The UNFCCC Secretariat is responsible for all administrative tasks to support the implementation of the Framework Convention and the Kyoto Protocol, as well as the rule-making process. This involves such diverse activities as organizing meetings, collecting and disseminating information from parties, and conducting training and capacity building.[47] It was heavily involved in the early work on the CDM, supporting the AIJ

[44] "About the Prototype Carbon Fund." Accessed at http://wbcarbonfinance.org/Router.cfm?Page=PCF&ft=About.

[45] Yamin, Interview.

[46] Reifsnyder, Interview.

[47] For a full elaboration of the tasks delegated to the Secretariat, see UNFCCC 1992, Article 8.

from 1995 onward. A small number of secretariat staff worked closely with parties developing AIJ projects, including the "Uniform Reporting Format"—the standardized methodology for documenting and reporting emissions reductions generated by AIJ projects.[48]

Given its experience with AIJ, and its long-standing knowledge about the climate change process, the UNFCCC Secretariat was also considered as a possible agent responsible for verifying offset projects. But it too had serious shortcomings. Negotiators were concerned about the *ex ante* transaction costs of this design choice. Expanding its responsibilities to include monitoring and verification in the CDM would require significant bureaucratic changes: more staff, a larger budget, and new oversight and reporting structures. These would all have to be negotiated before the CDM could become operational. This would not only prolong discussions at the outset but would also require repeated negotiations over the budget in the future.[49] One interviewee remarked that "if this [the role of the monitor] had been kicked to the UN, it would have never gotten off the ground."[50]

There was also the possibility that delegating verification would overwhelm the UNFCCC Secretariat—both because of the volume of projects anticipated and because there would be only one organization with a relatively small number of staff working on issues related to AIJ and the CDM at the time. A small staff coupled with a large workload would create bottlenecks and impede the timely approval of projects and issuance of credits. Finally, it was already clear that the secretariat would provide administrative support for the executive board and the project cycle more generally. It would be responsible for liaising with project developers and implementers, communicating views of the board, requesting documentation, and generally providing help to project developers. Being both the "helper" and the regulator would be complicated at best and could present potential conflicts.[51] For example, in its support capacity, the secretariat might help developers ensure that documentation conforms to reporting rules. In its monitoring capacity, it might fault the developer for this same issue. These three concerns ruled out the possibility of delegating to the UNFCCC Secretariat.

THE INTERNATIONAL ORGANIZATION FOR STANDARDIZATION (ISO)

The ISO is an international network of national standard-setting institutions. It is a private actor in the sense that its member institutes are not affiliated with governments (though often their standards are recognized by

    [48] Yamin, Interview.
    [49] Yamin, Interview.
    [50] John Drexhage, former negotiator, Canada. Interview by author, 15 October 2008.
    [51] Christine Zumkeller, former member of the UNFCCC Secretariat. Interview by author, 14 January 2010. Reifsnyder, Interview.

governments, and even IOs), and the standards promulgated are voluntary. ISO's long history—it was founded in 1947—and deliberative processes have transformed it into the pre-eminent international standard-setting organization. As such, when states recognized the need to develop a standardized approach to monitoring and verifying offset projects, the ISO seemed to be a plausible candidate for the task.

The ISO was involved in design discussions from the outset.[52] As one negotiator noted, ISO was "bandied about" as a possible agent since many of the monitoring and verification activities required in the CDM were similar to those of the ISO.[53] Because much of ISO's work focuses on accrediting other bodies to verify standards, it was considered not only as a potential monitor but also as a possible agent responsible for accrediting other monitors.[54] Indeed, the ISO set forth such a proposal, calling for a "global accreditation system," whereby it would be responsible for accrediting all third-party monitors.[55] In 1998 Brazil put forth the possibility of using the ISO as the body responsible for "pre-certifying" emissions reductions (i.e., estimating emissions reductions before the project is completed).[56] Other policy reports issued by governments and IOs made similar mentions of the ISO, but no concrete proposals appear to have been put forth.[57]

There were three objections to delegating monitoring authority to the ISO. The first was a technical objection: some negotiators felt that although ISO had experience in quality assurance, it had limited knowledge about carbon offset projects. Other negotiators emphasized the need to have an accreditation process tailor-made for the CDM, not one that was retrofitted from other areas. The second objection was political. States had a particular distaste for delegating to organizations outside of the UN system. Some of this sentiment came from the belief that climate change was different from other issues of international cooperation and therefore required specialized institutions.[58] Related to this was the concern that ISO standards favored conformity with *processes* over measurement of *outcomes*. Because environmental outcomes (i.e., emissions reductions) were the sole focus of the CDM, some felt that using the process-based ISO model was ill-conceived. Finally, and most importantly, states were concerned about the ability to control the agent carefully. The ISO is an

---

[52] John Kilani, former negotiator, South Africa. Interview by author, 5 November 2008; Maria Netto, UNFCCC Secretariat. Interview by author, 15 October 2008; Christiana Figueres, Executive Secretary, UNFCCC and former negotiator Costa Rica. Interview by author, 20 November 2008.

[53] Figueres, Interview.

[54] Gylvan Meira Filho 1998, 42.

[55] Netto, Interview.

[56] UNFCCC 1998a, 42. See also Gylvan Meira Filho 1998, 42.

[57] Environomics 1999; Earth Negotiations Bulletin 1999; Stewart et al. 2000, 72.

[58] Figueres, Interview.

independent organization, with its own funding and a diverse (and non-overlapping) set of stakeholders. It would therefore be subject to competing goals and would likely be more difficult to control.

In terms of the five benefits of delegation presented above, the ISO was able to deliver three (see table 4.1). Since the ISO is a private institution, it would be responsible for its own decisions about budgeting and matters of internal governance, thus shortening negotiating time. These issues were beyond the scope of parties to the protocol and therefore would not be an obstacle in the initial negotiations. In addition, any impartial third party—including the ISO—would keep both sides honest, reducing the likelihood of cheating. Finally, the ISO would reduce corruption by making it obvious if the executive board took decisions overruling the ISO's expert opinion. (Of course, a third-party verifier could also be corrupt or hand out favors, but the general consensus among states was that these technocratic organizations were more interested in preserving their reputation to ensure future business.)

However, despite its presence in the design discussions, and its experience with other types of monitoring, the ISO fell short on two key criteria. It lacked experience in carbon offset projects. It was also unclear whether the ISO would promote the efficient and speedy review of projects. The general model for the ISO is to develop standards and then deputize those in conformity with the standards to carry out the actual certification activities. In theory, the ISO could accredit a sufficient number of monitors to prevent bottlenecks in the approval process (though note that in this capacity the ISO would serve more as an accreditor than as a verifier). Ultimately, however, all projects would have to be reviewed by the ISO; thus, there was still potential for bottlenecks. None of the interviewees mentioned efficiency as a concern in considering the ISO as an agent. Given the potential for the ISO to meet this criterion, but lacking definitive evidence that it did, it receives half credit for efficiency in table 4.1.

THE PRIVATE SECTOR

In evaluating the alternatives, delegating to private firms to serve as third-party monitors appeared to be an attractive decision. Using multiple firms in the private sector offered several benefits that other potential agents could not. First, as noted in the previous section, private firms had been active in carbon offset projects and measurement since the mid-1990s. SGS developed the first third-party verification protocol for forestry offset projects and used it on a number of projects throughout the world. Other private actors, including Winrock and the World Business Council on Sustainable Development also had some experience in measuring carbon.[59] The Dutch government commissioned guidelines for monitoring

[59] Vine and Sathaye 1997.

and verification, which were drafted jointly with the conformity assessment firm (and future CDM monitor) Det Norske Veritas.[60] The view that the private sector was a source of expertise was widespread. An early report on design issues surrounding the CDM by the UN Conference on Trade and Development (UNCTAD) noted that "there are a variety of private entities with very substantial capacity and experience for certifying the performance of various goods and services and projects."[61]

Second, delegating to a nongovernmental third party made the negotiation process much simpler, mooting political issues that would inevitably arise with IOs. Third, there was much less concern about possibilities of corruption with private actors than with IOs or governments. Of course, any actor evaluating offset projects could be corrupt, but the consensus was that such an outcome was more likely among government bureaucrats and international civil servants than among expert technocrats. There was a widely held view that private firms had a vested interest in doing their job well to preserve their reputation and to garner repeat business. Such a reputation mechanism, states held, did not exist for public agents. One official involved in the negotiation said the choice between public and private agents came down to an issue of whom to trust more—politicians or technocrats.[62]

It is interesting that this reputational logic was both persuasive and largely unproblematic to states—even as the Enron scandal was unfolding.[63] As states were debating whether private agents would be better suited than an IO to keep buyers and sellers honest, one of the world's largest energy companies was collapsing, abetted by its accounting firm, Arthur Andersen, which was found to be complicit in the fraud that produced Enron's spectacular meltdown. Charged with ensuring its compliance with U.S. accounting and reporting regulations, Arthur Anderson not only helped hide Enron's massive debt but also obstructed the subsequent investigation by the Securities and Exchange Commission. Despite the almost contemporaneous unfolding of these events, all evidence suggests that negotiators in the CDM were much more concerned about inflation of credits by buyers and sellers than collusion between regulators and the regulated.[64] Many felt that any potential threats to the system could be controlled by careful oversight by the executive board, a point to which I return below.

Fourth, by deputizing many private firms to serve as verifiers, states could avoid the problems of the "one window" approach. One interviewee

---

[60] Ministry of Economic Affairs of the Netherlands 2000.

[61] Stewart et al. 2000, 70.

[62] Maurice LeFranc, EPA official. Interview by the author, 10 November 2008.

[63] For a useful study in variation of certifiers' credibility, see Starobin and Weinthal 2010.

[64] Figueres, Interview; Erik Haites, President, Margaree Consultants. Interview by the author, 7 October 2008.

likened using private agents to the model of home appraisals: when you get your home appraised, you do not expect the government to conduct the appraisal. Rather, you contract with a private appraiser, who has been licensed by the government.[65] By deputizing numerous "appraisers," the CDM would have multiple actors available to evaluate projects and, importantly, would promote competition among them.

Finally, there was a general sense among states and others involved in design discussions that a market solution would be the most efficient— both in terms of building on existing expertise and ensuring a competitive market in verifiers. This theme recurs in both interviews with negotiators and policy proposals. As the UNCTAD study notes, "Most analysts seem to agree that verification, monitoring, certification, insurance, and market-making functions should primarily be assigned to private sector institutions."[66] Several options papers in a 1998 UNDP study on CDM design issues share the same sentiment.[67] In sum, the private sector was viewed as an efficient solution to problems of transaction costs. Delegating to private agents would ensure that the CDM was up and running promptly, existing expertise was put to use, commitments between buyers and sellers were credible, the likelihood of corruption was minimized, and the monitoring and verification processes would run smoothly and without delay.

Explaining the Form of Private Authority

As I have argued throughout the book, understanding private authority requires explaining not only its emergence but also its form: delegated or entrepreneurial. The previous two sections of the chapter establish the demand for private authority: states were in search of an actor who could expedite implementation and lower transaction costs. Private actors were able to provide more of these benefits than other potential candidates. Yet this does not suffice to explain why private authority took a delegated rather than entrepreneurial form.

To complete the explanation, we turn to two key factors. First, agreement among powerful states facilitated the decision to delegate. The two most important negotiating blocs—the United States and its allies and the largest bloc of developing countries—agreed on the general structure and role of the CDM in the Kyoto Protocol and the need for independent verification of offset projects. Second, the presence of the executive board

---

[65] Reifsnyder, Interview.

[66] Stewart et al. 2000, 70.

[67] Siniscalco, Goria, and Janssen 1998; Panayotou 1998; Meijer and Werksman 2005.

assuaged concerns that agents could simply do what they pleased. As a strong focal point, the board could carefully screen agents before their accreditation and monitor their work throughout the project cycle.

Preferences of Key States

Between 1995 and 1997, various nations continued to develop and implement AIJ projects. At the same time, countries began negotiations on the Berlin Mandate—the legal document that lay the foundation for the Kyoto Protocol.[68] During these meetings, a variety of ideas were put forth to promote flexibility in the ways that developed countries could meet their reduction targets. The intricacies of these debates are beyond the scope of this chapter.[69] What is relevant, however, are the positions adopted by the United States and its allies (the so-called JUSCANNZ bloc) and the negotiating bloc representing the majority of developing countries, the Group of 77 and China (for brevity, henceforth the G-77). The evolution and eventual convergence of their views about the role of the CDM in the Kyoto Protocol shows that one of the two conditions for private delegated authority—homogeneous preferences of key states—was in place.

Although there were a variety of negotiating blocs in the climate regime at the time, JUSCANNZ and the G-77 are the most powerful states with respect to the CDM discussions. Each bloc had intense preferences. JUSCANNZ was the most adamant supporter of the CDM, while the G-77 was very skeptical. Given the intensity of preferences of each bloc, they would be the most likely to block an agreement that did not conform to their views. Arguably, JUSCANNZ was *the* most important group of countries in the Kyoto Protocol. It represented the majority of global emissions, so anything less than full participation would threaten the effectiveness, and even the entry into force, of the treaty—as was subsequently realized when the United States withdrew from Kyoto.

The European Union is *excluded* as a powerful group of states in this analysis. First, the European Union was most focused on emissions trading and, more specifically, limiting reliance on emissions trading as a means to achieve required reductions, rather than the other two flexibility mechanisms—the CDM and Joint Implementation. Second, the European Union was not unified in its views on the CDM. Publicly, it argued for strict limits on the amount of allowable reductions from the CDM.[70] However, throughout the negotiations, the European Union

---

[68] UNFCCC 1995.
[69] For a useful discussion, see Engels 2006.
[70] UNFCCC 1998a.

struggled to present a unified position on the CDM.[71] Third, although it represents a large part of the developed world, total emissions from the European Union were less than one-third of that of the JUSCANNZ group.[72] Fourth and finally, after the United States announced it would not attempt to ratify the protocol in March 2001, the European Union's position on the market mechanisms shifted. Thus, although it had a key role in determining the success of Kyoto, the European Union had neither strong nor consistent preferences on the CDM.

FROM DISAGREEMENT TO COMPROMISE

The United States, along with other members of JUSCANNZ, was generally very supportive of all market-based mechanisms being discussed for inclusion in Kyoto.[73] Although the United States was particularly focused on emissions trading (where countries who had met their reduction requirements could sell excess permits on the open market), it supported any market mechanism that would provide additional flexibility in meeting targets and, potentially, lower the cost of doing so. Indeed, a 1996 U.S. position paper on the future of Joint Implementation states:

> [A joint implementation regime] will encourage the rapid development and implementation of cooperative, mutually voluntary projects between partners . . . and provide an incentive through financial and technical assistance to further the development of non-Annex I country programs to limit increases in greenhouse gas emissions.[74]

Other members of JUSCANNZ aligned themselves with the United States and this view.[75]

The G-77, by contrast, was initially starkly opposed to North-South cooperation through carbon offset projects. Its primary concern was that such projects would constitute a first step toward imposing emissions limits on developing countries—a taboo that would violate the principle of common but differentiated responsibilities, codified in the Framework Convention and later in the protocol.[76]

The goal of the United States and JUSCANNZ to expand the role of market mechanisms in the Kyoto Protocol was furthered by Brazil's involvement in the negotiation process. A few short months before the

---

[71] Grubb and Yamin 2001; Jacoby and Reiner 2001, 302.

[72] Author's calculations, based on 2000 emissions, from http://cdiac.ornl.gov/trends/emis/tre_coun.html.

[73] JUSCANNZ has since evolved into the Umbrella Group.

[74] UNFCCC 1996a, 32.

[75] See, e.g., Australia's submission in UNFCCC 1996 and Russia's proposal in UNFCCC 1996b. Russia, though not a member of JUSCANNZ, was often a supporter.

[76] Werksman 1998, 148.

meeting in Kyoto, Brazil tabled a proposal for a "Clean Development Fund."[77] The proposal called for fines to be levied on those developed countries who failed to meet their reduction targets. The fines would then be distributed among developing countries to undertake adaptation and mitigation projects.[78]

The Brazilian proposal prompted the G-77 to reverse its opposition. Seeing opportunities for funds to be directed to the developing world, the G-77 endorsed the Brazilian proposal.[79] Although it did not yet bridge the gap about whether Joint Implementation would be restricted to developed nations, the proposal did create a basis of agreement upon which future negotiations could build. Participants in the post-Kyoto negotiations noted that the G-77 was focused more on the distributional issues surrounding the CDM than on the details of implementation.[80] Because the Clean Development Fund proposal addressed some of these concerns, a door toward compromise began to open. Werksman points out that "the brief history of the negotiations [of the CDM] in Kyoto can be characterized as a struggle that merged the US-backed proposals for project based Joint Implementation, and G-77 proposals for a fund fed by compliance penalties."[81]

The idea of a penalty-based system embodied in the Clean Development Fund was abandoned in favor of the incentive-based system that serves as the premise for the present-day CDM. Through a series of last-minute negotiations at Kyoto, both the JUSCANNZ and the G-77 signed on to the CDM in its current form.[82] The relatively quick decision making among key states is the first indication of their shared preferences about the general function of the CDM.

Once the incentive-based system was agreed upon, additional design features paved the way for further agreement on independent verification. First, rather than facilitating technology transfer or distributing funding, the CDM was focused exclusively on emissions reductions. Second, in a break from previous discussions of joint implementation, which were centered solely on the developed world, the CDM was to be a bilateral

---

[77] UNFCCC 1997, 3–58. Some involved with the process noted that the main contours of the Clean Development Mechanism were the product of a bilateral meeting between Brazil and the the United States in August 1997.

[78] Ibid., 9.

[79] Werksman 1998, 151; Grubb, Vrolijk, and Brack 1999, 101–3.

[80] Haites, Interview; Drexhage, Interview.

[81] Werksman 1998, 152.

[82] As further evidence that the European Union was not a key player in the debate on the CDM, Grubb and Yamin (2001, 274) note, "In the final dramatic night at Kyoto, it is well know that EU ministers were still locked in internal consultations while the plenary was in session: Chairman Estrada gaveled through the critical text on the CDM while EU ministers were still trying to establish a common position in another room."

mechanism between developing and developed nations. Once states had committed to these two design elements, the need for independent, third-party verification of projects became clear.[83] In subsequent debates about the design, developing countries in particular emphasized the importance of real, verifiable emissions. Moreover, all those involved recognized the opportunities for gaming. Both issues could be addressed by appointing an impartial third-party monitor.

At this point, the decision to delegate to private actors moved ahead quickly, yet another indication of key states' shared preferences. For reasons explained in the previous section, other potential agents were not desirable—either because they would not be sufficiently impartial or because they would not substantially lower the transaction costs of the CDM (or both). The notion of delegating such critical tasks to private actors was a new idea, and one former member of the UNFCCC Secretariat noted "there was a certain amount of nervousness" about using them as agents.[84] She also noted that the G-77 was especially wary, concerned about the possibility of oligopoly and of dominance by firms from the global North as well as what the cost implications of such dominance might be.

However, these concerns did not translate to strong objections. As one former negotiator put it, delegating to private firms was not "a make or break issue" for the G-77.[85] While the G-77 may have been appropriately wary about the use of private firms, like everyone else it also recognized that the third-party monitors would be central to the CDM's credibility.[86] Choosing an impartial agent was of utmost importance.

As early as 1999, country proposals for the future rules and modalities for the CDM contain references to the possibility that these monitors could be either public or private actors.[87] JUSCANNZ proposes the use of private actors in May 1999: "In order to ensure cost-effectiveness and efficiency, the operational entities could be drawn from private sector institutions (e.g., international accounting firms/certification bodies)."[88] Even the G-77, which had previously opposed market-based mechanisms, was on board with the possibility of using private actors for verification.

[83] Tattenbach, Interview.

[84] Christine Zumkeller, former member of the UNFCCC Secretariat. Interview by author, 14 January 2010.

[85] Drexhage, Interview.

[86] Zumkeller, Interview.

[87] UNFCCC 1999a. The JUSCANNZ proposal defines operational entities as "either a public or private entity" (p. 10).

[88] UNFCCC 1999b, para. 182. This proposal was made by Australia, Canada, Iceland, Japan, New Zealand, Norway, the Russian Federation, Ukraine, and the United States.

In a 1999 position paper, it notes: "Independent auditing of project activities may be done by public or private sector entities not involved in the identification, development or management of the project."[89]

In sum, the key negotiating blocs in the CDM—JUSCANNZ and the G-77—were initially in disagreement about how the new institution would evolve. However, once the distributional concerns of the G-77 were allayed, the basis for compromise was set. Moreover, having decided that the CDM would focus on emissions reductions and would involve both developed and developing countries, the need for impartial third-party verification—that is, delegation—became clear. The focus on emissions reductions (rather than funding, technology transfer, or capacity building), the possibility of gaming, and the incentive to overstate reductions all underscored the need for a third-party verification system. As documents from the post-Kyoto discussions make clear, both negotiating blocs were in agreement on this point.

Existence of a Strong Focal Institution

As argued in chapter 1, the existence of a strong focal institution is a key element in explaining private delegated authority. A strong focal institution—with sufficient capacity and authority—helps minimize the possibility of agency slack in two ways. First, it can undertake careful screening procedures to ensure that agents are qualified, and that their preferences are closely aligned with the principal. Second, with the proper oversight mechanisms, the focal institution can monitor agents' behavior to make sure they are carrying out their delegated functions properly. Given that the credibility of the third-party monitors was so crucial to the proper functioning of the CDM, the mechanisms for screening and monitoring them were equally important.

Article 12.4 of the Kyoto Protocol created a focal institution for the CDM, the executive board, but did not elaborate on its responsibilities. If the board was to be a strong focal institution, it would need independent rule-making authority on three issues: accreditation (i.e., agent screening), reviewing and auditing monitors' behavior, and delivering sanctions as needed—that is, a high degree of legalization, as described in chapter 1. As the subsequent analysis demonstrates, states agreed to endow it with these attributes, which in turn enabled sufficient oversight of private agents.

The decisions about how the executive board would function, who would staff it, and what its legal standing would be were debated after

---

[89] UNFCCC 1999c, para. 8.2.

Kyoto, between 1998 and 2001, with the final rules set forth in the Marrakesh Accords.[90] On the broadest level, the primary design issue was how much authority to delegate to the board. A 1998 UNDP report framed the question in legal-institutional terms: Was the board to be a subsidiary body of the Conference of the Parties (COP), or a principal organ? A subsidiary body, as its name suggests, is subordinate to the plenary body (the COP). However, a principal organ "may have a relationship which is hierarchical, parallel or a mixture of both . . . [It] may, for example, have some functions it is mandated to fulfill which the plenary organ is not entitled to take away or whose exercise it cannot control."[91] One member of the UNFCCC Secretariat pointed out that the biggest delegation issue was a concern not about the third-party monitors but rather about how much rule-making authority to transfer to the board.[92]

States were of two minds about this issue.[93] On one hand, they were generally wary of delegating to an international bureaucracy; in the climate change regime, this has traditionally been particularly true of developing countries. On the other, there was concern that requiring the COP to take all CDM decisions would be slow procedurally (the COP meets only once a year), and highly politicized. Given the anticipated volume of projects, many states recognized that some institution would have to oversee the day-to-day activities of the CDM. The debates about the CDM's design reflected this tension.

Discussions about the structure and function of the board began in 1998. From the outset, the G-77 was opposed to delegating rule-making authority. It tabled a document that outlined an "initial list of issues" of concern for the negotiating bloc. Among them was the following concern: "How to ensure that the executive board of the CDM shall function under the authority and guidance of the Conference of the Parties?"[94] This question set the stage for future comments and submissions by members of the G-77, which reiterated the need for the board to function under the authority of the COP without independent rule-making authority. Rather, it wanted all board "decisions" to be recommendations, which would ultimately be decided by the COP. Other developing countries shared this view.[95] Mexico and Bolivia both proposed that the board remain a subsidiary body and *not* be responsible for accreditation

[90] UNFCCC 2002c.
[91] Yamin 1998, 73.
[92] Netto, Interview.
[93] This bifurcation was communicated by a number of interviewees and is also reflected in the recurring language about oversight of both the executive board and of the monitors.
[94] UNFCCC 1998c, 9.
[95] UNFCCC 1998b.

or approval of methodologies.[96] Paraguay argued that the board should "intervene only when strictly necessary."[97]

However, JUSCANNZ, the European Union, and some developing countries thought that the board should have more independent authority. Brazil, largely viewed as one of the principal creators of the CDM, proposed that it serve as the accreditor for third-party monitors as early as 1998.[98] The following year, JUSCANNZ proposed that the board "function as a separate standing body."[99] The European Union further proposed that it be responsible for supervising the monitors, performing spot-checks of their work, and "decid[ing] independently" whom to monitor.[100] Moreover, it suggested that the board be able to recommend to the COP which monitors would lose the right to certify projects. India also supported an expanded role, proposing that the board be responsible for accrediting monitors, revoking accreditation as necessary, and overseeing the process of creating methodologies.[101]

These discussions culminated in a chairmen's text that formed the basis for negotiations in the lead-up to the Marrakesh meeting of the Conference of the Parties (COP), where final decisions about the rules and modalities of the CDM were taken. Although many of the disagreements described above are present in the chairmen's text, there are two important shifts toward a strong focal institution. First, the three key tasks for a strong executive board—accreditation, monitoring, and sanctioning of third-party monitors—were supported by a growing number of delegations.[102] Thus, some countries in the G-77 departed from their original objections to delegation to the board and espoused a more autonomous focal institution.

Second, JUSCANNZ made an important nod to the G-77, supporting language that stated, "The executive board shall be fully accountable to the COP/MOP."[103] The Conference of the Parties and the Meeting of the Parties (MOP) are the governing bodies of the Framework Convention and the Kyoto Protocol, respectively. Thus, this language granted broad authority to the highest governing authorities to intervene in the oversight and institutions of the CDM as it deemed appropriate. This

[96] UNFCCC 2000a; UNFCCC 2000b.
[97] UNFCCC 2000b, 55.
[98] UNFCCC 1998b.
[99] UNFCCC 1999b, para. 121. This proposal was also supported by Iceland, the Russian Federation, and Ukraine.
[100] Ibid., para. 131–34.
[101] UNFCCC 2000b, 41–42.
[102] Supporters included JUSCANNZ (plus Iceland, the Russian Federation, and Ukraine), Costa Rica, the European Union, India, Chile, and the African Group.
[103] UNFCCC 2000c, para 218.

compromise was cemented in the final text of the Marrakesh accords, which both notes that the board functions "under the authority and guidance of the COP" but also accords it independent power to accredit, monitor, spot-check, and sanction third-party monitors.[104]

Conclusion

This chapter has traced the emergence of private delegated authority in the CDM. The evidence presented here is consistent with the broader theory of private authority presented in chapter 1. Private authority emerged because private actors with existing expertise in monitoring carbon offset projects were able to provide benefits to states that other actors—primarily IOs—were not. They were able to lower the transaction costs of the CDM by reducing negotiating time, building on extant knowledge, reducing the likelihood of gaming and corruption, and ensuring the prompt review of projects. Because key negotiating blocs in the developed and developing worlds agreed on the need for impartial, independent monitoring, and because the executive board was a strong focal institution, capable of screening and supervising private agents, delegated private authority emerged.

The CDM has been an interesting institutional experiment in two ways. It represents one of the few instances in global environmental governance where private actors perform key regulatory functions. Moreover, despite its flaws, it is one of the best-developed institutions toward creating a global market for GHGs.[105] It success in each of these functions is mixed.

Some have called into question the performance of these private monitors that serve as the atmospheric police. Because they are paid by project developers, with an interest in maximizing the number of credits generated and sold, private monitors may have an incentive to "pad the numbers" on behalf of their clients. Because part of their job is to monitor the work of *other monitors*, they may have an incentive to let infractions slide, in the hopes that other firms will return the favor.[106] Indeed, the executive board temporarily suspended Det Norske Veritas's accreditation—which still monitors the largest share of CDM projects by far—in the wake of concerns about its performance and compliance with procedure.

Others have asked, quite rightly, whether the CDM has achieved the twin goals of reducing emissions and promoting sustainable development. Critics argue that reductions have not been additional and that

---

[104] UNFCCC 2002c, para. 5.

[105] It has also had a profound impact on the voluntary carbon market. See Green 2013a.

[106] Green 2008.

the focus on industrial gases has come at the price of a balanced regional distribution of activities and of projects that promote clean energy, technology-switching, and other aspects of sustainable development.[107] What's more, the absolute torrent of CDM credits has far outstripped demand, flooding the market and driving down price.

All of these problems will have to be addressed as the future of the CDM is decided along with the future of global climate change regulation. A recent high-level review of the CDM has acknowledged these and other shortcomings and called for extensive reforms, among the reforms in how the CDM is structured and governed.[108] Although it is unlikely that the verification model will be eliminated, private actors may see their role change, along with new rules and enhanced oversight mechanisms.

What is clear, however, is that the future of any climate change regime is tied to carbon markets and therefore to the CDM. Scholars have argued that *carbon* governance, which relies on both public and private authority rather than *climate* governance, which occurs primarily in the intergovernmental arena, seems to be the future approach to managing climate change.[109] Despite the uncertain future of the CDM, it is likely that some form of carbon offsets will persist in the future. To the extent that these offsets—whether public (under some future intergovernmental regulation) or private (within the voluntary carbon market)—require third-party monitoring, we can expect that private authority will also persist, in some form or another.

[107] See, e.g., Lohmann 2006; Wara 2007; Boyd et al. 2009.

[108] High Level Panel on the CDM Policy Dialogue 2012.

[109] Bernstein et al. 2010; Biermann 2010; Newell, Boykoff, and Boyd 2012; Green 2013a. Newell and Paterson 2010 go even further, arguing that responding to climate change is not simply a matter of governing carbon, but reimagining the global economy.

CHAPTER FIVE

Atmospheric Accountants: Entrepreneurial Authority and the Greenhouse Gas Protocol

JUST AS FINANCIAL ACCOUNTING measures the inflow and outflow of money, greenhouse gas (GHG) accounting provides an inventory of the gases that are put into and removed from the atmosphere. The Greenhouse Gas Protocol, which was created by two NGOs, the World Resources Institute (WRI) and the World Business Council on Sustainable Development (WBCSD), is now the world leader in firm-level greenhouse gas accounting procedures.[1] In extensive consultation with numerous firms, government agencies and other NGOs, WRI and WBCSD created the *Greenhouse Gas Protocol Corporate Accounting and Reporting Standard*. The protocol can be viewed as a successful example of private entrepreneurial authority: it is a set of standards that governs the behavior of actors in world politics without explicit delegation of authority by states. Virtually all GHG registries—which do not trade emissions but require participants to report them—use some version of the protocol, as do numerous other emissions reporting initiatives.

This chapter explains the success of WRI and WBCSD in creating the *de facto* standard for GHG emissions accounting at the firm (or "corporate") level. Earlier work on financial accounting has shown that despite its technical nature, standard setting is an inherently political process.[2] The creation of the GHG Protocol is similarly political, involving negotiation among myriad actors, including states. Although the protocol is a case of *private* authority, the chapter shows that states played an important role in its creation: their inability to come to an agreement about the related issue of emissions trading created a regulatory vacuum, which nonstate actors filled through the creation of the protocol.

I demonstrate that the emergence of the GHG Protocol is broadly consistent with the theory of private authority presented in chapter 1. The protocol emerged as *the* standard for corporate-level greenhouse gas emissions accounting because its creators were able to deliver three

---

[1] This chapter is based on Green 2010b.
[2] Mattli and Büthe 2003; Mattli and Büthe 2005.

benefits to potential rule takers that were not offered by other actors: reduced transaction costs, first-mover advantage, and enhanced reputation. Standardized "off the shelf" reporting procedures created by the protocol made it relatively easy for individual firms interested in adopting voluntary reporting measures to do so. In addition, the protocol provided technical support and ensured a consistent standard across actors. Adopting the protocol also helped users prepare for international regulation of GHG emissions, potentially giving them a competitive advantage with respect to other firms. Although the Kyoto Protocol had yet to enter into force when the GHG Protocol was published in 2001, many firms believed that some form of climate regulation was likely; implementing GHG accounting was viewed as a way to begin to prepare for such an event. Finally, although primarily motivated by the threat of regulation, firms adopting the GHG Protocol could also burnish their reputations as corporate citizens by positioning themselves as climate leaders (indeed, one such program was called "Climate Savers").

The chapter also explains the form of private authority—that is, why we see entrepreneurial authority projected by NGOs. Here, I argue that the inability of public authorities (governments or international organizations) to address the issue of firm-level emissions, combined with the lack of a strong focal institution to screen and monitor agents, foreclosed the delegation of regulatory authority and also created an opening for entrepreneurial private authority.

The most powerful states with respect to the issue of emissions trading—European Union and the JUSCANNZ negotiating bloc—had vastly different views on the appropriate role for this policy tool. Dissent among these states about the role of emissions trading, and thus, the possible *uses* of GHG emissions accounting standards, took the issue of corporate-level accounting methodologies off the agenda for intergovernmental cooperation. This deprived the Secretariat of the UNFCCC, the international public actor most likely to take on such as role, of any political mandate to do so. Moreover, even with such a mandate, the lacked the human resources to work on this issue. Thus, the ostensible focal institution was weak both politically and in terms of its capabilities.

At the same time, many firms, including those in JUSCANNZ countries, expected that climate change regulation would eventually be enacted. For these companies, the uncertainty created by governmental deadlock about the form of such "inevitable" future regulation was undesirable. The lack of public regulation meant continued uncertainty about the level of exposure, the risk of higher costs if large changes would have to be made quickly, and ambiguity about baselines, which is the metric against which future emissions would be evaluated. These concerns about the future were compounded by the risk that undertaking voluntary efforts to lower their GHG emissions would put them at a competitive disadvantage rather than provide them with an opportunity to receive financial or reputational credit for early efforts. Regulatory uncertainty thus provided a window of opportunity for the two NGOs, who were willing to supply (or, more precisely, provide an institutional structure to foster) private regulation out of a genuine desire to reduce GHG emissions, but with a savvy eye toward managing future risks. As a result, WRI and the WBCSD were able to provide a set of benefits that were valued by various stakeholders, and which led to the widespread adoption of these private rules.

The emergence of the GHG Protocol is consistent with my theory of private authority. Because of the divergent preferences of states, and the relative weakness of the likely focal institution, entrepreneurial NGOs were able to meet a demand for benefits that other actors were not. Consequently, public and private actors around the world chose to adopt the GHG Protocol to measure their greenhouse gas emissions.

Primer on GHG Accounting and the GHG Protocol

GHG Accounting

Greenhouse gas accounting provides a detailed and replicable report of the GHG emissions generated by a specific site or actor. The technical and scientific aspects of GHG accounting are complex, but two concepts must be introduced before discussing the specifics of the protocol. First, like financial accounting, GHG accounting can be conducted for either voluntary or regulatory purposes. Firms may be required to file financial accounting reports with the government, but they also create them for purposes of planning and management. Similarly, GHG accounting can be voluntary or linked to a regulatory regime. Some firms choose to track their emissions in order to be transparent to their shareholders or to reduce energy consumption. Others, such as large power producers in the European Union, are required by law to report their emissions levels, so governments can evaluate whether they are in compliance with regulations. The general term "GHG program" refers to both voluntary initiatives and regulatory programs that measure and report GHG emissions.[3] Although many GHG programs are voluntary, they are widely viewed as the logical precursor to emissions trading. One cannot buy or sell emissions without first quantifying them; in this sense, many firms

[3] World Resources Institute and World Business Council on Sustainable Development 2004, 98.

view GHG accounting as the first step in preparing for mandatory emissions trading.[4]

Second, just as financial accounts can be kept at the level of a project, firm, or country, so can GHG accounting occur on multiple levels. GHGs are generally measured and reported at one of four different levels: national, installation, corporate, or project. National-level reporting tracks emissions by sector and then aggregates them to present data for GHG emissions at the level of the nation-state. The UNFCCC requires national level reporting, and the methodology for such reporting was created by the Intergovernmental Panel on Climate Change.[5]

Installation-level reporting (also referred to as the facility-level reporting) measures emissions from a specific entity—such as a power plant, a paper mill, or cement factory. This type of measurement scheme was used in the now defunct U.K. Emissions Trading Scheme, and now in the EU Emissions Trading Scheme. As we will see in the following section, emissions trading schemes tend to use the facility level as the basis for reporting.

Corporate-level reporting occurs at the level of the organization. Any private firm, government agency, or NGO that wishes to track its emissions would use a corporate accounting scheme. Corporate-level accounting is distinct from the facility-level measures because it requires making decisions about organizational boundaries. For firms with joint operations or subsidiaries, corporate accounting requires deciding how these sources will be measured. Moreover, corporate accounting also calls for the calculation of "indirect emissions" from purchased electricity use, as well as emissions generated, for example, from purchased materials, waste disposal, and travel.[6] Generally, corporate-level reporting is used by individual firms as well as in some voluntary reporting schemes. By contrast, project-level reporting is used for calculating the emissions reductions generated by carbon offset projects, such as reforestation, wind farms, or methane capture. The GHG Protocol also developed a project-level standard, which was released in 2005. This chapter focuses exclusively on the corporate standard, which was released in 2001, and has become the "gold standard" for corporate-level reporting.[7] The project standard competes with a crowded landscape of offset standards and is less widely used.

---

[4] This view is expressed not only in the GHG Protocol but also by a number of participants in the protocol. See also Meckling 2011, 95.

[5] Intergovernmental Panel on Climate Change 2006.

[6] WRI and WBCSD launched a "Corporate Value Chain" standard in October 2011, which measures GHG emissions of a product from its creation to its disposal.

[7] Rebecca Eaton, former director, Climate Savers Program, World Wildlife Fund. Interview by author, 21 May 2009.

What Is the WRI/WBCSD Protocol?

The GHG Protocol is a multifaceted institution. It is at once a consultative standard-setting process, a conceptual framework, and a set of standards. I explain each of these aspects of the institution for two purposes: to acquaint the reader with the different functions of the protocol, for the purpose of conceptual clarity; and to distinguish between its different components.

The GHG Protocol is first and foremost a standard-setting process. It describes itself as "a multi-stakeholder partnership of businesses, nongovernmental organizations, governments, and others convened by the World Resources Institute and the World Business Council for Sustainable Development."[8] These two organizations convened hundreds of experts from business, government, and NGOs to create a methodologically rigorous standard. The process has dedicated staff at WRI and WBCSD, as well as partner institutions and public and private funders.

The protocol is also a framework for thinking about how to measure emissions. As one of the WRI staff involved with its creation explains, "The *GHG Protocol* corporate accounting and reporting standard is intended to be a 'GHG GAAP' – the GHG equivalent of generally accepted accounting practices for financial reporting."[9] To this end, it has created a number of conceptual tools. For instance, the protocol provides concepts for dividing up emissions into different "scopes." Scope 1 emissions are those that come from sources owned or controlled by the company. Scope 2 includes those emissions that come from purchased electricity. Scope 3 subsumes all other indirect emissions (such as transportation or extraction of purchased materials). The concept of scopes has become pervasive in the language and practice of GHG programs. Another key conceptual contribution of the GHG Protocol has been to provide conceptual frameworks for thinking about how to decide which emissions to include or exclude in the accounting (known as equity vs. control boundaries), an all-important issue for accounting at the corporate level.

Third, the protocol is a set of rules, comprised of three components: standards, guidelines, and calculation tools. In order for a firm to state that it has conducted its accounting in accordance with the protocol, there are a minimum number of requirements that it must meet.[10] The authors of the protocol signal that they use "shall" to specify required activities. In this sense, it is similar to treaty language that distinguishes

[8] World Resources Institute and World Business Council on Sustainable Development 2004, 2.

[9] Sundin and Ranganathan 2002, 141–42.

[10] Note that the protocol is voluntary, so there is no monitoring of compliance or sanction for noncompliance. Some organizations choose to have their GHG reporting independently audited, but this is not required by the protocol.

between should and shall—activities that are recommended versus those that are required. However, the protocol also suggests certain practices without requiring them. These guidelines range from recommendations about general principles to specific how-to guidance on gathering data and calculating emissions. One main author of the protocol identified the how-to guidance as a key contribution, walking new users through the process of creating a GHG inventory.[11]

Finally, the protocol offers specific tools and formulae for calculating actual emissions. These include how to calculate emissions from activities such as combustion or energy use (applicable to all entities that use the protocol) to "sector-specific" tools for aluminum, iron and steel, oil and gas, and other sectors. These calculation tools are peer reviewed in the sense that they were developed collaboratively with expertise from the requisite sector.[12]

The Emergence of the GHG Protocol

WRI, WBCSD, and the other organizations involved in the creation and vetting of the GHG Protocol were not the first to develop procedures for measuring greenhouse gases. However, they were among the first to develop ways to measure carbon emissions at the corporate level. In this section, I briefly review earlier efforts to measure and report GHG emissions and offsets, showing that the GHG Protocol was one of the earliest and certainly the most transparent efforts to develop a firm-level accounting tool.[13] The expertise concentrated within the protocol process is a key factor in understanding its uptake. The process was, quite simply, the first effort to bring together actors with experience and knowledge about corporate-level GHG accounting. Previously, what limited knowledge existed about corporate-level accounting was scattered across numerous firms, governments, and other organizations. WRI and WBCSD were the first to pool the resources of these actors through a multi-stakeholder consultative process.

Early GHG measurement efforts began in 1995, when the IPCC released GHG inventory guidelines. The UN Framework Convention on Climate Change requires Annex I countries—those with binding targets

[11] Michael Gillenwater, former EPA official. Interview by author, Washington, DC, 21 May 2009.
[12] Some tools also draw on measures created by the Intergovernmental Panel on Climate Change.
[13] I use "firm level" and "corporate level" interchangeably for standards that seek to provide measures of GHG emissions at the level of aggregation of a firm, whether or not it is legally a corporation.

under the Kyoto Protocol—to report annually on their emissions in six sectors: energy, industrial processes, solvents, agriculture, land use and land use change and waste. The IPCC guidelines, revised in 1996 and re-released in 2006, are to be used by Annex I countries when calculating their national-level emissions. These guidelines have been revised and refined since their initial release and are widely used for calculating emissions within a national territory.[14]

The same year, the parties to the UNFCCC agreed to undertake the pilot program called Activities Implemented Jointly (AIJ), whereby states could experiment with carbon offset projects.[15] Although it was agreed that states could not earn credits for these pilot projects, the prospect of project-based credits raised awareness about the need for measuring the amount of carbon removed in different types of offset activities. As experiments with offset projects began, so did work on measuring them. In 1997 a working paper drafted by the Lawrence Berkeley Laboratory in the United States cited seven existing protocols and guidelines, created by governments, IOs, NGOs, and private firms.[16] These represented various attempts to measure and report on different types of offset projects. Most of the protocols were rudimentary at best. The Uniform Reporting Format created by the UNFCCC was little more than a two-page questionnaire to describe the activities of the offset project. The key event of that year was the signing of the Kyoto Protocol, which institutionalized the practice of carbon offset projects, making the need for well-developed measurement tools quite urgent.

Thus, by 1997, there was considerable activity surrounding GHG measurement. However, almost all of it was related to intergovernmental agreements, with states as the primary actors. Moreover, these efforts were focused almost exclusively on the national and project levels and were still very basic tools. There is little evidence of equivalent methodologies for the facility or firm levels.

The focus on climate change at the corporate level began in 1997, when British Petroleum (BP) announced an ambitious plan to create an internal emissions trading program. The goal was to reduce BP's emissions by 10 percent below 1990 levels by 2010.[17] However, such a goal first required that BP develop a system for measuring and reporting. Victor and House describe these initial steps:

> Until the decision to pursue the ETS [emissions trading scheme], the company had no uniform standard for reporting greenhouse gas emissions. BP developed a CO_2 reporting protocol within months of Browne's speech [announcing

[14] Intergovernmental Panel on Climate Change 2006.
[15] UNFCCC 1995.
[16] Vine and Sathaye 1997, 8–16.
[17] Browne 1997.

BP's new initiative], and by the end of 1997 had inventoried GHG emissions for 1990, 1994, 1995, and 1996 . . . *The lack of reliable inventories was normal in the industry at the time.*[18]

Thus, the BP experiment was not only the first in corporate-level emissions trading; it was necessarily one of the first in corporate-level emissions measurement.

As BP was implementing its pilot trading scheme, other organizations began to recognize the need for a corporate-level emissions reporting scheme. Shortly after BP announced its plans, four future members of the GHG Protocol called businesses to action for the same purpose.[19] BP, along with Monsanto, General Motors, and WRI published *Safe Climate, Sound Business: An Action Agenda* in October 1998. The document challenges businesses to address their contributions to climate change and to "measure, track, and openly report greenhouse gas emissions from their operations."[20] Moreover, the signatories to the document pledge to cooperate to "develop a joint protocol for measuring and reporting greenhouse gas emissions and the eco-efficiency of our global operations."[21]

The steps for action set forth in *Safe Climate, Sound Business* laid the foundations for the GHG Protocol. NGOs and firms alike had identified the need for such a tool, and the existing expertise was minimal. Only a few forward-looking firms and NGOs had any experience with measuring GHGs at the firm level, and even these efforts were fairly new. Because existing experience on corporate-level accounting was minimal, early movers had an opportunity to shape measurement rules and practices. Although there was no guarantee that such rules would become binding, many firms felt that a proactive stance was a way to avoid undesirable regulatory outcomes. One former representative of the WBCSD who was involved in the early stages of the WBCSD noted that input at the early stages of developing a measurement tool was a much easier way to shape future rules. He noted, "If you [i.e., the business community] don't do anything and just leave it to the regulators, you're stuck with whatever comes out."[22] By contrast, he noted, it is "much easier to influence regulation at the early stages [than to] undo something that's already been presented."[23]

To follow up on the pledge laid out in *Safe Climate, Sound Business*, WRI began talking to leaders in business as well as NGOs and government actors. It did not want to present a measurement protocol as a *fait*

[18] Victor and House 2004, 2102, emphasis added.
[19] Monsanto was not involved in the consultations and drafting of the GHG Protocol.
[20] The Climate Protection Initiative 1998, 6.
[21] Ibid., 16.
[22] Dave Moorcroft, former director, Climate and Energy Programme, World Business Council for Sustainable Development. Interview by author, 17 November 2009.
[23] Moorcroft, Interview.

accompli, but rather wanted to create a consultative multi-stakeholder process both to produce a rigorous product and to cultivate future users of the protocol. It soon discovered that the WBCSD had a similar initiative in mind. After some discussion, each organization realized that "two different efforts are tantamount to a distandard."[24] Each side realized that the other had something to bring to the table. WRI provided a considerable amount of technical expertise; WBCSD had extensive reach into the business world via its membership. These members were potential users of the protocol. Moreover, each side realized that the legitimacy and credibility of any measurement scheme would be greatly enhanced by having both NGOs and industry groups involved.[25] One representative of the WBCSD noted that there was suspicion on both sides at the outset, but there was also agreement on the need for a "quality product"[26] as well as something that was "implementable."[27] Both of these goals could be achieved through a rigorous, transparent and participatory rule-making process.

The cooperation between WRI and WBCSD did not occur seamlessly. Despite initial wariness, there were three factors that facilitated their collaboration. First, all major participants in the process stressed the importance of the deliberative process. This commitment to deliberation and revision addressed the concern that some views might not be adequately considered and that the end product would favor one group of interests over another.[28] Because participants felt that all points of view were seriously discussed, there was less reason for one group to "take their ball and go home" by starting a competing standard.

Second, particularly at the early stages of the process, the participants— including those from the private sector—were largely leaders (or aspiring leaders) on climate change. (Unsurprisingly, in some cases, these were firms that needed some good publicity.) This self-selecting group was committed to creating a meaningful outcome—a workable standard— rather than creating a lowest-common-denominator standard. To promote good-faith negotiation, members of the protocol participated in their individual capacity. As a result, people did not simply negotiate on behalf of their organization but rather focused on contributing their

[24] Janet Ranganathan, Vice President for Science and Research, World Resources Institute. Interview by author, 19 May 2009.

[25] Meckling 2011 identifies the legitimacy conferred by business-NGO coalitions as a key source of their influence in emissions trading policies.

[26] Moorcroft, Interview.

[27] Antonia Gawel, World Business Council for Sustainable Development, Interview by author, 8 November 2008.

[28] Ranganathan, Interview; Pankaj Bhatia, Director, GHG Protocol, Interview by author, 11 November 2008, and with Rob Frederick, former manager of corporate social, responsibility, Ford Motor Companies, 8 May 2009.

expert knowledge to the process.[29] This is not to say that the discussions were not without contention but that that they were governed by the collective desire to create a rigorous methodology rather than one that would favor certain groups.

Third, the vision for the final corporate standard was to create a framework for GHG accounting, in which individual users could use only the parts they wanted or that suited their objectives. In other words, the protocol was not designed to be an "all or nothing" standard. While basic elements are required to maintain the intent and integrity of the standard, there was some degree of flexibility in its application. Understandably, this lowered the stakes for many groups; if certain nonessential parts of the standard were objectionable, they could simply choose not to implement them. With this common ground in mind, WRI and WBCSD agreed to join forces rather than create competing standards.

Because WBCSD had a large member base of multinational firms, one of its key contributions was to ensure participation and support from the private sector, which came in two forms. Many WBCSD members expressed interest in the process, and some were willing to contribute funds or staff time to developing the project. Moreover, by bringing these corporate actors into the fold and encouraging their input and buy-in, WBCSD helped prevent the creation of a competing standard promulgated solely by business interests.

Another important development in consolidating the authority of the WRI/WBCSD collaboration occurred in 2001, when the U.S. Environmental Protection Agency (EPA) became a major funder and participant.[30] Given the uncertainty surrounding U.S. regulatory responses to climate change, the EPA's involvement served to reassure firms that the protocol's rules would be taken seriously by the U.S. government. This further reinforced the perceived legitimacy and potential high level of future usefulness of the protocol to business groups, lowering the payoff of creating a competing standard. Importantly, the EPA also pledged to use the protocol in its own voluntary reporting program—again demonstrating recognition of the protocol by the government. Moreover, other core advisers to the protocol were heavily involved with separate efforts to create trading schemes or measurement protocols. The process convened by WRI and the WBCSD provided a natural focal point for these various efforts.

WRI and WBCSD also fostered commitment to the new standards by setting up the creation of the protocol as an extensive multi-stakeholder process. One member of the project management team described it as "a

[29] Ranganathan, Interview.

[30] Cynthia Cummis, former EPA official, Washington, DC. Interview by Author, 19 May 2009.

big tent initiative," where anyone who was interested could participate.[31] When the first edition of the protocol was published in September 2001, it listed more than three hundred contributors from some two hundred organizations.[32] Through the drafting process, many participants became invested in the implementation of the protocol. As one member of the WRI project team put it, the GHG Protocol "became theirs too."[33] In short, the multi-stakeholder process was a key strategy for building constituencies for the protocol.[34]

WRI and WBCSD also employed other strategies to build these constituencies and commit future users to the protocol. After the first draft was completed, some firms agreed to "road-test" the protocol, to see what worked and what did not.[35] Their experiences resulted not only in improving the final product but also in creating more users. Preliminary drafts were peer reviewed by accounting firms and KPMG, to ensure consistency and replicability.[36] Similarly, WRI and WBCSD worked with industry associations to help tailor the protocol to specific sectors such as aluminum, cement, and wood products. There are now a dozen such tools, many of which have become standard for each industry. These iterative reviews had three beneficial effects: they improved the quality of the standard, increased the legitimacy of the process, and created buy-in among participants. All of these efforts helped prevent the creation of a competing standard. However, success is not merely measured by the absence of competition; we must also look at the breadth of the protocol's adoption.

Adoption of the Standard

The definition of private authority is purposefully broad about which actors in world politics must defer to private actors in order to create private authority. *Any actor* who adopts privately created rules or standards without coercion creates an instance of private authority. Entrepreneurs may persuade only a few like-minded actors to defer, or the uptake of their rules and practices may be widespread. In this section, I show that the uptake of the protocol's standards has been very widespread:

[31] Ranganathan, Interview.

[32] World Resources Institute and World Business Council on Sustainable Development 2001.

[33] Ranganathan, Interview.

[34] This is consistent with Bernstein and Cashore 2007, who describe a support-building phase for nonstate market-driven governance systems.

[35] For a similar phenomenon in financial accounting standards, see Mattli and Büthe 2005.

[36] World Resources Institute 2001.

numerous GHG registries have adopted the protocol, as have pilot programs, industry organizations, and even one emissions trading scheme.

One might argue that the widespread use of the protocol does not demonstrate private regulatory authority but is simply "business as usual" for those who adopt it. However, I maintain that adopting the protocol involves real, measurable costs. Implementation requires purposeful and sustained action: choosing organizational boundaries, setting a baseline to compare emissions over time, identifying and calculating emissions, gathering company-wide data, and assessing the accuracy of the data collected. In other words, we can be confident that adopting the protocol requires meaningful and costly changes in the behavior and practices of adopters and thus conforms to the definition of private authority.[37]

WRI and WBCSD are projecting entrepreneurial authority in two ways. First, I show how other emissions trading schemes and reporting registries have adopted some or all of the protocol in their measurement and reporting methodologies.[38] I chose to examine all extant trading schemes and four of the largest reporting schemes and evaluate the extent to which they adopt various components of the protocol.[39] Second, I supply additional evidence illustrating its influence over other standard-setting processes. I examine the involvement of the GHG Protocol as an institution in discussions surrounding the creation and design of other accounting and trading programs. I also provide evidence showing that participants in the protocol process were able to influence the position of previously resistant actors, persuading them to adopt the protocol as well as a pro-active strategy toward GHG measurement.

Before turning to the specific programs that have adopted the GHG Protocol, some discussion of the universe of cases is in order. Unfortunately, it is infeasible to generate a complete list of all of the firms and GHG registries that measure and report their emissions, and then calculate the percentage that do *not* use the protocol. However, a review of the corporate users shows that 18 percent of U.S. Fortune 100 companies have adopted the protocol and 12 percent of the Global Fortune 100 are users. These statistics are neither insignificant nor overwhelming. Roughly 70

[37] Dahl 1957, 202–3.

[38] Figuring out who has adopted the protocol is a difficult matter. The GHG Protocol website lists those users who either use the protocol or whose own measurement scheme is compatible with the protocol. However, it does not distinguish between these two. I have tried to triangulate, by consulting not only with the GHG Protocol staff but also with staff at relevant reporting schemes to ask them the extent to which they rely on the WRI/WBCSD protocol for their own reporting requirements.

[39] The trading schemes were selected on the basis of trade volume as reported by Capoor and Ambrosi 2008. The voluntary reporting schemes were selected on the basis of the number of participating firms and the geographic breadth of participants, as well as information gleaned from interviews about which reporting programs are most widely used.

percent of S&P 500 firms now report their emissions through the Carbon Disclosure Project, which estimates that more than half of the participating firms use the protocol.[40] This suggests that through the organizational auspices of the Carbon Disclosure Project, roughly 35 percent of S&P500 firms use the GHG Protocol. This is a rough measurement, but it provides a sense that using this methodology is not simply on the margins of the private sector.

Estimating the proportion of GHG registries that use the protocol (or are based on the protocol) is more challenging because there is no established list of all extant registries. To define the universe of cases, I began with the list of protocol users listed on the GHG Protocol website.[41] I supplemented this list with web searches and references to other registries in the literature and in websites about carbon accounting. In sum, I tried to establish as complete a list as possible using multiple sources.

Virtually every registry in the set of cases I compiled has either adopted the protocol, created its own methodology based in whole or in part on the protocol, recommended using the protocol (or another methodology based on it), or stated that its method for measuring GHG emissions is "consistent" with the protocol. Some programs were merely "compatible with" the protocol; these were excluded from the list of adopters (see table 5.1). Also excluded were programs that focus primarily on one type of energy provision or exclusively on carbon offset projects. In other words, I have focused only on registries (as opposed to other types of carbon management or abatement methodologies) and set a stringent standard for those that I designate as protocol adopters.

Despite using these strict criteria, the high level of uptake of the protocol is clear. There is no real competition among standards. The Greenhouse Gas Protocol is *the* standard for corporate-level measurement. The one competing standard that exists was created by the UN Environment Program (UNEP) in 2000.[42] The UNEP GHG Indicator was created around the same time as the protocol. The indicator was not intended to serve as a substitute or a complement to the protocol but rather was to be a "stand-alone" tool for users that might not have the capacity to implement the more complex procedures in the Greenhouse Gas Protocol.[43] The intended users were small and medium-sized enterprises with

[40] PricewaterhouseCoopers 2012. The 50 percent figure was provided by Joanna Lee via email communication. The Carbon Disclosure Project has also adopted the use of more recent standards created by the GHG Protocol for its reporting purposes, including the Product Life Cycle standard and the Corporate Value Chain standard.

[41] This list is available from http://www.ghgprotocol.org/standards/corporate-standard/users-of-the-corporate-standard

[42] See http://www.uneptie.org/energy/information/tools/ghg/

[43] Mark Radka, UNEP Division of Technology, Industry and Economics. Interview by author, 14 April 2009.

a preference for an internal management tool, rather than an external reporting standard. However, according to one of its creators, it was never widely publicized, and UNEP takes only minimal steps to update it.

Evaluating the universe of cases of emissions trading schemes is much more straightforward; of the ten functional schemes, one uses the protocol. As I discuss below, only one emissions trading scheme decided to measure emissions at the corporate level. Given that the decision about the level of aggregation (corporate, facility, or national) is prior to the selection of the measurement standard, the conclusions to be drawn from this fact are mixed. In sum, the distribution of uptake of the standard is varied, with the highest concentration by far taking place in voluntary registries. I turn now to the specifics of adoption rates in GHG registries and emissions trading schemes.

Adoption of the Protocol in GHG Registries

GHG registries differ from emissions trading schemes in that they are nonregulatory and generally are not linked to the purchase or sale of emissions allowances. Although some have government participants, almost all are run by private actors. More importantly, unlike emissions trading schemes, which tend to focus at the facility level, the majority of reporting programs occur at the corporate level. Space constraints preclude a detailed discussion of all of the GHG reporting programs that have adopted the protocol for their methodologies, but table 5.1 provides an overview of the main programs by sector.[44] Importantly, some twenty-five major reporting programs worldwide use the protocol, including four key programs: the standard promulgated by the International Organization for Standardization (ISO), the Carbon Disclosure Project, the North American–focused Climate Registry, and the U.S.-based Climate Leaders program. In the remainder of this section, I briefly describe these, two of which are global and two of which are in the United States.

By far, the biggest success of the protocol has been its wholesale adoption by ISO. ISO is a network of national standards institutes that creates standards for a vast range of products and processes. After the release of the GHG Protocol in 2001, ISO proposed developing its own methodology, despite the fact that firms, NGOs, and reporting programs were already using the protocol. Nonetheless, ISO forged ahead. Those involved in the negotiations with ISO have differing explanations of its desire to create its own scheme. Two participants in the process attributed ISO's insistence on a separate standard to the active participation of the oil and

[44] This table is an "edited version" of the GHG Protocol website, including all of those programs that explicitly say they are based on the protocol or have adopted it wholesale, but excluding those programs that are merely "compatible with" the protocol.

gas industry, which was generally opposed to action on climate change, let alone the adoption of a measurement scheme created without their input.[45] Another key participant attributed ISO's reluctance to adopt the protocol to its "mind set [and] mental model" as well as the "defensive behavior of the ISO organization."[46]

In an effort to prevent the creation of a competing scheme, participants of the GHG Protocol sought out the ISO and tried to persuade them to adopt the extant standard as their own. A protracted set of discussions between ISO and the main authors of the protocol followed. The protocol used its support from WBCSD and the business community to persuade ISO that establishing a competing standard would be a disservice to all. Many of those involved in the process of drafting the protocol became vocal supporters and thus persuasive ambassadors to skeptics. In the end, there was "a little luck involved" because some of the most vocal opponents were not present at the final ISO vote.[47] After approximately five years of negotiation, ISO finally adopted a standard for GHG measurement and reporting that is almost identical to the protocol, called ISO-14064, Part 1.[48] Thus, the ISO has deferred to the methods set forth in the protocol and has repackaged them as its own. Given the ISO's broad reach and high level of legitimacy among business and industry, its decision to adopt the protocol has translated to a much wider reach to these communities.

A second global user of the protocol is the Carbon Disclosure Project (CDP). An independent nonprofit organization, the CDP collects data on GHG emissions on behalf of institutional investors. CDP is organized on the principle that investors are in a better position to evaluate the risks and potential areas for improvement of the companies they invest in if they know their emissions and exposure to future regulation. In 2012, 81 percent of companies from the Global 500 provided GHG emissions data to the CDP, representing US$78 trillion in investor assets.[49] The Carbon Disclosure Project relies on participating companies to report their emissions in a manner that is transparent, rigorous, and compatible with its program. Although it does not require a particular GHG accounting methodology, it strongly recommends that participants use the protocol. One interviewee at CDP reported that more than 50 percent use the protocol in responding to the survey. She added that the protocol was chosen because "it has international recognition as being thorough and robust,

[45] Bhatia, Interview; Ranganthan, Interview.

[46] Moorcroft, Interview.

[47] Bhatia, Interview.

[48] The primary difference is that ISO requires third-party verification, which the protocol does not.

[49] https://www.cdproject.net/en-US/Pages/global500.aspx.

and we believe it to be the most appropriate."[50] In addition, for so-called scope 3 emissions, which account for emissions all along the value chain, the protocol is the only accepted standard.[51]

There are two key adopters of the protocol in the United States that also demonstrate the breadth of adoption. The first is the EPA's voluntary reporting program, called Climate Leaders. Climate Leaders was created in 2001 to help participating companies to measure and reduce their GHG emissions. It was phased out in late 2010, following the creation of national reporting requirements for large emitters. Like ISO-14064, Climate Leaders adopted the protocol in its entirety. It became involved in the early consultations about creating the protocol and decided to fund the initiative as well as to use the newly created standard in its own program.[52] The motivations for using the protocol were three. First, existing voluntary reporting protocols developed by the U.S. Department of Energy (DoE) did not provide a useful model, because they were focused on project-level rather than corporate-level reporting.[53] Thus, at the time, there were no other models to draw upon—save for the process emerging from WRI and WBCSD. Second, the international reach of the standards was appealing. Because multinational corporations were the primary target market for Climate Leaders, using an international standard such as GHG Protocol assured compatibility with other users and facilitated consistent accounting practices across worldwide operations of a given company. Third, the transparency and inclusiveness of the GHG Protocol process bolstered the legitimacy of the standards and helped to ensure buy-in from a broad range of stakeholders.

The policy landscape has changed since Climate Leaders was created in 2001. New EPA regulations require power plants, refineries, and other large emitters to report their GHG emissions.[54] Subnational compliance-based initiatives such as the Regional Greenhouse Gas Initiative and the new California market have also emerged. However, Climate Leaders' use of the protocol was a significant contribution to its widespread uptake. The EPA's funding and adoption of the protocol lent legitimacy to the efforts of WRI and WBCSD; with the active support of future regulators, potential users of the protocol saw the value of getting a seat at the table.

[50] Joanna Lee, Carbon Disclosure Project. Email communication with the author, 14 April 2009.

[51] PricewaterhouseCoopers 2012, 55.

[52] Cynthia Cummis, former director, Climate Leaders Program, U.S. Environmental Protection Agency. Interview by author, 19 May 2009.

[53] Cummis, Interview.

[54] See http://www.epa.gov/ghgreporting/index.html for data and information on reporting requirements.

The second program, the Climate Registry, is a voluntary GHG program used by organizations in forty U.S. states, six Mexican states, and eleven Canadian provinces and territories, as well as four Native Sovereign Nations. Its goal is to promote the use of a single set of measurement tools to calculate, report, and verify GHG emissions and to establish a common data infrastructure for reporting. The Climate Registry states that it draws on four sources in the creation of its own measurement protocol: the WRI/WBCSD GHG Protocol, ISO-14064, the United States' EPA Climate Leaders, and the California Climate Action Registry. As table 5.1 indicates, the California Climate Action Registry has also adopted the protocol. In this sense, *all* of the methodologies that contributed to the Climate Registry's methodology are products of the protocol. The geographic breadth of the Climate Registry, as well as its position that any federal GHG regulation should use its accounting and calculation methodologies shows the broad uptake of the protocol and the potential for even more expansion.

Adoption of the GHG Protocol in Emissions Trading Schemes

Currently, there are ten emissions trading schemes in their operation phase.[55] Table 5.2 lists them in the order of their founding date.[56] A first glance at the table suggests that the adoption rate of the protocol is low—only one in ten. However, such a conclusion presupposes that each trading scheme makes the choice about the level of aggregation (national, facility, corporate) *simultaneously* with the choice of measurement standard. In fact, this is not the case. Rather, the first design choice is the level of aggregation, followed by the choice of measurement standard *for a given level of aggregation*. Put another way, only one emissions trading scheme has opted to conduct trading among firms (rather than, say, nation-states or facilities); once it did so, it selected the protocol as its measurement standard.

The Chicago Climate Exchange (CCX) was a voluntary but legally binding program to reduce and trade greenhouse gas emissions among

[55] Betsill and Hoffmann 2011. According to their work, in 2008, there were seven active schemes. Twenty-six additional schemes that are either now defunct or are in the preliminary planning stages. I exclude the former because many were created before the protocol was published, and thus are not plausible candidates for adopting it. I exclude the latter because they have yet to create specific rules about accounting and reporting. I also include the Clean Development Mechanism, since it is linked to the cap-and-trade scheme under Kyoto, and the emissions trading schemes in California and Australia, which have come on line since Betsill and Hoffman's work was published.

[56] The last year of the comprehensive survey of emissions trading by Betsill and Hoffmann 2011 is 2008. I have updated their work to include emissions trading schemes that have become operational since then.

TABLE 5.1
GHG Programs Using the Protocol

Voluntary Governmental Programs	Industry Associations and National Industry Initiatives	Nongovernmental Programs	Other
Australian National Greenhouse and Energy Reporting Guidelines	Association des entreprises pour la réduction des gaz à effet de serre	Business Leaders Initiative on Climate Change	ISO 14064-Part I
Brazil GHG Protocol Program	International Council for Forest and Paper Association	Carbon Disclosure Project	United Nations GHG Calculator
Canadian GHG Challenge Registry	International Petroleum Industry Environmental Conservation	Carbon Trust Standard	
China Corporate Energy Conservation and GHG Management Program	New Zealand Business Council for Sustainable Development	Climate Neutral Network	
India GHG Inventory Program	Taiwan Business Council for Sustainable Development	WWF Climate Savers	
Mexico GHG Program	WBCSD Sustainable Cement		
New Mexico GHG Mandatory Emissions Reporting	World Economic Forum Global GHG Registry		
Philippine Greenhouse Gas Accounting and Reporting Program			
The Climate Registry			
US EPA Climate Leaders Program[a]			

[a] US EPA Climate Leaders was phased out at the end of 2010.

TABLE 5.2
Emissions Trading Schemes, by Founding Date

Trading Scheme	Founding Date	Level of Reporting
Chicago Climate Exchange[a]	2003	Corporate
New South Wales[b]	2003	Facility
European Union Emissions Trading Scheme	2005	Facility
Japan Voluntary Emissions Trading Scheme	2005	Facility
Clean Development Mechanism	2006	Project
Kyoto Protocol	2008	Nation
New Zealand	2008	Facility
Regional Greenhouse Gas Initiative	2009	Facility
Australia[c]	2012	Facility
California	2013	Facility

[a] The CCX has since abandoned its trading scheme to focus solely on offsets.

[b] The New South Wales trading scheme has been incorporated into a new federal carbon policy in Australia.

[c] The Australian policy begins as carbon tax, but will become a fully operational cap-and-trade scheme in 2015.

North American firms. In 2011 it transitioned from an emissions trading scheme to an offsets program. Credits were earned through abatement projects and then could be traded among its members. In Phase II, which ran from 2007 to 2010, members committed to reduce emissions 6 percent below a baseline level. The baseline could be either the average of annual emissions between 1998 and 2001 or the single year 2000. Allowances were allotted to each member equal to the emissions reduction target. Members that did not meet their annual target were required to buy allowances equal to the amount of the overage. The CCX grew rapidly, doubling its trading volume in between 2006 and 2007.[57] However, it declined in value and volume almost as rapidly, once it was clear that there would be no comprehensive U.S. climate legislation.

The paucity of trading schemes at the corporate level raises a broader question about the applicability of the protocol to compliance-based trading. The general perception is that corporate-level reporting is not well suited for compliance-based trading.[58] Because judgments are required to decide which emissions should be included and excluded for

[57] Capoor and Ambrosi 2009, 1.

[58] Several interviewees confirmed that this is a widely held view, though it was not necessarily clear when discussions about corporate-based accounting first began.

a given organization's report, possibilities of double counting arise. The protocol notes that "whether or not double counting occurs depends on how consistently direct and indirect emissions are reported."[59] The possibility of double counting raises two challenges for GHG markets: the overall amount of emissions may be inflated as a result of inaccurate counting, and two companies could potentially claim ownership of the same "piece" of emissions. Both problems would impede the proper functioning of a trading market. For this reason, "compliance regimes are more likely to focus on the 'point of release' of emissions"—that is, when a given ton of GHG can be physically tied to its producer at the facility level.[60] Since the CCX was a voluntary market, which had no mandate to account for all emissions, issues surrounding double counting were not pertinent.

However, this observation does not render corporate accounting entirely irrelevant for regulation; the new EPA regulations require some entities to report at the corporate level.[61] In the European Union, the accounting methods for cement production are consistent with the sector-based tool developed by cement firms and the GHG Protocol.[62] Moreover, as the European Union moves forward with its trading scheme, it has been relying upon the existing cement-sector tool to establish benchmarks for future allowances. Finally, it is important to note that corporate accounting can be disaggregated to track emissions from individual facilities.[63] In a word, there have been some regulatory applications of the protocol, and one can move from corporate to facility levels of accounting if policies so require. Nonetheless, as the following section illustrates, the majority of actors deferring to the protocol do so for voluntary GHG registries.

The Broad Authority of the GHG Protocol

As stated earlier, tracing the number and size of the organizations that have adopted the GHG Protocol gives an incomplete picture of the authority of the protocol as an institution. In addition to persuading others to adopt the rules it created, the protocol as an institution helped shape other discussions of GHG measurement and reporting in three ways. It served as a technical adviser, contributed to a general shift in attitude by

[59] World Resources Institute and World Business Council on Sustainable Development 2001, 21.

[60] Ibid.

[61] US EPA 2009.

[62] Bruno Vanderborght, Senior Vice President of Climate Protection, Holcim Industries. Interview by author, 26 November 2009.

[63] World Resources Institute 2007.

previously resistant actors, and continues to influence the institutional landscape through its "progeny"—other firm-level standards that have adopted some or all of the protocol's rules.

Staff from the protocol served as technical advisers to GHG programs as they were being created.[64] Although in many cases, new registries adopted large parts of the protocol, many also have requirements that depart from the protocol in various ways. Thus, staff at WRI and WBCSD worked closely with the California Climate Action Registry (now part of the Climate Registry) and the ISO, as each worked to create a reporting methodology based on the protocol, but with some additions or amendments. For example, the most recent version of the Climate Registry standard adopts many of the reporting requirements and standards set forth in the protocol, but also encourages members to report at the facility level—a measurement standard not included in the protocol.[65]

Protocol staff members were also involved in the discussions around the Regional Greenhouse Gas Initiative (RGGI), one of two government-sanctioned compliance-based emissions trading scheme in the United States (the other one, in California, began trading in January 2013). They have played a similar role in the Western Climate Initiative, which is in the process of creating an emissions trading scheme in the western United States and Canada and in early discussions of the governors in midwestern states in the United States to reduce GHG emissions. Neither RGGI nor the Western Climate Initiative could adopt the protocol wholesale, because both have chosen to conduct reporting at the facility rather than at the corporate level. However, protocol staff worked closely with RGGI on a sector-based tool for stationary combustion, as well as on verification and software issues.

At the federal level, the protocol worked with an outside firm to develop a version of the standard tailored for use by government agencies.[66] A 2009 U.S. executive order requires government agencies to report and eventually reduce their emissions; the version of the protocol created specifically for the U.S. public sector provides the tools to implement this regulation. Protocol staff members at WRI and WBCSD have also provided technical expertise to the U.S. Department of Energy's voluntary GHG reporting program as it sought to revise its guidelines; the new version is now consistent with the protocol. Protocol staff also consulted on discussions of monitoring and reporting requirements during the design phase of the EU emissions trading scheme. Like RGGI, the EU scheme

[64] Information on the ongoing interactions between the GHG Protocol and these various other programs and trading schemes is documented in regular updates of the protocol's newsletter. These details are drawn from seven years of newsletter updates, available from http://www.ghgprotocol.org/newsletter/newsletter-archives.

[65] http://www.theclimateregistry.org/downloads/2013/03/TCR_GRP_Version_2.0.pdf.

[66] World Resources Institute and LMI 2011.

requires measurement and reporting at the facility level; the protocol is therefore of limited applicability. However, in the case of the United Kingdom's now-defunct emissions trading scheme, methods for estimating emissions from electricity use and joint-ventures relied heavily on the protocol.[67] Thus, in each of these cases, registries and trading schemes developing measurement standards sought out and deferred to the expertise of staff at the GHG Protocol.

Second, the protocol helped facilitate a shift from no action on climate change to various efforts to measure GHG in two previously resistant groups of actors—energy-intensive industries and large developing nations. The production of cement is extremely energy intensive and thus produces considerable GHG emissions. Many cement firms have mobilized against domestic legislation on GHG emissions because of the heavy costs that the industry would incur. One firm—Holcim—has been decidedly ahead of the curve. It began considering the possibility of monitoring its GHG emissions in 1999.[68] A quick internal survey of Holcim holdings revealed seven different methodologies for measuring emissions, each of which yielded widely varied calculations for the same activities. Upon discovering the work of the protocol, and seeing the large gap between Holcim's work and the emerging protocol, Holcim opted to work with WRI and WBCSD, both because of their reputations and "to facilitate further acceptance by other cement companies and other organizations."[69] The early work undertaken by Holcim was thus incorporated into the standards developed through the protocol process.

The involvement of Holcim as one of the core advisers in the GHG Protocol and its commitment to implementing the standard resulted in two important outcomes. First, the protocol created a sector-based tool (first released in 2002), tailored specifically to the needs of the cement industry. Second, Holcim spent considerable time and energy refining the tool and then promoting it within the industry. In 2002 eleven cement firms agreed to "road test" the tool, and revisions were made based on their experiences. In addition, Holcim was involved in the creation of the Cement Sustainability Initiative, which requires signatories to use the protocol. It has also conducted an extensive capacity-building campaign in developing nations to help firms implement the measurement and reporting standard. The result of all of these activities is that the cement sector version of the protocol is used in nearly 100 percent of cement production in the United States and European Union, and 65 percent in Latin America. Globally, the adoption rate is estimated to be near 65 percent, not including China.[70]

[67] Ranganathan. Interview.
[68] Vanderborght, Interview.
[69] Bruno Vanderborght. Email communication with author, 2 December 2009.
[70] Vanderborght, Interview.

These efforts have not been without objections. Bruno Vanderborght, senior vice president of Climate Protection at Holcim, was a core adviser to the first draft of the protocol. He noted that some firms in Asia have resisted adopting the protocol, in part because measurement systems already in place worked differently. Their eventual adoption of the protocol can be attributed to continued discussion and peer pressure from industry leaders such as Holcim.[71]

The protocol has also established small GHG programs in developing countries in an effort to promote the idea of GHG measurement and build the capacity to do so. To date, it has established programs in Mexico, China, Brazil, India and the Philippines. In these instances, WRI, WBCSD and other participants in the creation of the standard have been successful in inducing others to adopt the protocol. Perhaps more importantly, the protocol has also started a broader conversation about the need to monitor GHG emissions. Developing countries have in general been resistant to such efforts because they are not required to reduce their emissions under the Kyoto Protocol.

These examples show that the protocol was able to provide a nonthreatening way for a variety of actors to participate in technical (i.e., nonpolitical) discussions about policy action. As one interviewee put it, the protocol provided a venue and the technical expertise for actors who wanted to get involved in GHG measurement.[72] In short, the protocol became a focal point for activity on corporate GHG standards where previously there had been none.

Third, the protocol continues to promote GHG measurement practices without being actively involved in them. As demonstrated in this section, most GHG programs that function at the corporate level state that they are based on the WRI/WBCSD Corporate Protocol as well as the ISO-14064 standard. In other words, the protocol either directly or through its "progeny" has become the *de facto* standard on which almost all other corporate standards are based. This is well illustrated by the evolution of the Climate Registry, which is based on four different sources, all of which are derived from the protocol.

Explaining the Emergence of the GHG Protocol

The model of private authority argues that it can be explained as a function of supply and demand, which accounts for both the emergence and form of private authority. The supply side posits that private expertise is

[71] Vanderborght, Interview.
[72] Gillenwater, Interview.

a necessary but not sufficient condition for emergence. The demand side posits that private actors are able to project authority when they can provide benefits that others cannot. The entrepreneurial form of private authority can be explained by two independent variables: the divergent preferences of key powerful states in the climate negotiations, and the relatively weak capacity of the regime's focal institution, the UNFCCC Secretariat.

As noted above, there was a limited supply of private expertise, scattered across firms and NGOs. As a multi-stakeholder process, WRI and WBCSD assembled this extant knowledge into one place. Moreover, it drew upon outside experts in government and elsewhere throughout the drafting, revision, and road-testing phases.

There was clearly a demand for entrepreneurial authority to create a corporate-level GHG standard. The protocol offered three key benefits to those who chose to adopt it. First, it created the possibility for first-mover advantage, giving firms that implemented GHG reporting a head start on managing emissions before national and intergovernmental rules were put in place. These early adopters would be better prepared for future regulation. Moreover, they could establish credible baselines to ensure that future emissions restrictions were not based on unrealistic expectations and possibly secure credits for early action.[73] The protocol refers to this as "baseline protection"—a clear way to insulate against regulatory risk.[74] Second, the protocol reduced transaction costs in two ways. It provided companies who wanted to implement GHG accounting with a ready-made way to do so, complete with software, a how-to guide, and technical support. Moreover, as use of the protocol expanded, it reduced the possibility of switching to a new standard in the future. Third, the protocol provided an opportunity for firms who used it to promote themselves as responsible global citizens. In other words, it was a tool for improving their reputation. I address each in turn.

As carbon regulation became an increasingly likely outcome, many firms began to recognize that it was time to prepare for this eventuality. Key participants in the protocol from the private sector acknowledged the potential advantages of early action through GHG reporting. One participant in the revised edition of the protocol from Ford Motor Companies noted that the firm understood that carbon regulation was coming, and it wanted to be prepared.[75] It viewed two advantages to early action on GHG measurement and reporting: the ability to reduce

[73] Recall that although the Kyoto Protocol was signed in 1997, it did not enter into force until 2005; thus, any action that firms took on climate change when the protocol was released in 2001 was *in anticipation* of binding Kyoto rules.

[74] World Resources Institute 2007, 8.

[75] Frederick, Interview.

risk exposure preemptively, thus gaining an advantage over competing firms, and the ability to help shape the rules that might eventually become binding. Others who worked on the protocol and related GHG registries acknowledged that particularly in the United States, there was frustration with the uncertainty of the future of regulation. Adopting a credible measurement scheme was a way for firms to protect themselves and potentially receive credits for reductions made before regulation was enacted.[76] Indeed, this is the stated reason for the creation of the California Climate Action registry (based on the protocol). It describes itself as a response to the request of CEOs who began taking early action to combat climate change and wanted "to protect their early actions to reduce emissions by having a credible and accurate record of their profiles and baselines."[77]

In addition to the promise of benefits through first-mover action, the protocol provided a second benefit—reduced transaction costs. As states and businesses began to recognize the need for a credible and robust measurement scheme, they also realized the costs of creating one. The protocol recognized this demand; one of its main objectives is "to simplify and reduce the costs of compiling a GHG inventory."[78] When the director of the EPA Climate Leaders program began to move forward on program design, she quickly realized the time and effort needed to create a usable GHG measurement scheme. After talking with staff at WRI, she noted that "it just made sense" to use the protocol. Not only would this address the costs of creating a new standard, but it would ensure that the standard adopted by the EPA was internationally consistent.[79] The protocol could reduce transaction costs in another way: to the extent that the standard became widely adopted, it would eliminate the need for (and the costs associated with) switching to another standard in the future.[80] Again, the protocol was cognizant of this material benefit and cited it as a reason to use the tool: "Both business and other stakeholders benefit from converging on a common standard."[81] Moreover, the protocol not only reduced transaction costs by providing a ready-made standard but also furnished the tools for firms to find ways to save money through improved efficiency. By measuring the energy flows of the organization, protocol users could identify sources of waste and areas for improvement— reducing the financial transaction costs of doing business.

[76] Eaton, Interview.

[77] Climate Action Registry, n.d., available from http://www.climateregistry.org/about .html/.

[78] World Resources Institute and World Business Council on Sustainable Development 2004, 3.

[79] Cummis, Interview.

[80] Mattli and Büthe 2003.

[81] World Resources Institute and World Business Council on Sustainable Development 2004, 3.

Finally, the protocol allowed adopters to publicize their good deeds, thereby burnishing their reputations as responsible corporate citizens. Using the protocol was a way to join a "green club," which offers the excludable benefits to members who have taken progressive action.[82] For firms that had suffered from bad publicity in the past, this was a particularly attractive option. For example, in the wake of bad publicity surrounding its operations in Nigeria and the sinking of the Brent Spar, Shell also sought to incorporate social objectives into its strategy. CEO Mark Moody-Stuart noted that "being seen as helping to deliver solutions that are common to society is also good for business."[83] One interviewee noted that businesses wanted to reduce their emissions for two reasons: to get credits for early action or "for PR reasons"—in other word, to be able to say that they are doing their part.[84]

The demand for private authority in the form of the protocol is quite clear: participants stood to benefit materially and enhance their reputations. WRI and WBCSD recognized the opportunity to provide these benefits and stepped forward. However, explaining the emergence of entrepreneurial authority is incomplete without a discussion of why other actors did not step forward as suppliers of authority. Why didn't states cooperate to create a corporate accounting protocol? Alternatively, why wasn't this type of tool created by an international organization? I show that the preferences of powerful states and the relative weakness of the likely focal institution explain why *entrepreneurial* private authority was able to emerge in this case.

Heterogeneous Preferences

As stated earlier, greenhouse gas accounting can serve as a tool for transparency and management, but it can also serve as the basis for emissions trading. Thus, when considering which state preferences are most relevant with respect to the GHG Protocol, we must look at the distribution of positions on emissions trading. Key actors in the climate regime could not agree on the appropriate role for emissions trading in the Kyoto Protocol; as a result, efforts to create subnational measurement tools—a necessary precursor to a trading system—could not move forward.

The most influential states in the Kyoto negotiations were developed countries—those that faced binding targets and timetables under the new agreement. (Without ratification by states representing 55 percent of the world's emissions—which had to include a substantial portion of the

[82] Prakash and Potoski 2006.

[83] Hamilton 1998.

[84] Vicki Arroyo, former vice president, Domestic Policy Analysis and General Counsel, Pew Center on Global Climate Change. Inteview by author, 12 November 2008.

developed world—the Kyoto Protocol would not enter into effect.) They were in deep disagreement about the role of emissions trading. In the run-up to Kyoto, the two key negotiating blocs of developed countries were the European Union and the JUSCANNZ group.

The schism over emissions trading was evident from the beginning of the Kyoto negotiations. In general, the European Union was pushing for aggressive domestic action. It was skeptical about emissions trading and, as a leader on the global stage in climate change policy, objected to the possibility that developed countries could buy their way out of domestic reductions through trading.[85] One account of the European Union's position on climate change states quite plainly, "Emissions trading was not part of the EU negotiating position in the Kyoto negotiations."[86]

JUSCANNZ, by contrast, pushed hard for market mechanisms and opposed any cap on the amount of reductions that could be used to meet reduction targets. In the wake of what was viewed as a politically and environmental successful implementation of an emissions trading scheme for nitrogen and sulfur oxides in the Clean Air Act, the United States was a particularly resolute advocate for emissions trading in Kyoto.[87] It argued that market mechanisms were an appropriate and feasible policy.[88]

This division between the European Union and JUSCANNZ persisted through 1997, when states met for the final negotiations of Kyoto. JUSCANNZ, led by the United States, wanted maximum flexibility in the ways that each state could meet its targets and continued to push for emissions trading. The European Union, with no experience in trading, felt strongly that reductions should be made domestically, without the "back door" of trading.[89] In the end, the final text at Kyoto created trading mechanisms, but there was no agreement about how they would be used.[90] In other words, the divergence in preferences had perhaps been mitigated, but was yet to be fully resolved. As late as 2000—well after Kyoto was signed (though before it entered into force), the European Union insisted that at least 50 percent of emissions reductions should be achieved domestically, while the United States argued that there should be no limit on the use of emissions trading mechanisms to reach national targets.

[85] Depledge 2006; Skjaerseth and Wettestad 2008.
[86] Skjaerseth and Wettestad 2008, 67.
[87] Grubb, Vrolijk, and Brack 1999, 90; Meckling 2011, 56.
[88] Schreurs 2004.
[89] There are numerous accounts of the history of the Kyoto negotiations. This summary draws on Werksman 1998; Schreurs 2004; and Yamin 2005, which focus particularly on the flexibility mechanisms.
[90] Articles 6, 12, and 17.

The impasse on emissions trading was not resolved until 2001. After the election of George W. Bush, the United States announced that it would not ratify Kyoto. Because the United States was no longer actively negotiating in 2001, Japan became a key player—both as a member of JUS-CANNZ and as a close ally of the United States. It continued to push for unrestricted use of trading and offsets. Many argue that the United States withdrawal, combined with the pilot trading program in the United Kingdom, shifted the European Union toward a more open attitude toward emissions trading.[91] The European Union finally agreed that there would be no cap on the use of emissions trading to meet domestic targets.[92]

The reasons for the shift in the European Union's position and the trading scheme it developed between 1998 and 2003 are beyond the scope of the inquiry here.[93] The key point is that while WRI and WBCSD were drafting the Greenhouse Gas Protocol, the two largest negotiating blocs in the developed world were feuding over whether and how emissions trading would be part of an intergovernmental agreement on climate change. Thus, preferences of powerful states were clearly heterogeneous, providing an important condition for the supply of entrepreneurial private authority.

The U.S. withdrawal from the Kyoto process created another layer of divergent preferences: between the United States and states that supported Kyoto. In the United States, the decision not to move forward with ratification resulted in a slowing of federal activity on climate change and great uncertainty about future regulation. This uncertainty, coupled with little action by the government provided a perfect window for private actors to fill the gap through private standards and a compelling reason for firms to adopt those standards. As one interviewee noted, uncertainty was a key motivator for business involvement in the protocol.[94] Although the protocol could not be a substitute for federal regulation, it served as a plausible and legitimate interim measure until government policy took shape. Moreover, private standards were a way to circumvent government inaction. Indeed, one person at the EPA said that working with WRI "gave them cover" to advance a policy agenda that was not consistent with the Bush administration's view.[95] In this sense, the protocol

---

[91] See, for example, Zapfel and Vainio 2002.

[92] The consensus text was presented at COP-6, part 2 in July 2001, but not formally adopted until COP-7 in November 2001 in Marrakesh, Morocco.

[93] For a detailed timeline of domestic discussions of emissions trading within the EU, see Lefevere 2005.

[94] Eaton, Interview.

[95] Maurice LeFranc, Climate Change Division, Office of Air and Radiation, U.S. Environmental Protection Agency. Interview by author, 10 November 2008.

emerged at a key moment, providing an opportunity for forward looking firms and organizations to take some action toward preparing for future regulation.

Focal Institution

I have argued that when there is a strong focal institution capable of screening and monitoring agents, delegated authority will emerge. However, with respect to emissions trading, the focal institution, the UNFCCC Secretariat, had neither the capability nor the mandate to oversee a GHG accounting system.

The UNFCCC Secretariat was clearly *the* focal institution for greenhouse gas methodologies and thus a potential agent for states. The main purpose of the secretariat is to assist in the implementation of the Framework Convention and the Kyoto Protocol.[96] In this capacity, it has supported the implementation of methodologies for national accounting and for offset projects.[97] It is also responsible for coordination of reporting and review processes. It compiles and disseminates mountains of data on states' emissions and oversees technical reviews of GHG inventories. Thus, although it is primarily (though not exclusively) focused at the national level, it is the main hub for carbon-related accounting and reporting and therefore the logical focal institution to consider. (The other possible focal institution, the executive board, had not yet fully developed.)

During the creation of the protocol, the UNFCCC Secretariat was focused on two types of GHG measurement: project-based accounting and national reporting. By the mid-1990s, states were beginning to design and implement carbon-offset projects in anticipation of the Clean Development Mechanism. These activities focused on project-based emissions measurement: how much CO_2 would have been emitted without a given offsetting project? The secretariat was also tasked with helping parties measure and report national-level emissions, as required under Article 12 of the Framework Convention. Thus, parties had been quite specific about the tasks for which the secretariat was responsible, and firm-level accounting was clearly not one of them. For these reasons, the secretariat can be considered a weak focal institution with respect to corporate accounting.

Even assuming that the focal institution would try to work on corporate-level accounting "on the side," there were very few resources to do so. One interviewee said that in the early stages of the Clean Development

---

[96] UN Framework Convention on Climate Change, Article 8.

[97] Primarily through Activities Implemented Jointly, and only indirectly through the Clean Development Mechanism.

Mechanism, there were only two staff members assigned to the issue.[98] More broadly, when the protocol was published in 2001, the UNFCCC Secretariat reported a total of fifty-eight professional-level staff employed in the entire organization.[99] The Greenhouse Gas Protocol, by contrast, had twenty-two staff serving on the project team, as well as *hundreds* of contributors involved in the drafting, peer review, and revising of the first edition. Even with a political mandate, the secretariat would be lacking in capacity—both in number and in expertise.

CONCLUSION

The GHG Protocol is a successful case of entrepreneurial authority, which serves as the basis for the ISO standard on GHG reporting, as well as countless voluntary reporting registries. It has been adopted by numerous firms and large swaths of a few industries and is being piloted in developing countries. In a word, the accounting practices created by WRI, WBCSD, and the participants in the protocol process have become the standard of choice for corporate reporting of GHG emissions worldwide.

The success of the GHG Protocol is due in part to its timing: it became the focal institution for corporate-level reporting simply because at the time there was no organization—public or private—with the expertise to fulfill the same role. Although there had been considerable work on carbon accounting at the national and project levels, WRI and WBCSD were among the first to gather existing expertise on corporate-level accounting. What little work had been done on the corporate level was fragmented across firms and governments that had developed pilot programs. The protocol process was able to draw on these efforts, and bring the actors involved in them into one room.

But timing alone does not provide a complete account of the success of why WRI and WBCSD were successful in attaining regulatory authority, or why targets of these privately set standards chose to adopt them. The success of these two institutions in becoming *the* private regulator for corporate-level GHG accounting is further explained by several factors. First, the disagreement among the EU and JUSCANNZ bloc on the appropriate role for emissions trading in the climate regime gave rise to a vacuum of government action.[100] As a result, there were few resources earmarked for the UNFCCC Secretariat (or other international organizations, for that matter) to pursue the development of measurement

---

[98] Christiana Figueres, Climate Change Negotiator, Costa Rican Delegation. Interview by author, 20 November 2008.

[99] UNFCCC 2001, p. 20.

[100] Arroyo, Interview.

methodologies to implement emissions trading—which could have included corporate-level standards. The overwhelming focus was on offsets. This provided a window of opportunity for private actors to create their own standards without much opposition. Second, the focal institution most likely to develop such rules did not have the expertise or capacity to do so. Third, the transparency of the rule-making process and the willingness by WRI and WBCSD to include all interested parties endowed the process and, eventually, the rules with a high level of legitimacy. Indeed, interviewees described the reputation and legitimacy of WRI, WBCSD, and the protocol process as reasons for adopting the GHG Protocol standards. Fourth, the transparency also demonstrated the rigor and iterative nature of the process; subjecting the rules to peer review, road testing, and revision reinforced the notion that the rules produced were of high quality.

Because authority is a relational concept, an adequate explanation of the regulatory authority of the GHG Protocol must also account for why potential targets of this form of private regulation chose to adopt them. The protocol was able to provide both material and reputational benefits to its users. It provided a way to reduce transaction costs by standardizing reporting practices and providing technical support to its users. It also helped early adopters get a head start on preparing for future regulation. Regulatory uncertainty surrounding emissions reporting and trading was clearly an important motivating factor for many firms. Early adopters could not only begin to measure and manage their emissions; they could also potentially receive credits for reductions made before regulation was implemented. At the same time, the protocol allowed users to tout their environmental responsibility through the use of a rigorous and vetted reporting protocol. Finally, the involvement of many of the adopters in the rule-making process is also a key element in explaining why so many actors voluntary chose to comply with these private standards. Involvement in the rule-making process had two beneficial influences. It allowed participants to shape the final outcomes (presumably, somewhat in accordance with their own preferences), and thereby created buy-in for those involved—a further incentive to use the standards.

CHAPTER 6

Conclusion

HOW ARE PRIVATE RULE MAKERS contributing to the management of global environmental problems? As I have argued, the answer to this question lies in rethinking the meaning of private authority. When the concept is properly disaggregated, it becomes clear that private authority is not simply evidence of the erosion of state authority; public and private authority are not "zero-sum." Rather, I have argued that a revised conceptualization of private authority demonstrates that it is diffused through and among a diverse set of actors, creating multiple loci for rule making and governance.

Rethinking private authority means distinguishing between two separate phenomena: delegated and entrepreneurial forms of private authority. Delegated authority occurs when states, acting collectively, delegate tasks to private actors. Entrepreneurial authority, by contrast, requires no *ex ante* transfer of authority; private actors simply create rules that others choose to adopt. Without this conceptual refinement, our collective understanding is necessarily incomplete. Moreover, a refined understanding of the concept of private authority allows for a clearer theory, because each form of private authority occurs under different conditions.

To be clear: mine is not an argument about the "retreat of the state."[1] It is an argument about the changing role of states as a collective governing body and the increasing complexity of governance arrangements. The scope of global environmental governance is expanding and so are the types of actors involved in governing. This finding is clearly demonstrated in chapter 2. There are more environmental treaties than ever before. Indeed, Mitchell's work on environmental treaty making shows just how much more governing is occurring: since 1990, the total number of multilateral environmental agreements has doubled, from 502 in 1990 to 1,029 in 2010.[2] In the same time period, the number of bilateral agreements has increased by 60 percent.[3] Put simply, there is more governance,

---

[1] Strange 1996. See also Ohmae 1995; Mathews 1997.

[2] Mitchell 2002–13. See http://iea.uoregon.edu/page.php?query=summarize_by_year& yearstart=1950&yearend=2010&inclusion=MEA.

[3] Mitchell 2002–13. See http://iea.uoregon.edu/page.php?query=summarize_by_year& yearstart=1950&yearend=2010&inclusion=BEA.

and as a consequence more governors are responsible for doing it. This explains the relatively steady proportion of delegation to private actors, despite the overall growth in functions delegated. The *amount* of delegation to private actors is increasing, but the proportion is not. Private actors are just doing their share of a larger workload.

The data show the growing role of states as a collective governing body in another way: more actors are responsible for the same task. The international political arena is broadening and deepening. As a result, the way that states are governing appears to be changing: they are enlisting more actors (including IOs and private actors) to undertake the same task. This finding reinforces the notion that governance is expanding: there are multiple loci of authority rather than a single locus that rests with the state. As Nye notes, it is more useful to conceptualize power as positive-sum, where actors have power to accomplish goals *with* others rather than power *over* them.[4]

To investigate these multiple loci of authority, I have offered a historical review of their role in environmental politics. Private authority is not new; scholars have shown the prominence of private authority in premodern times.[5] Yet this book has offered two "exploratory missions" to understand their breadth and variation in contemporary environmental politics. These add to existing historical work and, more importantly, provide much needed context to contemporary debates about the role of the state in an era of increasing globalization. Chapters 2 and 3 show that private authority in the environmental arena is not a new phenomenon. Both delegated and entrepreneurial authority first appeared in the 1950s. However, the absolute amount has increased in the past two decades. In the case of delegated authority, this is an indication of a power share: states are doing more governing and enlisting private actors to help in this endeavor. The recent spike in transnational environmental civil regulations—one form of entrepreneurial authority—shows that this is a new and fast-growing phenomenon in environmental politics.

The very existence of entrepreneurial authority speaks to an expansion of governance tools and governing actors, as demonstrated by chapter 3. Its rapid growth demonstrates that in some areas of environmental politics, private actors are offering additional or alternative rules to those promulgated by states. To understand more clearly the ways in which the proliferation of civil regulation contributes to the fragmentation of governance, I distinguish between *de novo* and amended civil regulations. The former category includes those comprised of entirely new sets of rules

[4] Nye 2011, xvii.

[5] Milgrom, North, and Weingast 1990; Greif, Milgrom, and Weingast 1994; Cutler 2003; Greif 2006.

and standards. By contrast, amended rules appropriate some aspects of existing civil regulation in the creation of their own standards. This information aims to capture the extent to which entrepreneurial authority is fragmenting, by creating ever greater numbers of unrelated schemes, or converging, by reproducing the content of some rules through appropriation or recognition.

The shrinking ratio of *de novo* schemes offers additional evidence of the expansion of governing authority. As time progresses, the number of civil regulations continues to grow; however, these rules are increasingly based on existing private rules. Thus, although the *number* of civil regulations has grown over time, their *substance* is increasingly reproducing itself. This finding clearly shows that the loci of authority are growing, though we have yet to understand the conditions under which this leads to increased fragmentation or convergence among multiple civil regulations.[6]

These exploratory missions provide two important insights. First, private authority is a fixture of contemporary environmental politics. In the case of entrepreneurial authority, it is growing rapidly. Skeptics have rightly criticized work on the role of nonstate actors in world politics for being overly focused on the positive cases and success stories. The data presented here contextualizes these positive cases within a much larger picture of the extent of and changes in delegated and entrepreneurial private authority. This allows me to argue, with ample evidence, that private authority is not a fluke; it is a persistent phenomenon. Second, the data show that there are multiple loci of authority in environmental politics, which occur in various configurations. Thus, to speak of a zero-sum relationship between public and private authority is simply not instructive. Rather, we must turn to a more nuanced set of questions and ask: When does private authority emerge and what are its effects on world politics?

Beyond the demonstration of the persistence and growth of private authority, this book advances our theoretical understanding of this phenomenon. Many works simply take the presence of nonstate actors in world politics as a given. As interdependence grows, it follows that we will need more institutions and more actors to manage its accompanying challenges. But this assertion is underspecified. What kinds of institutions? What kinds of actors? Perhaps we can assume that the Internet and other information technologies have facilitated the growth of transnational networks. However, this does not explain the emergence of private actors as rule makers.

---

[6] Cashore, Auld, and Newsom 2004; Overdevest 2010; Fransen 2011; Green 2013a. All provide accounts of why convergence or divergence has occurred with respect to a specific group of environmental standards, yet none provides a generalizable theory.

To this end, I offer a model of *why* private authority emerges and, when it does, whether it will be delegated or entrepreneurial in form. The emergence of private authority can be broadly understood as a function of supply and demand. Expertise is a necessary, but not sufficient, condition for private authority. By virtue of their knowledge, private actors must be able to provide some benefit to potential rule takers; without such expertise, adoption of private rules is unlikely. Private actors developed early expertise in carbon measurement and accounting for two related reasons: fear and profit. Some private actors smelled profit. Société Générale de Surveillance (SGS), one of the firms charged with monitoring projects in the CDM, knew there was a market not only for selling carbon, which required measuring it, but also for verifying emissions-reducing activities. As early as 1997, SGS noted an "emerging need" for verification services to support the multiple carbon offset schemes that had begun to appear.[7] Another part of the explanation of early private-sector expertise is clearly the fear of regulation. Preparation could not only lessen the risk of regulatory exposure but, ideally, afford an opportunity to shape future rules and regulations.

As a result of this expertise, private actors were able to offer potential rule takers benefits that others, especially international organizations, could not—creating a demand for private authority. Chapters 4 and 5 demonstrate these benefits quite clearly. Following the logic of principal-agent theory, private agents, delegated authority by states acting collectively, were able to lower the transaction costs of governing. The designers of the Clean Development Mechanism chose to delegate authority to private actors rather than any of the IO candidates in part because they already had experience measuring carbon. This avoided the need to build capacity within an IO, which might have been an "obvious" choice, save for the lack of knowledge. Moreover, delegating to private actors simplified the negotiating process enormously. This choice preempted brewing turf wars between contending IOs over which one would be the best monitor of the CDM, and as a result, it facilitated a fast start to the new mechanism—a political priority for key states. Delegating to private agents also simplified questions of the legal relationship between the governing bodies of the Kyoto Protocol and the IO selected to monitor.

In the case of the GHG Protocol, private actors with expertise offered two important benefits. One was reputational enhancement, of two different kinds. Firms that adopted the GHG Protocol could claim that they cared about climate change and had taken (at least preliminary) steps toward reducing their emissions. Of course, the GHG Protocol is a management tool for emissions mitigation, not a set of regulations. But there was

---

[7] Moura-Costa, Stuart, and Trines 1997.

a belief among the protocol's creators that it was a first important step toward future reductions. After all, as the business mantra goes, "you cannot manage what you do not measure." In addition, because the protocol was a collaboration between a business NGO (the World Business Council on Sustainable Development) and a "green" NGO (the World Resources Institute), the standards were viewed as credible by both sides and by users. The product of collaboration and an open process, the final standards were seen as legitimate and robust, since WRI would not lend its name to anything less than what it believed to be a rigorous standard.[8]

The second benefit was the potential for first-mover advantage. Many of the creators and adopters of the protocol believed that emissions' regulation was inevitable. Early action was a way to get a head start on the competition and potentially to shape future rules. Chapter 5 demonstrates that companies were worried about regulatory uncertainty and that the protocol provided them a way to prepare for the future. Moreover, the broad uptake of the protocol shows that it is has been incorporated or adopted almost wholesale by myriad reporting schemes around the world. This affords an additional potential advantage for early movers: the avoidance of future switching costs. As more users adopted the protocol, the risk that companies would have to switch to a new standard in the future diminished. In the United States, this gamble has paid off. The 2008 U.S. EPA federal reporting regulations are based on a variant of the GHG Protocol, the EPA Climate Leaders program. Despite its focus on the facility level, these federal rules share common elements with the GHG Protocol. In sum, the demand for private authority is based in instrumental logic: actors are willing to recognize privately created rules when they stand to benefit in some way.

The form, or supply, of private authority, by contrast, is a more complex story. Explaining whether entrepreneurial or delegated authority will emerge depends upon the configuration of powerful states' preferences and the presence or strength of a focal institution. Here, I am realistic about the constraining role of state power: powerful states with strong preferences will not be overruled by private actors. When strong states have shared views and a way to control agents, the likelihood of entrepreneurial authority is low. Under these conditions (and given a demand for private authority), states will choose to delegate to private agents, who can be carefully screened and monitored by a focal institution. However, if strong states disagree, and they have no reliable focal institution, then private agents will be able to insert themselves into the policy process, creating rules that fill the unmet demand for regulation.

---

[8] Newell 2001 refers to NGOs' choice to engage with businesses as one of "liberal governance," which privileges responsible management over ideological confrontation.

In a word, in the theory of private authority presented here, both states and private actors act in strategic and self-interested ways. When states choose to delegate to private actors, they are selecting agents that are best equipped to provide the benefits they require. Similarly, when private actors successfully project entrepreneurial authority, they are capitalizing on an unmet demand for benefits. The divergence in states' preferences provides an opportunity to insert themselves into the regulatory landscape.

THEORETICAL IMPLICATIONS: HOW PRIVATE AUTHORITY MATTERS

The findings presented in this book show that under certain conditions, the rule-making activities of private actors have autonomous effects on global environmental politics. In this section, I offer a framework for understanding precisely how private authority matters. Here, I seek a theoretical middle ground between realists, who argue that the effects of private authority are always a function of state power,[9] and constructivists, who emphasize that nonstate actors can help change identities and interests through the organization and dissemination of knowledge and the diffusion of norms.[10] The reinterpretation of these two views hinges on our collective understanding of the roles of agency and structure in world politics. I argue that instead of the realist focus on outcomes, or the constructivist focus on processes, a more useful evaluation of the effects of private authority should focus on outputs. I conclude with a brief discussion of the generalizability of the theory to other issues in world politics.

Assessing Effects

In his work on global regulation, Drezner argues that nonstate actors may affect the *processes* of global rule making but not the final regulatory outcomes. Outcomes are always, and exclusively, the product of state preferences. The dichotomous distinction he creates between processes and outcomes in such arguments is flawed and impedes our ability to answer the question: Does private authority matter?[11] In this section, I first discuss the meaning of this distinction and how it applies to private

---

[9] Drezner 2007, chap. 3. A softer version of this argument, articulated by O'Brien et al. 2000, is that nonstate actors may change the context in which states operate, but not the content of their policies. See also Weiss 1998.

[10] See, e.g., P. Haas 1990; Litfin 1994; Keck and Sikkink 1998; Barnett and Finnemore 1999.

[11] Wendt 1992, 393, finds the "dichotomous privileging of structure over process" to be problematic, "since transformations of identity and interest through process are transformations of structure."

authority. On the basis of these revised definitions, it is problematic to argue that private authority does not affect governance outcomes, since this is often not the appropriate metric for evaluating the effects of private authority. With this adjustment in mind, I show that private authority can in fact "matter"—in the sense of having an impact on environmental outcomes and regulatory outputs. Finally, I suggest that private authority can provide an important political function that may serve to facilitate further action with lasting effects—a view consistent with constructivist arguments about the power of individual agents.

Outcomes can be broadly understood as real-world effects. In the scholarship on international institutions, outcomes allow us to answer the question, Has the actor, policy, or institution taken action that successfully alleviates the problem? With respect to the environmental arena, a successful outcome is one that improves environmental quality.[12] Processes, by contrast, can be understood as activities focused on specific tasks or narrow functions.[13] A successful process might be one that accurately gathers or completely disseminates data, or thoroughly monitors all actors with respect to a specific behavior.

With these definitions in mind, it is clear that there are three flaws in the argument that private authority does not affect outcomes. The first flaw emerges once the definition of outcomes is clarified: some forms of entrepreneurial authority *are* improving outcomes—they are positively affecting environmental quality.[14] Carbon certification schemes are generating offsets that reduce the amount of carbon dioxide emitted into the atmosphere and, in some cases, also produce environmental co-benefits, such as improved biodiversity. Organic certification promotes the production of agricultural goods that do not use pesticides, which can contribute to environmental problems. Forestry certification helps mitigate the damage done to forests through the process of extraction, producing healthier, more sustainable forests. One may legitimately ask if these effects are better or worse than other kinds of institutional arrangements (namely, public ones), but this is certainly different from claiming that they have no effect at all.

Second, when one disaggregates private authority into its constituent forms, it is clear that impact on outcomes is not always an appropriate metric. In the case of delegated authority, for instance, it seems that the effect on the regulatory process is a more instructive way to evaluate effectiveness. For example, if private actors are delegated a narrow, discrete

[12] Haas, Keohane, and Levy 1993.
[13] Gutner and Thompson 2010, 237.
[14] As I note in chapter 4, we could know much more about *how much* civil regulations are improving environmental outcomes, but there is at least some evidence that they have some positive environmental effects.

task, such as reporting to states about the health of a specific set of fisheries in a regional fisheries agreement, it makes no sense to expect that they will "solve" the problem of overfishing in that region. In other words, evaluating their impact on outcomes is a category error. In this particular instance, private actors were not tasked with solving the overfishing problem; thus we should not expect them to achieve a goal so far beyond the purview of their delegated authority. Rather, to assess adequately whether private delegated authority matters, we must use metrics appropriate to the task with which they were charged.[15] The important point here is that it is inapt to dismiss the potential effects of private authority by saying that processes are less important than outcomes and that all forms of private authority should be gauged by a standard of whether they affect outcomes. In many cases, private authority will not, *by definition*, have any effect on regulatory outcomes. Thus, to measure the effects of private authority against that standard is illogical.

Third, forcing a dichotomy between process and outcome overlooks an important intermediary potential effect of private authority—on regulatory *outputs*. Outputs can be understood as occupying a middle ground between process and outcome. Haas et al. operationalize outputs with respect to international institutions as "observable political effects."[16] Gutner and Thompson suggest that outputs for international organizations might include political impacts, behavior and compliance, and policy agendas.[17] In other words, outputs can be conceived of as both concrete behaviors (such as the level of adoption of private rules or compliance with them) and more diffuse effects (such as social learning or greater understanding about the nature of the problem).[18] Outputs are an additional possible measure for gauging the impact of both types of private authority.

To be clear, I am not arguing that private authority *always* has an effect on outcomes, outputs, or processes. Rather, I maintain that the way in which other scholars have approached this question often creates the foregone conclusion that they will not. In the case of the Clean Development Mechanism, private authority affects both regulatory processes and outputs. Private actors are charged with a specific task that is part of the regulatory process—deciding whether carbon offset projects fulfill the requirements set out by the executive board. But their activities also have an impact on a regulatory output: whether the CDM produces

[15] A discussion of the appropriate measures of process effectiveness is well beyond the scope of this book. On the challenges of measuring regime effectiveness, see, e.g., Young 1999; Young 2001; Hovi, Sprinz, and Underdal 2003.

[16] Haas, Keohane, and Levy 1993, 7.

[17] Gutner and Thompson 2010, fig. 1.

[18] Young 2001.

carbon reductions via offset projects. According to the process-outcome dichotomy, we would say that private authority has little to no impact on combatting climate change. Yet, this is not their explicit task: private actors are supposed to monitor only whether a project will reduce the amount of emissions it promises and whether those reductions actually take place. That is the extent of its authority. Certainly, the degree to which they succeed or fail may eventually contribute to the slowing of climate change, but so will myriad other factors, many of which are well beyond the control of those private agents. Thus, it is more appropriate to ask, Does delegated private authority affect the functioning of the CDM, and if so, how? In other words, what is the effect of private agents on outputs?

The Greenhouse Gas Protocol provides further evidence for the utility of regulatory outputs when evaluating the impact of private authority. The creators of the GHG Protocol deliberately decided that it would be nonbinding. It does not require third-party certification, nor does it ask its users to report their emissions to a centralized body. It is very simply a tool that individual firms can use for management purposes. Thus, its aim was not to reduce emissions but rather to help firms begin to think systematically about their carbon footprints. By design, there should be no improvement in environmental quality, unless firms choose to do so. Outcomes are therefore not an instructive measure.

However, in terms of *outputs*, chapter 5 shows that the GHG Protocol has had considerable effects. First, it has influenced the behavior of thousands of firms, which are now more aware of their emissions habits. Second, it has diffused through different environmental standard-setting processes to become the gold standard for firm-level emissions' accounting. A group of private actors created a set of rules that are now used worldwide and recognized by the International Organization for Standardization. Third, private actors involved with the GHG Protocol persuaded previously reluctant firms to engage in measurement activities. For example, the cement industry, a huge emitter of greenhouse gases, had been very resistant to the idea of preparing for emissions regulation. However, the leading cement firm Holcim was a core adviser in the creation of the GHG Protocol and then an advocate for its use among cement producers. It later spearheaded the Cement Sustainability Initiative, which requires signatories to use the GHG Protocol and conducts capacity building to help firms implement the standard. The result has been both increased awareness and change in behavior of cement producers globally. These longer-term consequences of the GHG Protocol on outputs point to a constructivist account of the effects private authority, showing how it may help change the identity and therefore the interests of actors in world politics.

In sum, although there are limits to private authority,[19] to argue that private actors have no effect on world politics is fundamentally misleading. First and foremost, private authority is contributing to improvements in outcomes—furthering the production of global public goods, in the form of enhanced environmental quality. Moreover, in many cases, it is inappropriate to judge the effects of private authority against a standard of outcomes. Agents delegated a narrow function cannot reasonably be expected to exceed their mandate; a more appropriate evaluation of their effectiveness would be to ask if they are successfully executing the tasks with which they are charged. Finally, there is a case to be made for measuring the effects of private authority in terms of outputs. Here, the appropriate question is, Have private rules changed the behavior of other actors—which may or may not include states? In the case of climate change, for instance, Hoffmann's work offers some compelling evidence; a variety of nonstate actors have abandoned efforts to influence the intergovernmental process and instead are devising their own rules and practices to promote emissions mitigation and adaptation.[20] In answering this question, we must also keep in mind that changes may occur over long periods of time; thus, private authority can promote learning or new approaches to a problem that shift behavior in the long term.[21] This view is consistent with constructivist approaches to changes in world politics that emphasize "unit-level" origins to structural changes.[22] Appropriate revisions to skeptics' arguments would be to identify private authority as a governance *output* and then compare it to like outputs, that is, public arrangements. In general, this adjustment seeks to expand the breadth of inquiry to understand the effects of private authority over time.

Moving beyond Environmental Politics

The discussion of how to assess the extent to which private authority matters raises broader questions about the generalizability of the theory beyond the area of environment. Of course, this is ultimately an empirical question requiring further investigation. Preliminary evidence presented in this book suggests support for the model in explaining delegated and private authority beyond the case of climate change to the broader en-

---

[19] Graz and Nölke 2008b; Mayer and Gereffi 2010. For a more optimistic interpretation, see Lake 2010, 607, who notes that credit rating agencies are a form of private authority that is "robust, deeply institutionalized, and unlikely to be challenged."

[20] Hoffman 2011.

[21] This is similar to the deliberative process described in the experimentalist literature. See, e.g., Sabel and Zeitlin 2008; Sabel and Zeitlin 2010; Overdevest and Zeitlin 2012. See also Auld and Green 2012; Green 2012.

[22] Ruggie 1983.

vironmental arena. States' preference for delegating implementation tasks to private actors shown in chapter 2 supports the logic of reducing transaction costs, as does the finding that most delegation at the post-treaty level calls for some type of expert input. Chapter 3 shows that civil regulations have emerged to govern various technical environmental problems, such as indoor air pollution, building standards, and industrial production. These focus on *managing* environmentally harmful behavior, which demands more expertise than creating rules that simply require *abstaining* from them. Moreover, many of these civil regulations occur in areas where public institutions are fragmented, diffuse, or simply non-existent, supporting the argument that weak focal institutions are a key element in explaining the emergence of entrepreneurial authority.

Despite these findings, to understand the degree to which the theory generalizes outside of environment requires, in the first instance, more descriptive work about variation across issues and over time. Koremenos's work on international delegation is a useful departure point; her findings suggest that delegation to private actors is more frequent in the areas of human rights and economic agreements and least prevalent in security.[23] In terms of entrepreneurial authority, there is a limited amount of cross-case analysis; more work here would be useful.[24] I am unaware of any equivalent large-N work that examines variation in entrepreneurial authority across multiple issue areas.[25] This is clearly an important first step.

Second, further small-N research will help test whether the model helps explain private authority with respect to other issues. Because delegated private authority is more prevalent at the post-treaty level, there is a definite need for further work to examine why states and IOs select private actors as agents once treaties enter into force.[26] Extant work on private agents, notably in the areas of financial and technical standards,[27] military force,[28] and humanitarian aid,[29] could provide a useful starting point for cross-issue analysis.

Third, and more challenging is the need to find hard cases with which to test the theory—instances in which we would expect private authority to emerge, though it does not. With respect to entrepreneurial authority, a close approximation would be to find areas in which civil regulations emerged and then collapsed or merged with other extant private

[23] Koremenos 2007; Koremenos 2008, fig. 1.

[24] Bartley 2007; Auld et al. 2009.

[25] Abbott and Snidal 2009 examine entrepreneurial authority in the areas of labor and environment, but there do not appear to be works that include other issue areas in world politics.

[26] This view is echoed by Lake and McCubbins 2006.

[27] Kerwer 2005; Singer 2010; Büthe and Mattli 2011; Richardson and Eberlein 2011.

[28] Singer 2004; Avant 2005; Chesterman and Lehnardt 2007.

[29] Cooley and Ron 2002; Cooley 2010.

rules. With respect to delegated authority, instances in which states chose to create a new focal institution rather than delegating to a private actor with expertise would constitute a hard case. Here, private actors would be able to provide benefits that an IO could not, and yet states selected either to create a new institution or to develop the capacity of an existing one.

THE ROLE OF PRIVATE AUTHORITY IN THE FUTURE CLIMATE CHANGE REGIME

This book has shown that there are multiple loci of authority in global environmental politics, and that some of these include regulatory roles for private actors. I have shown why this is important for theories of global governance and regulation; I now turn to a discussion of how these findings matter for rule making in the real world with respect to climate change. In this section, I discuss four ways that private actors can contribute to creating effective solutions to address climate change. I also point to some of the potential ways in which private authority can retard the production of public goods.

First, private entrepreneurial authority can promote experimentation.[30] In the climate change regime, the growth of carbon offset standards has provided multiple ways to produce both emissions reductions and additional social and environmental "co-benefits," such as enhanced biodiversity and local economic development. The Clean Development Mechanism has put emissions reductions at the forefront, to the detriment, many have argued, of other environmental priorities. Private standards have sought ways to square this circle, by reinserting other public goals into the design of offset projects. Numerous other initiatives, such as the Carbon Disclosure Project and the Walmart Sustainability Index, offer additional evidence of experimentation *outside* the multilateral arena.

Because entrepreneurial authority does not require resources or oversight by states, it is a potentially low-cost way to generate new policy options. There are clear political benefits to this approach. States can simply "let 1,000 flowers bloom" and see which rules appear robust. If and when public actors deem it beneficial, they can then choose to recognize privately created standards. For example, the Australian government now recognizes two private carbon standards—the Verified Carbon Standard and the Gold Standard—as acceptable credits in their voluntary offset scheme. In this way, entrepreneurial authority could be a useful addition

---

[30] Hoffmann 2011 is an excellent and thorough example of experimentation with respect to climate change. Avant, Finnemore, and Sell 2010a, 9, recognize the innovative capacity of global governors. See also McNamara 2010; Green 2012.

to states' tool kit for addressing public goods problems. The language of "public-private partnerships" suggests a more institutionalized way of harnessing private innovation and is potentially a logical extension of the approach offered here.[31]

Second, entrepreneurial authority may help promote normative shifts, when public actors are unwilling to assume the political costs of imposing regulation. The Greenhouse Gas Protocol and the Carbon Disclosure Project are both examples of such a shift. In 2001, when these were both nascent initiatives, many leading corporations were fighting climate regulation. The Global Climate Coalition, a U.S. lobbying organization composed of energy companies and other large emitters, was still expending considerable resources to deny the existence of climate change. Now some of those previously intransigent firms have adopted private rules to measure and report emissions. The emission-intensive cement industry described in chapter 5 is but one example. Certainly, measurement and reporting are not the same as emissions abatement; nonetheless, it is a pronounced shift from earlier positions. These examples illustrate the potential political utility of entrepreneurial authority. Under the guise of voluntary action, private actors may help lessen the political costs of implementing regulation in the future.

Relatedly, it appears—at least in the case of climate change—that private actors are successful at effecting normative changes when the group of rule makers includes both "green" NGOs and business actors. In both theory and policy, we tend to treat these two groups as distinct. They are different actors and often have very different interests. Yet chapter 5 provides evidence that under certain conditions "baptist and bootlegger" coalitions may emerge, to the benefit of both groups. Both sides boost their legitimacy by cooperating with an unlikely ally.[32] The effect is a broader audience and larger group of rule adopters. This book shows that there is utility in considering the causes and effects of when "world civic politics meets private governance."[33]

Third, private authority can help inform existing policy debates. Both forms of private authority are predicated on expertise. Private actors can contribute knowledge and practical experience to evolving policy processes. A recent example from within the multilateral arena comes from REDD: reducing emissions from deforestation and forest degradation. Essentially, the North has promised to pay the South to keep its forests—and the carbon dioxide they contain—in the ground. Within the

[31] Some research has shown that in the realm of the UN, these partnerships are most frequently a way for international organizations to further their agendas, rather than fundamentally reorganize their approach. See Andonova and Levy 2004; Hale and Mauzerall 2004; Andonova 2010.

[32] DeSombre 2000.

[33] Ruggie 2004, 509.

multilateral arena, countries are now discussing how to create baselines against which to measure reductions, and whether reductions should be measured at national, subnational, or project levels. They are funding demonstration efforts and pilot projects to work out the details of implementation.

Entrepreneurial authority is contributing actively to these efforts. Private offset standards have been created for REDD projects. Indeed, REDD projects now dominate the voluntary market and far outpace the number of forestry projects in the CDM.[34] More recently, the Verified Carbon Standard—a private carbon offset standard—has paved the way for further innovations in REDD policy. To date, both public and private REDD activities have occurred at the project level. However, there is an emerging consensus that REDD activities are ideally undertaken across a jurisdiction rather than as a discrete, geographically delimited project. Jurisdictional REDD reduces the likelihood of "leakage"—simply pushing deforestation from inside the project area to elsewhere. Recognizing the lack of rules and tools to implement "jurisdictional REDD," the Verified Carbon Standard has just launched the first accounting standards to help states and other subnational actors undertake such activities. Both of these examples demonstrate how innovation by private regulators is pushing forward multilateral policy.

Fourth, private authority can help promote competition among rules, a potential driver of upward harmonization. In spite of seeming progress at the climate talks in Durban and Doha, the future of the Kyoto process is uncertain. As long as regulatory uncertainty persists, there will be a demand for ways to hedge against future compliance costs. The proliferation of privately created standards can give hedgers choices. However, they will have to distinguish among the quality of different products. Smart hedgers will seek robust, well-respected standards, in the hopes that they will "count" once regulation kicks in. In other words, we should expect to see competition produce some leaders in the market—standards that are used more frequently than others. Indeed, some research indicates that this process is already underway.[35] Thus, private authority can potentially help ratchet up standards toward higher quality.

Of course, these are all *potential* contributions that private authority can make to future progress on climate change. This is not to say that private authority is categorically a positive influence on the production of public goods. There is also evidence to the contrary, to which I now turn.

First, as with public authority, the relationship between the rule maker and the rule taker may create undesired outcomes. The CDM has been

[34] Diaz, Hamilton, and Johnson 2011.
[35] Green 2013a.

criticized on several fronts.[36] Among other problems, the relationship between the project developer and the project verifier (the private agents discussed in chapter 4) is likely to produce incentives for cheating. Project verifiers are paid by those whom they are supposed to monitor—the project developers. Thus, private agents have conflicting goals. States have delegated to them to act as impartial monitors, but clients want them to rule in their favor. It is impossible to know the degree to which verifiers have chosen clients over their monitoring duties, but some evidence suggests that this relationship has produced some perverse outcomes.[37] Of course, this is not an insoluble problem; realigning verifiers' incentives would go a long way to avoiding approvals on projects that do not merit them.[38] The point here is that one must delegate with care—and with oversight mechanisms. Trust, but verify.

This lesson is particularly important since countries agreed in Durban to create a new, yet-to-be-defined market mechanism for the future climate regime. One of the key reasons for delegating to private actors was expediency: states wanted to get the CDM up and running quickly. Delegating to private agents would not only solve monitoring issues but avoid protracted political battles. Because there is always urgency attached to multilateral climate policy (though this rarely corresponds to rapid action), one could easily imagine similar arguments being made with respect to the new market mechanism: should an agent be required, choose the one that is best qualified and least controversial. Given that private actors are even better established in their expertise than they were a decade ago, a repeat scenario is not implausible. In this case, a robust mechanism for watching the watchers is needed.

Second, private authority may aim to reap the reputational benefits of producing public goods without actually doing so. In lieu of stringent standards, it is just as easy, if not easier, to imagine very weak privately created standards that make inflated claims about their effects. Such is the nature of greenwashing. Even worse, instead of stringent standards driving a ratcheting-up effect, we might observe weak ones promoting a race to the bottom. As others have pointed out, private rule making has distributional consequences and may favor the most powerful actors involved, at the expense of achieving desired policy outcomes.[39]

The potential adverse effects of private authority highlighted here raise important questions about accountability. Ostensibly, the issue of

[36] Wara 2007; Green 2008; Wara and Victor 2008; Lovbrand 2009; Lund 2010.

[37] Green 2008.

[38] Lund 2010 suggests several steps to effect this outcome.

[39] See, e.g., Mattli and Büthe 2003. Mosley 2009 is wary of enhancing the role of private regulation in the financial sector for fear of greater skewing toward the interests of organized finance.

accountability is less problematic in cases of delegated authority, where oversight comes from states and is accompanied by powerful incentives for compliance: revocation of authority. Indeed, when the CDM monitoring firm Det Norske Veritas was found to be lax in its implementation of standard procedures, the executive board revoked its accreditation.

Much trickier, however, is ensuring the accountability of those who project entrepreneurial authority—those who are not ultimately bound by the oversight of the state. Slaughter has dubbed this "the governance tri-lemma": the need for "global rules without centralized power" and "actors who can be held to account through a variety of political mechanisms."[40] In Slaughter's world, those actors are regulators, judges, and legislators—government actors in the "disaggregated state." In the portrait of world politics presented here, rule makers are not necessarily government actors, and so accountability mechanisms must come from diverse sources.[41] Unpacking the "democratic deficit" and its associated challenges of accountability is well beyond the scope of this book, though, undoubtedly, very relevant to the policy implications set forth here. Scholars have already begun to tackle this issue.[42] To the extent that private authority grows, questions of accountability will become increasingly important.

In sum, this book is not about the wonder or shame of private actors in world politics. I have refrained from making normative pronouncements about the desirability of private authority. Instead, I have outlined the potential roles of private actors in the climate regime—as both a help *and* a hindrance. There is no *a priori* reason to think that private actors are "good" or "bad" for effective climate governance—or other global issues. Rather, we must consider the conditions under which they can contribute to managing global problems (or stymie effective management) through the roles outlined above.

The Research Frontier: International Cooperation across Actors

This book can only be the beginning of a much more complicated story about the ways in which rule makers of all kinds—states, international organizations, NGOs, private firms, and transnational networks comprising all of the above—manage globalization. The dense landscape of

[40] Slaughter 2004, 10.

[41] Grant and Keohane 2005 outline multiple approaches to accountability in global governance, which are not necessarily contingent on state authority.

[42] Bruhl 2005; Bass and Gueneau 2007; Bernstein and Cashore 2007; Bäckstrand 2008; Auld and Gulbrandsen 2010.

multiple types of global rule makers suggests that the nature of sovereignty is changing. It is no longer instructive to restrict sovereignty to territorial sanctity, as in the Westphalian sense, or with mutual recognition, as in the international legal sense.[43] Certainly, I am not the first to make such an assertion. Chayes and Chayes refer to a "new sovereignty" which is characterized by membership and participation in international legal regimes.[44] More recently, and following in the Chayes' tradition, Slaughter has argued that under current conditions of interdependence "sovereignty-as-autonomy makes no sense."[45] Even realists like Stephen Krasner acknowledge that sovereignty is "organized hypocrisy."[46]

These arguments, and those of other theorists of transgovernmentalism,[47] emphasize the interconnections among states—through legal agreements and networks of state actors. Future research should push this avenue of inquiry one step further, to include the interconnections between states and private actors.[48] If the sovereignty of states is to become more "flexible and practical," as Slaughter suggests, it must also leverage the ability of private authority to contribute to global governance.[49] As I have argued repeatedly, this need not come at the "cost" of state authority but rather can be considered as one mode for enhancing it.

This implies two strands of inquiry for future research. The first is to use this reconceptualization of private authority to understand the conditions under which each form of private authority produces positive effects—whether measured in processes, outcomes, or outputs. Here, there is a great need for more study of entrepreneurial authority. We know very little about its impact on outcomes and nothing terribly systematic about outputs or processes. Moreover, my emphasis on outputs—the observable political effects of private authority—underscores the need to study private authority longitudinally. The data and theory presented here largely focus on the moment of emergence, but a fuller understanding of the role of private authority in world politics should examine its effects on rules and actors over time.

Nor do we have much understanding about how private actors fit into the world of international treaty making and implementation as agents. Chapter 2 shows some interesting trends. First, states tend to delegate to

[43] Krasner 1999 lists four types of sovereignty: domestic, Westphalian, international legal, and interdependence. The last of these refers to the ability of states to control transborder movements: it is a refutation of sorts of the effects of globalization on the state.
[44] Chayes and Chayes 1995.
[45] Slaughter 2004, 267.
[46] Krasner 1999.
[47] Raustiala 2002; Newman 2008; Eberlein and Newman 2008.
[48] See, e.g., Abbott and Snidal 2009; Milner 2009; Avant, Finnemore, and Sell 2010b; Whytock 2010; Abbott 2012.
[49] Slaughter 2004, 268.

private actors for their expertise, suggesting some functions for which they have a comparative advantage. At the treaty level, this translates to selection of private agents to aid in implementation; at the post-treaty level, they are used for rule making—usually to make specific decisions about species management. Thus, one avenue for further inquiry would be to compare governance outcomes when IOs or private agents are selected for the same policy functions. Do private agents really have a comparative advantage in certain areas, and if so, when? Second, the data show that private agents are more active at the post-treaty level. Thus, to understand better how delegated authority contributes to global governance, it is clear that we need to look more carefully at what happens *after* treaties enter into force—when states and international organizations wrestle with the political and policy challenges of translating law into practice. Lake and McCubbins suggest tentatively that private actors might be especially useful as information providers whose input can help principals decide whether delegation is advantageous.[50] While the intuition here is useful—private actors can contribute to states' decision-making processes—it fails to recognize their potential role as agents. More research on the role of private agents at the post-treaty level would greatly advance our collective understanding of the relative governing strengths of private actors.

The second area of inquiry is to understand when and how private and public authority interact, and the effects of these interactions. Once we do away with the notion that authority is zero-sum, we must ask, How does authority operate in world politics? Again, this introduces the key dimension of effects over time. Like states, private actors are faced with similar questions about exercising institutional control in the face of interdependence. How can private rule makers effectively project authority? Since authority is relational, and because private actors lack the right to rule that states enjoy, the answer to this question necessarily includes other actors. Private actors can be delegated authority by states. Or, they can seek to project authority on their own. In some cases, this requires that they strategically relinquish control, as was the case in the Greenhouse Gas Protocol. Combining forces with other organizations, who are perhaps unlikely allies, can greatly enhance the pool of expertise, collective legitimacy, and thus the ability to supply rule-making authority. Powell observes this trend among firms. He notes that "many firms are no longer structured like medieval kingdoms, walled off and protected from outside forces. Instead, we find companies involved in an intricate latticework of collaborative ventures."[51] For this reason, he argues that under

[50] Lake and McCubbins 2006.
[51] Powell 1990, 301.

some conditions, networks can be more desirable than the organizational forms of markets and hierarchies.

Young has suggested that "we are in the midst of . . . a paradigm shift in our thinking about governance." This is because scholarly work now approaches governance as a "social function" rather than as constituted solely by the behavior of governments.[52] The result of this shift is a move not only away from states as the sole locus of power, as I have suggested, but also, as he suggests, away from political science as the primary discipline addressing matters of governance.[53] As interdependence produces an "opening effect," we can expect, and indeed have already observed, more complex interrelationships among actors and institutions. An understanding of the causes and effects of these interrelationships—described as polycentricity, regime complexity, and institutional interplay in the political science literature—will require theoretical tools that range across disciplines.[54] The research frontier lies in understanding not only the interactions among different types of actors but also the *systemic* effects of complexity. The contribution that political science can make—understanding the dynamics of authority among actors and across institutions—is critical to discovering ways to tackle effectively global threats like climate change.

In sum, interdependence is contributing to a growth in the amount of governance and changes in who governs and how, rendering states and private actors more permeable to the influence and authority of others. It is changing our understanding of the concept of authority—redefining it as a way to engage with other actors rather than as an impetus to insist upon separation or domination. Yet to understand this shift fully, we must look to the entire spectrum of engagement—beyond states to private actors. Private actors are engaging with each other and with states in order to project authority in world politics. The challenge now is to understand how this willingness to engage—from both sides—can enhance our collective ability to tackle global problems.

[52] Young 2009, 37.
[53] Young 2009.
[54] Young 2002; Raustiala and Victor 2004; Ostrom 2010; Oberthur and Stokke 2011.

Bibliography

Abbott, Kenneth W. 2012. The Transnational Regime Complex for Climate Change. *Environment and Planning C: Government and Policy* 30 (4): 571–90.

Abbott, Kenneth W., Jessica F. Green, and Robert O. Keohane. 2013. Organizational Ecology in World Politics: Institutional Density and Organizational Strategies. Paper presented at the 2013 annual convention of the International Studies Association, 3–6 April 2013, San Francisco.

Abbott, Kenneth W., Robert O. Keohane, Andrew Moravcsik, Anne-Marie Slaughter, and Duncan Snidal. 2000. The Concept of Legalization. *International Organization* 54 (3): 401–19.

Abbott, Kenneth W., and Duncan Snidal. 1998. Why States Act through Formal International Organizations. *Journal of Conflict Resolution* 42 (1): 3–32.

———. 2000. Hard and Soft Law in International Governance. *International Organization* 54 (3): 421–56.

———. 2001. International "Standards" and International Governance. *Journal of European Public Policy* 8 (3): 345–70.

———. 2009. The Governance Triangle: Regulatory Standards Institutions and the Shadow of the State. In *The Politics of Global Regulation*, edited by Walter Mattli and Ngaire Woods, 44–88. Princeton, NJ: Princeton University Press.

———. 2010. International Regulation without International Government: Improving International Organization Performance through Orchestration. *Review of International Organizations* 5 (3): 315–44.

Alchian, Armen A., and Harold Demsetz. 1972. Production, Information Costs and Economic Organization. *American Economic Review* 62 (5): 777–95.

Alter, Karen. 2008. Delegation to International Courts: Self-Binding vs. Other-Binding Delegation. *Law and Contemporary Problems* 71 (1): 37–76.

Alter, Karen J., and Sophie Meunier. 2009. The Politics of International Regime Complexity. *Perspectives on Politics* 7 (1): 13–24.

Andonova, Liliana B. 2010. Public-Private Partnerships for the Earth: Politics and Patterns of Hybrid Authority in the Multilateral System. *Global Environmental Politics* 10 (2): 25–53.

Andonova, Liliana B., and Marc A. Levy. 2004. Franchising Global Governance: Making Sense of the Johannesburg Type II Partnerships. *Yearbook of International Cooperation on Environment and Development* 2003–04: 19–31.

Andonova, Liliana B., and Ronald B. Mitchell. 2010. The Rescaling of Global Environmental Politics. *Annual Review of Environment and Resources* 35 (1): 255–82.

Auld, Graeme. 2008. Contested Trajectories of Private Governance: How Program Origins Affect Processes of Adaptation and Change. Vancouver, Canada.

Auld, Graeme, Cristina Balboa, Steven Bernstein, and Benjamin Cashore. 2009. The Emergence of Non-state Market-Driven Global Environmental Governance: A Cross-Sectoral Assessment. In *Governance for the Environment: New*

Perspectives, edited by Magali A. Delmas and Oran R. Young, 183–215. Cambridge: Cambridge University Press.

Auld, Graeme, Steven Bernstein, and Benjamin Cashore. 2008. The New Corporate Social Responsibility. *Annual Review of Environment and Resources* 33 (1): 413–35.

Auld, Graeme, and Jessica F. Green. 2012. Unbundling the Regime Complex: The Effects of Private Authority. Osgoode Hall Law School Comparative Research in Law and Political Economy Research Paper No. 15/2012, TBGI Project Subseries No. 3. Available from http://ssrn.com/abstract=2116296.

Auld, Graeme, and Lars H. Gulbrandsen. 2010. Transparency in Nonstate Certification: Consequences for Accountability and Legitimacy. *Global Environmental Politics* 10 (3): 97–119.

Auld, Graeme, Lars H. Gulbrandsen, and Constance McDermott. 2008. Certification Schemes and the Impacts on Forests and Forestry. *Annual Review of Environment and Resources* 33: 1–25.

Avant, Deborah D. 2005. *The Market for Force: The Consequences of Privatizing Security*. Cambridge: Cambridge University Press.

Avant, Deborah D., Martha Finnemore, and Susan K. Sell. 2010a. Who Governs the Globe? In *Who Governs the Globe?*, edited by Deborah D. Avant, Martha Finnemore, and Susan K. Sell, 1–34. Cambridge: Cambridge University Press.

———, eds. 2010b. *Who Governs the Globe?* Cambridge: Cambridge University Press.

Bäckstrand, Karin. 2008. Accountability of Networked Climate Governance: The Rise of Transnational Climate Partnerships. *Global Environmental Politics* 8 (3): 74–102.

Baldwin, David A. 2002. Power and International Relations. In *Handbook of International Relations*, edited by Walter Carlsnaes, Thomas Risse, and Beth A. Simmons, 177–91. London: Sage.

Barnett, Michael N., and Martha Finnemore. 1999. The Politics, Power, and Pathologies of International Organizations. *International Organization* 53 (4): 699–732.

Barrientos, Stephanie, and Sally Smith. 2007. Do Workers Benefit from Ethical Trade? Assessing Codes of Labour Practice in Global Production Systems. *Third World Quarterly* 28 (4): 713–29.

Bartley, Tim. 2003. Certifying Forests and Factories: States, Social Movements, and the Rise of Private Regulation in the Apparel and Forest Products Fields. *Politics & Society* 31 (3): 433–64.

———. 2007. Institutional Emergence in an Era of Globalization: The Rise of Transnational Private Regulation of Labor and Environmental Conditions. *American Journal of Sociology* 113 (2): 297–351.

———. 2010. Transnational Private Regulation in Practice: The Limits of Forest and Labor Standards Certification in Indonesia. *Business and Politics* 12 (3). Available from http://www.degruyter.com/view/j/bap.2010.12.3/bap.2010.12.3.1321/bap.2010.12.3.1321.xml?format=INT.

Bass, Stephen, and Stephane Gueneau. 2007. Global Forest Governance: Effectiveness, Fairness and Legitimacy of Market-Driven Approaches. In *Participation for Sustainability in Trade*, edited by Sophie Thoyer and Benoît Martimort-Asso, 161–82. Aldershot: Ashgate.

Beck, Ulrich. 1992. *Risk Society: Towards a New Modernity*. London: Sage.

Bendor, Jonathan, A. Glazer, and T. Hammond. 2001. Theories of Delegation. *American Political Science Review* 95 (4): 235–69.

Bernstein, Steven. 2001. *The Compromise of Liberal Environmentalism*. New York: Columbia University Press.

———. 2002. Liberal Environmentalism and Global Environmental Governance. *Global Environmental Politics* 2 (3): 1–16.

Bernstein, Steven, Michele Betsill, Matthew J. Hoffmann, and Matthew Paterson. 2010. A Tale of Two Copenhagens: Carbon Markets and Climate Governance. *Millennium—Journal of International Studies* 39 (1): 161–73.

Bernstein, Steven, and Benjamin Cashore. 2007. Can Non-state Global Governance Be Legitimate? An Analytical Framework. *Regulation and Governance* 1 (4): 347–71.

Betsill, Michele M., and Harriet Bulkeley. 2006. Cities and the Multilevel Governance of Global Climate Change. *Global Governance: A Review of Multilateralism and International Organizations* 12 (2): 141–59.

Betsill, Michele M., and Elisabeth Corell, eds. 2008. *NGO Diplomacy: The Influence of Nongovernmental Organizations in International Environmental Negotiations*. Cambridge, MA: MIT Press.

Betsill, Michele M., and Matthew J. Hoffmann. 2011. The Contours of "Cap and Trade": The Evolution of Emissions Trading Systems for Greenhouse Gases. *Review of Policy Research* 28 (1): 83–106.

Biermann, Frank. 2010. Beyond the Intergovernmental Regime: Recent Tends in Global Carbon Governance. *Current Opinion in Environmental Sustainability* 2: 284–88.

Biermann, Frank, and Klaus Dingwerth. 2004. Global Environmental Change and the Nation State. *Global Environmental Politics* 4 (1): 1–22.

Biermann, Frank, and Philipp Pattberg. 2008. Global Environmental Governance: Taking Stock, Moving Forward. *Annual Review of Environment and Resources* 33 (1): 277–94.

Biermann, Frank, Philipp Pattberg, Harro van Asselt, and Fariborz Zelli. 2009. The Fragmentation of Global Governance Architectures: A Framework for Analysis. *Global Environmental Politics* 9 (4): 14–40.

Blowfield, Michael. 2007. Reasons to Be Cheerful? What We Know about CSR's Impact. *Third World Quarterly* 28 (4): 683–95.

Börzel, Tanja A., and Thomas Risse. 2010. Governance without a State: Can It Work? *Regulation & Governance* 4 (2): 113–34.

Boyd, Emily, Nate Hultman, J. Timmons Roberts, Esteve Corbera, John Cole, Alex Bozmoski, Johannes Ebeling, et al. 2009. Reforming the CDM for Sustainable Development: Lessons Learned and Policy Futures. *Environmental Science & Policy* 12 (7): 820–31.

Bradley, Curtis A., and Judith G. Kelley. 2008. The Concept of International Delegation. *Law and Contemporary Problems* 71 (1): 1–36.

Braithwaite, John, and Peter Drahos. 2000. *Global Business Regulation*. Cambridge: Cambridge University Press.

Brown Weiss, Edith. 1993. International Environmental Law: Contemporary Issues and the Emergence of a New World Order. *Georgetown Law Journal* 81 (3): 675–710.

Browne, John. 1997. Addressing Global Climate Change. Stanford University, Stanford, CA.

Broz, J. Lawrence, and Michael Brewster Hawes. 2006. Congressional Politics of Financing the International Monetary Fund. *International Organization* 60: 367–99.

Bruhl, Tanja. 2005. The Privatization of Governance Systems: On the Legitimacy of International Environmental Policy. In *Governance and Democracy Comparing National, European and International Experiences*, edited by Arthur Benz and Yannis Papadopolous, 228–51. Abingdon: Routledge.

Bulkeley, Harriet, Liliana Andonova, Karin Bäckstrand, Michele Betsill, Daniel Compagnon, Rosaleen Duffy, Ans Kolk, et al. 2012. Governing Climate Change Transnationally: Assessing the Evidence from a Database of Sixty Initiatives. *Environment and Planning C: Government and Policy* 30 (4): 591–612.

Busch, Marc L. 2007. Overlapping Institutions, Forum Shopping, and Dispute Settlement in International Trade. *International Organization* 61 (4): 735–61.

Büthe, Tim. 2010a. Global Private Politics: A Research Agenda. *Business and Politics* 12 (3). Available from http://www.degruyter.com/view/j/bap.2010.12.3 /bap.2010.12.3.1345/bap.2010.12.3.1345.xml?format=INT.

———. 2010b. Private Regulation in the Global Economy: A (P)Review. *Business and Politics* 12 (3). Available from http://www.degruyter.com/view/j /bap.2010.12.3/bap.2010.12.3.1328/bap.2010.12.3.1328.xml.

Büthe, Tim, and Walter Mattli. 2011. *The New Global Rulers: The Privatization of Regulation in the World Economy*. Princeton, NJ: Princeton University Press.

Cafaggi, Fabrizio, ed. 2012. *Enforcement of Transnational Regulation: Ensuring Compliance in a Global World*. Cheltenham: Edward Elgar.

Cafaggi, Fabrizio, and Agnieszka Janczuk. 2010. Private Regulation and Legal Integration: The European Example. *Business and Politics* 12 (3). Available from http://www.degruyter.com/view/j/bap.2010.12.3/bap.2010.12.3.1320/bap .2010.12.3.1320.xml.

Capoor, Karan, and Philippe Ambrosi. 2008. *State and Trends of the Carbon Market, 2008*. Washington, DC: World Bank.

———. 2009. *State and Trends of the Carbon Market, 2009*. Washington, DC: World Bank.

Carpenter, R. Charli. 2007. Studying Issue (Non)-Adoption in Transnational Advocacy Networks. *International Organization* 61 (3): 643–67.

Cashore, Benjamin. 2002. Legitimacy and the Privatization of Environmental Governance: How Non-state Market Driven Systems Gain Rule-Making Authority. *Governance* 15 (4): 508–29.

Cashore, Benjamin, Graeme Auld, Steven Bernstein, and Constance McDermott. 2007. Can Non-state Governance "Ratchet Up" Global Environmental Standards? Lessons from the Forest Sector. *Review of European Community & International Environmental Law* 16 (2): 158–72.

Cashore, Benjamin, Graeme Auld, and Deanna Newsom. 2004. *Governing through Markets: Forest Certification and the Emergence of Non- state Authority*. New Haven: Yale University Press.

Cerny, Philip G. 1995. Globalization and the Changing Logic of Collective Action. *International Organization* 49 (4): 595–625.

Chayes, Abram, and Antonia Handler Chayes. 1993. On Compliance. *International Organization* 47 (2): 175–205.

———. 1995. *The New Sovereignty: Compliance with International Regulatory Agreements*. Cambridge, MA: Harvard University Press.

Chesterman, Simon, and Chia Lehnardt. 2007. *From Mercenaries to Market: The Rise and Regulation of Private Military Companies*. Oxford: Oxford University Press.

Clapp, Jennifer. 1998. The Privatization of Global Environmental Governance: ISO 14000 and the Developing World. *Global Governance* 4 (3): 295–316.

Clark, Margaret. 1994. The Antarctic Environmental Protocol: NGOs in the Protection of Antarctica. In *Environmental NGOs in World Politics: Linking the Local and the Global*, edited by Thomas Princen and Mattias Finger, 160–85. London: Routledge.

The Climate Protection Initiative. 1998. *Safe Climate, Sound Business: An Action Agenda*. Washington, DC: World Resources Institute.

Coase, R. H. 1960. The Problem of Social Cost. *Journal of Law and Economics* 3: 1–44.

Cochrane, Kevern L., and David J. Doulman. 2005. The Rising Tide of Fisheries Instruments and the Struggle to Keep Afloat. *Philosophical Transactions of the Royal Society of London. Series B, Biological Sciences* 360 (1453): 77–94.

Commission on Global Governance. 1995. *Our Global Neighbourhood: The Report of the Commission on Global Governance*. New York: Oxford University Press.

Conroy, Michael E. 2007. *Branded! How the "Certification Revolution" Is Transforming Global Corporations*. British Columbia: New Society Publishers.

Constance, Douglas H., and Alessandro Bonanno. 2000. Regulating the Global Fisheries: The World Wildlife Fund, Unilever, and the Marine Stewardship Council. *Agriculture and Human Values* 17: 125–39.

Cooley, Alexander. 2010. Outsourcing Authority: How Project Contracts Transform Global Governance Networks. In *Who Governs the Globe?*, edited by Deborah D. Avant, Martha Finnemore, and Susan K. Sell, 238–65. Cambridge: Cambridge University Press.

Cooley, Alexander, and James Ron. 2002. The NGO Scramble: Organizational Insecurity and the Political Economy of Transnational Action. *International Security* 27 (1): 5–39.

Cortright, David, and Ron Pagnucco. 1997. Limits to Transnationalism: The 1980s Freeze Campaign. In *Transnational Social Movements and Global Politics: Solidarity beyond the State*, edited by Jackie G. Smith, Charles Chatfield, and Ron Pagnucco, 159–74. Syracuse, NY: Syracuse University Press.

Cutler, A. Claire. 2003. *Private Power and Global Authority: Transnational Merchant Law in the Global Political Economy*. Cambridge: Cambridge University Press.

Cutler, A. Claire, Virginia Haufler, and Tony Porter. 1999a. Private Authority and International Affairs. In *Private Authority and International Affairs*, edited by A. Claire Cutler, Virginia Haufler, and Tony Porter, 3–30. Albany: SUNY Press.

Cutler, A. Claire, Virginia Haufler, and Tony Porter. 1999b. The Contours and Significance of Private Authority in International Affairs. In *Private Authority and International Affairs*, edited by A. Claire Cutler, Virginia Haufler, and Tony Porter, 333–76. Albany: SUNY Press.

Dahl, Robert A. 1957. The Concept of Power. *Behavioral Science* 2: 201–16.

Dai, Xinyuan. 2000. Information Systems in Treaty Regimes. *World Politics* 54 (4): 405–36.

Dauvergne, Peter, and Jane Lister. 2012. Big brand sustainability: Governance Prospects and Environmental Limits. *Global Environmental Change* 22 (1): 36–45.

Delmas, Magali, and Ivan Montiel. 2008. The Diffusion of Voluntary International Management Standards: Responsible Care, ISO 9000, and ISO 14001 in the Chemical Industry. *Policy Studies Journal* 36 (1): 65–93.

Depledge, Johanna. 2006. The Opposite of Learning: Ossification in the Climate Change Regime. *Global Environmental Politics* 6 (1): 1–22.

DeSombre, Elizabeth. 2000. *Sources of International Environmental Policy: Industry Environmentalists and US Power*. Cambridge, MA: MIT Press.

Diaz, David, Katherine Hamilton, and Evan Johnson. 2011. *State of the Forest Carbon Markets, 2011: From Canopy to Currency*. Washington, DC: Ecosystem Marketplace.

Dimitrov, Radoslav. 2003. Knowledge, Power, and Interests in Environmental Regime Formation. *International Studies Quarterly* 47: 123–50.

Dingwerth, Klaus, and Margot Eichinger. 2010. Tamed Transparency: How Information Disclosure under the Global Reporting Initiative Fails to Empower. *Global Environmental Politics* 10 (3): 74–96.

Dingwerth, Klaus, and Philipp Pattberg. 2009. World Politics and Organizational Fields: The Case of Transnational Sustainability Governance. *European Journal of International Relations* 15 (4): 707–43.

Djelic, Marie-Laure, and Kerstin Sahlin-Andersson. 2006. *Transnational Governance: Institutional Dynamics of Regulation*. Cambridge: Cambridge University Press.

Downs, George W., David M. Rocke, and Peter N. Barsoom. 1996. Is the Good News about Compliance Good News about Cooperation? *International Organization* 50 (3): 379–406.

Drezner, Daniel W. 2004. The Global Governance of the Internet: Bringing the State Back In. *Political Science Quarterly* 119 (3): 477–98.

———. 2007. *All Politics Is Global: Explaining International Regulatory Regimes*. Princeton, NJ: Princeton University Press.

Earth Negotiations Bulletin. 1999. *Summary Report: Technical Workshop on Mechanisms under Articles 6, 12 and 17 of the Kyoto Protocol*. Bonn, Germany. Available from http://www.iisd.ca/vol12/enb1298e.html.

Eberlein, Burkard, and Abraham L Newman. 2008. Escaping the International Governance Dilemma? Incorporated Transgovernmental Networks in the European Union. *Governance* 21 (1): 25–52.

Eckstein, Harry. 1975. Case Studies and Theory in Political Science. In *Handbook of Political Science. Political Science: Scope and Theory*, edited by Fred I. Greenstein and Nelson W. Polsby, 7: 94–137. Reading, MA: Addison-Wesley.

Engels, Anita. 2006. Market Creation and Transnational Rule Making: The Case of CO2 Emissions Trading. In *Transnational Governance: Institutional Dynamics of Regulation*, edited by Marie-Laure Djelic and Kerstin Sahlin-Andersson, 329–48. Cambridge: Cambridge University Press.

Environomics. 1999. *Options for Process and Institutional Arrangements for Conformity Assessment for the Clean Development Mechanism*. Bethesda, MD.

Epstein, David, and Sharyn O'Halloran. 1999. *Delegating Powers: A Transaction Cost Politics Approach to Policy Making under Separate Powers*. Cambridge: Cambridge University Press.

Esbenshade, Jill Louise. 2004. *Monitoring Sweatshops: Workers, Consumers, and the Global Apparel Industry*. Philadelphia: Temple University Press.

European Environment Agency. 2011. *Greenhouse Gas Emission Trends and Projections in Europe, 2011: Tracking Progress towards Kyoto and 2020 Targets*. Copenhagen, Denmark.

Falkner, Robert. 2003. Private Environmental Governance and International Relations: Exploring the Links. *Global Environmental Politics* 3 (2): 72–87.

Florini, Ann. 2000. *The Third Force: The Rise of Transnational Civil Society*. Tokyo and Washington, DC: Japan Center for International Exchange; Carnegie Endowment for International Peace. Distributed in the U.S. by Brookings Institution Press.

Fransen, Luc. 2011. Why Do Private Governance Organizations Not Converge? A Political-Institutional Analysis of Transnational Labor Standards Regulation. *Governance* 24 (2): 359–87.

———. 2012a. *Corporate Social Responsibility and Global Labor Standards: Firms and Activists in the Making of Private Regulation*. New York: Routledge.

———. 2012b. The Politics of Meta-standard Interactions in Private Sustainability Governance: Institutional Design, Actor Strategies and Organizational Embedding. Paper presented at the 2012 convention of the American Political Science Association, September 2013. New Orleans, LA.

Friedman, R. B. 1990. On the Concept of Authority in Political Philosophy. In *Authority*, edited by Joseph Raz, 56–92. New York: New York University Press.

Fuchs, Doris A. 2007. *Business Power in Global Governance*. Boulder, CO: Lynne Rienner.

Fuchs, Doris, and Agni Kalfagianni. 2010. The Causes and Consequences of Private Food Governance. *Business and Politics* 12 (3). Available from http://www.degruyter.com/view/j/bap.2010.12.3/bap.2010.12.3.1319/bap.2010.12.3.1319.xml?format=INT.

Gale, Fred P. 1998. *The Tropical Timber Trade Regime*. London: Palgrave Macmillan.

Garcia-Johnson, Ronie. 2000. *Exporting Environmentalism: US Multinational Chemical Corporations in Brazil and Mexico*. Cambridge, MA: MIT Press.

Garrett, Geoffrey, and Barry Weingast. 1993. Ideas, Interests and Institutions: Constructing the European Community's Internal Market. In *Ideas and Foreign Policy: Beliefs, Institutions, and Political Change*, edited by Judith Goldstein and Robert O. Keohane, 173–206. Ithaca, NY: Cornell University Press.

Gereffi, Gary, Ronie Garcia-Johnson, and Erika Sasser. 2001. The NGO-Industrial Complex. *Foreign Policy* 125 (July–August): 56–65.

Gereffi, Gary, John Humphrey, and Timothy Sturgeon. 2005. The Governance of Global Value Chains. *Review of International Political Economy* 12 (1): 78–104.

Grant, Ruth W., and Robert O. Keohane. 2005. Accountability and Abuses of Power in World Politics. *American Political Science Review* 99 (1): 29–43.

Graz, Jean-Christophe, and Andreas Nölke. 2008a. Introduction: Beyond the Fragmented Debate on Transnational Private Governance. In *Transnational Private Governance and Its Limits*, edited by Jean-Christophe Graz and Andreas Nölke, 1–26. New York: Routledge.

———, eds. 2008b. *Transnational Private Governance and Its Limits*. New York: Routledge.

Green, Jessica F. 2008. Delegation and Accountability in the Clean Development Mechanism: The New Authority of Non-state Actors. *Journal of International Law and International Relations* 4 (2): 21–55.

———. 2010a. Private Authority on the Rise: A Century of Delegation in Multilateral Environmental Agreements. In *Transnational Actors in Global Governance: Patterns, Explanations and Implications*, edited by Jonas Tallberg and Christer Jönsson, 155–76. New York: Palgrave Macmillan.

———. 2010b. Private Standards in the Climate Regime: The Greenhouse Gas Protocol. *Business and Politics* 12 (3). Available from http://www.degruyter.com/view/j/bap.2010.12.3/bap.2010.12.3.1318/bap.2010.12.3.1318.xml?format=INT.

———. 2012. From Green to REDD: How Private Authority Shapes Public Rules on Carbon Sinks. Paper presented at Ohio State University, Mershon Center for International Security Studies, Globalization Speaker Series, 16 May.

———. 2013a. Order Out of Chaos: Public and Private Rules for Managing Carbon. *Global Environmental Politics* 13 (2): 1–25.

———. 2013b. Global administrative law and the emerging framework for carbon accounting. Unpublished Manuscript.

Green, Jessica F., and Jeff Colgan. 2013. Protecting Sovereignty, Protecting the Planet: State Delegation to International Organizations and Private Actors in Environmental Politics. *Governance* 26 (3).

Greif, Avner. 1993. Contract Enforceability and Economic Institutions in Early Trade: The Maghribi Traders' Coalition. *American Economic Review* 83 (3): 525–48.

———. 2006. *Institutions and the Path to the Modern Economy: Lessons from Medieval Trade*. Cambridge: Cambridge University Press.

Greif, Avner, Paul Milgrom, and Barry R. Weingast. 1994. Coordination, Commitment, and Enforcement: The Case of the Merchant Guild. *Journal of Political Economy* 102 (4): 745–76.

Grubb, Michael, Christian Vrolijk, and Duncan Brack. 1999. *The Kyoto Protocol: A Guide and Assessment*. London: Royal Institute of International Affairs.

Grubb, Michael, and Farhana Yamin. 2001. Climatic Collapse at The Hague: What Happened, Why, and Where Do We Go from Here? *International Affairs (Royal Institute of International Affairs 1944–)* 77 (2): 261–76.

Gulbrandsen, Lars H. 2004. Overlapping Public and Private Governance: Can Forest Certification Fill the Gaps in the Global Forest Regime? *Global Environmental Politics* 4 (2): 75–99.

———. 2005. Sustainable Forestry in Sweden: The Effect of Competition among Private Certification Schemes. *Journal of Environment & Development* 14 (3): 338–55.

Gupta, Aarti. 2010. Transparency in Global Environmental Governance: A Coming of Age? *Global Environmental Politics* 10 (3): 1–9.

Gutner, Tamar, and Alexander Thompson. 2010. The Politics of IO Performance: A Framework. *Review of International Organizations* 5: 227–48.

Gylvan Meira Filho, Luiz. 1998. Ideas for Implementation. In *Issues and Options: The Clean Development Mechanism*, edited by Jose Goldemberg, 39–44. New York: United Nations Development Programme.

Haas, Ernst. 1990. *When Knowledge Is Power: Three Models of Change in International Organizations*. Berkeley: University of California Press.

Haas, Peter M. 1989. Do Regimes Matter? Epistemic Communities and Mediterranean Pollution Control. *International Organization* 43 (3): 377–403.

———. 1990. *Saving the Mediterranean: The Politics of International Environmental Cooperation*. New York: Columbia University Press.

———. 1992. Introduction: Epistemic Communities and International Policy Coordination. *International Organization* 46 (1): 1–35.

Haas, Peter M., Robert O. Keohane, and Marc A. Levy. 1993. *Institutions for the Earth: Sources of Effective International Environmental Protection*. Cambridge, MA: MIT Press.

Hale, Thomas N., and Denise L. Mauzerall. 2004. Thinking Globally and Acting Locally: Can the Johannesburg Partnerships Coordinate Action on Sustainable Development? *Journal of Environment and Development* 13 (3): 220–39.

Hall, Rodney Bruce, and Thomas J. Biersteker. 2002. The Emergence of Private Authority in the International System. In *The Emergence of Private Authority in Global Governance*, edited by Rodney Bruce Hall and Thomas J. Biersteker, 3–22. Cambridge: Cambridge University Press.

Hamilton, Katherine, Milo Sjardin, Molly Peters-Stanley, and Thomas Marcello. 2010. *Building Bridges: State of the Voluntary Carbon Markets, 2010*. New York and Washington, DC: Bloomberg New Energy Finance and Ecosystem Marketplace. Available from http://www.forest-trends.org/documents/files/doc_2434.pdf.

Hamilton, Katherine, Milo Sjardin, Allison Shapiro, and Thomas Marcello. 2009. *Fortifying the Foundation: State of the Voluntary Carbon Market, 2009*. New York: Ecosystem Marketplace and New Carbon Finance. Available from http://www.ecosystemmarketplace.com/documents/cms_documents/StateOfThe VoluntaryCarbonMarkets_2009.pdf.

Hamilton, Martha. 1998. Shell's New Worldview; At Helm of Oil Titan, Moody-Stuart Sees Profit in Principles. *Washington Post*, 2 August, sec. H.

Hasenclever, Andreas, Peter J. Mayer, and Volker Rittberger. 1997. *Theories of International Regimes*. Cambridge: Cambridge University Press.

Haufler, Virginia. 2001. *A Public Role for the Private Sector*. Washington, DC: Carnegie Endowment for International Peace.

———. 2009. Transnational Actors and Global Environmental Governance. In *Governance for the Environment: New Perspectives*, edited by Magali A. Delmas and Oran R. Young, 119–43. Cambridge: Cambridge University Press.

Haufler, Virginia. 2010. Disclosure as Governance: The Extractive Industries Transparency Initiative and Resource Management in the Developing World. *Global Environmental Politics* 10 (3): 53–73.

Hawkins, Darren G., David A. Lake, Daniel L. Nielson, and Michael J. Tierney. 2006a. *Delegation and Agency in International Organizations.* Cambridge: Cambridge University Press.

———. 2006b. Delegation under Anarchy: States, International Organizations and Principal-Agent Theory. In *Delegation and Agency in International Organizations,* edited by Darren G. Hawkins, David A. Lake, Daniel L. Nielson, and Michael J. Tierney, 3–38. Cambridge: Cambridge University Press.

High Level Panel on the CDM Policy Dialogue. 2012. *Climate Change, Carbon Markets and the CDM: A Call to Action.* Luxembourg: CDM Policy Dialogue.

Hobbes, Thomas. 1996. *Leviathan.* Edited by Richard Tuck. Cambridge: Cambridge University Press.

Hoffmann, Matthew J. 2011. *Climate Governance at the Crossroads.* Oxford: Oxford University Press.

Hovi, Jon, Detlef F. Sprinz, and Arild Underdal. 2003. The Oslo-Potsdam Solution to Measuring Regime Effectiveness: Critique, Response, and the Road Ahead. *Global Environmental Politics* 3 (3): 74–96.

Humphreys, David. 1996. *Forest Politics: The Evolution of International Cooperation.* London: Earthscan.

Hunt, Colin A.G. 2009. *Carbon Sinks and Climate Change: Forests in the Fight against Global Warming.* Cheltenham: Edward Elgar.

Hurd, Ian. 1999. Legitimacy and Authority in World Politics. *International Organization* 53 (2): 379–408.

Intergovernmental Panel on Climate Change. 2006. *Revised 1996 Guidelines for National Greenhouse Gas Inventories.* London: IPCC WGI Technical Support Unit.

———. 2007. *Climate Change, 2007: Synthesis Report.* Geneva: Intergovernmental Panel on Climate Change.

Jacobsson, Bengt. 2006. Regulated Regulators: Global Trends of State Transformation. In *Transnational Governance: Institutional Dynamics of Regulation,* edited by Marie-Laure Djelic and Kerstin Sahlin-Andersson, 205–24. Cambridge: Cambridge University Press.

Jacobsson, Bengt, and Kerstin Sahlin-Anderson. 2006. Dynamics of Soft Regulations. In *Transnational Governance: Institutional Dynamics of Regulation,* edited by Marie-Laure Djelic and Kerstin Sahlin-Andersson, 247–65. Cambridge: Cambridge University Press.

Jacoby, Henry D., and David M. Reiner. 2001. Getting Climate Policy on Track after The Hague. *International Affairs (Royal Institute of International Affairs 1944-)* 77 (2): 297–312.

Jordan, Lisa, and Peter Van Tuijl. 2000. Political Responsibility in Transnational NGO Advocacy. *World Development* 28 (12): 2051–65.

Jordana, Jacint, and David Levi-Faur, eds. 2004. *The Politics of Regulation: Institutions and Regulatory Reforms for the Age of Governance.* Cheltenham: Edward Elgar.

Joyner, Christopher C. 1998. *Governing the Frozen Commons: The Antarctic Regime and Environmental Protection.* Columbia: University of South Carolina Press.

Keck, Margaret E., and Kathryn Sikkink. 1998. *Activists beyond Borders: Advocacy Networks in International Politics.* Ithaca, NY: Cornell University Press.

Kell, Georg, and David Levin. 2003. The Global Compact Network: An Historic Experiment in Learning and Action. *Business and Society Review* 108 (2): 151–81.

Keohane, Robert O. 1982. The Demand for International Regimes. *International Organization* 36 (2): 325–55.

———. 1984. *After Hegemony: Cooperation and Discord in the World Political Economy.* Princeton, NJ: Princeton University Press.

Keohane, Robert O., Andrew Moravcsik, and Anne Marie Slaughter. 2000. Legalized Dispute Resolution: Interstate and Transnational. *International Organization* 54 (3): 457–88.

Keohane, Robert O., and Joseph S. Nye Jr. 1977. *Power and Interdependence in World Politics.* 2nd ed. Boston: Little Brown.

Keohane, Robert O., and David G. Victor. 2011. The Regime Complex for Climate Change. *Perspectives on Politics* 9 (1): 7–23.

Kerwer, Dieter. 2005. Rules That Many Use: Standards and Global Regulation. *Governance* 18 (4): 611–32.

Khanna, Madhu, and Keith Brouhle. 2009. The Effectiveness of Voluntary Environmental Initiatives. In *Governance for the Environment: New Perspectives,* edited by Magali A. Delmas and Oran R. Young, 144–82. Cambridge: Cambridge University Press.

King, Andrew. 2007. Cooperation between Corporations and Environmental Groups: A Transaction Cost Perspective. *Academic Management Review* 32 (3): 889–900.

King, Andrew, and Michael J. Lenox. 2000. Industry Self-Regulation without Sanctions: The Chemical Industry's Responsible Care Program. *Academy of Management Journal* 43 (4): 698–716.

King, Andrew, and Michael W. Toffel. 2009. Self-Regulatory Institutions for Solving Environmental Problems: Perspectives and Contributions from the Management Literature. In *Governance for the Environment: New Perspectives,* edited by Magali A. Delmas and Oran R. Young, 98–115. Cambridge: Cambridge University Press.

King, Gary, Robert O. Keohane, and Sidney Verba. 1994. *Designing Social Inquiry.* Princeton, NJ: Princeton University Press.

Kingsbury, Benedict, Nico Krisch, and Richard B. Stewart. 2005. The Emergence of Global Administrative Law. *Law and Contemporary Problems* 68 (15): 15–61.

Kirton, John J., and Michael John Trebilcock. 2004. *Hard Choices, Soft Law: Voluntary Standards in Global Trade, Environment and Social Governance.* Aldershot: Ashgate.

Knill, Christoph, and Dirk Lehmkuhl. 2002. Private Actors and the State: Internationalization and Changing Patterns of Governance. *Governance* 15 (1): 41–63.

Kobrin, Stephen J. 2002. Economic Governance in an Electronically Networked Global Economy. In *The Emergence of Private Authority in Global Governance*, edited by Rodney Bruce Hall and Thomas J. Biersteker, 43–75. Cambridge: Cambridge University Press.

Kolk, Ans, and Rob van Tulder. 2002. *International Codes of Conduct: Trends, Sectors, Issues and Effectiveness*. Rotterdam: SCOPE.

Kolk, Johanna Elisabeth Maria, Rob van Tulder, Robertus Johannes Maria Tulder, and Carlijn Welters. 1999. *International Codes of Conduct and Corporate Social Responsibility: Content and Context of a New Wave in Voluntary Regulation*. Erasmus Universiteit Rotterdam, Faculteit Bedrijfskunde/Rotterdam School of Management.

Kollmuss, Anja, Helge Zink, and Clifford Polycarp. 2008. *Making Sense of the Voluntary Carbon Market: A Comparison of Carbon Offset Standards*. Stockholm Environment Institute and Tricorona. Available from http://assets.panda.org/downloads/vcm_report_final.pdf.

Koppell, Jonathan G. S. 2003. *The Politics of Quasi-Government*. Cambridge: Cambridge University Press.

———. 2010. *World Rule: Accountability, Legitimacy, and the Design of Global Governance*. Chicago: University of Chicago Press.

Koremenos, Barbara. 2007. If Only Half of International Agreements Have Dispute Resolution Provisions, Which Half Needs Explaining? *Journal of Legal Studies* 36: 189–212.

———. 2008. When, What and Why Do States Choose to Delegate? *Law and Contemporary Problems* 71 (1): 151–91.

Koremenos, Barbara, Charles Lipson, and Duncan Snidal. 2001. The Rational Design of Institutions. *International Organization* 55 (4): 761–99.

Kossoy, Alexandre, and Philippe Ambrosi. 2010. *State and Trends of the Carbon Market, 2010*. Washington, DC: World Bank.

Kossoy, Alexandre, and Pierre Guigon. 2012. *State and Trends of the Carbon Market, 2012*. Washington, DC: World Bank.

Krasner, Stephen D. 1999. *Sovereignty: Organized Hypocrisy*. Princeton, NJ: Princeton University Press.

Lake, David A. 2009. *Hierarchy in International Relations*. Ithaca, NY: Cornell University Press.

———. 2010. Rightful Rules: Authority, Order, and the Foundations of Global Governance. *International Studies Quarterly* 54 (3): 587–613.

Lake, David A., and Mathew McCubbins. 2006. The Logic of Delegation to International Organizations. In *Delegation under Anarchy: States, International Organizations and Principal-Agent Theory*, edited by Darren G. Hawkins, David A. Lake, Daniel L. Nielson, and Michael J. Tierney, 341–68. Cambridge: Cambridge University Press.

Lederer, Markus. 2011. From CDM to REDD+—What Do We Know for Setting Up Effective and Legitimate Carbon Governance? *Ecological Economics* 70 (11): 1900–1907.

Lefevere, Jurgen. 2005. The EU Greenhouse Gas Emissions Allowance Trading Scheme. In *Climate Change and Carbon Markets: A Handbook of Emissions Reduction Mechanisms*, edited by Farhana Yamin, 75–148. London: Earthscan.

Lenox, Michael J., and Jennifer Nash. 2003. Industry Self-Regulation and Adverse Selection: A Comparison across Four Trade Association Programs. *Business Strategy & the Environment* 12 (6): 343–56.

Levi-Faur, David, ed. 2012. *Handbook on the Politics of Regulation*. Cheltenham: Edward Elgar.

Linacre, Nicholas, Alexandre Kossoy, and Philippe Ambrosi. 2011. *State and Trends of the Carbon Market, 2011*. Washington, DC: World Bank.

Lipschutz, Ronnie D. 1992. Restructuring World Politics: The Emergence of Global Civil Society. *Millennium* 21 (3): 389–420.

Lipschutz, Ronnie D., and Cathleen Fogel. 2002. "Regulation for the Rest of Us?" Global Civil Society and the Privatization of Transnational Regulation. In *The Emergence of Private Authority in Global Governance*, edited by Rodney Bruce Hall and Thomas J. Biersteker, 115–40. Cambridge Studies in International Relations, 85. Cambridge: Cambridge University Press.

Lister, Jane, and Genevieve LeBaron. 2012. *Shopping for Sustainability at the Canton Fair: The Political Economy of Transnational Retail Governance in China*. Vancouver: Liu Institute for Global Issues.

Litfin, Karen. 1994. *Ozone Discourses: Science and Politics in Global Environmental Cooperation*. New Directions in World Politics. New York: Columbia University Press.

Locke, Richard M., Qin Fei, and Alberto Brause. 2007. Does Monitoring Improve Labor Standards? Lessons from Nike. *Industrial & Labor Relations Review* 61 (1): 3–31.

Lohmann, Larry. 2006. *Carbon Trading: A Critical Conversation on Climate Change, Privatisation and Power*. Uddevalla, Sweden: Development Dialogue.

———. 2009. Regulatory Challenges for Financial and Carbon Markets. *Carbon & Climate Law Review* 3 (2): 161–71.

Lovbrand, Eva. 2009. Revisiting the Politics of Expertise in Light of the Kyoto Negotiations on Land Use Change and Forestry. *Forest Policy and Economics* 11: 404–12.

Loya, Thomas A., and John Boli. 1999. Standardization in the World Polity: Technical Rationality over Power. In *Constructing World Culture: International Nongovernmental Organizations since 1875*, 169–96. Stanford, CA: Stanford University Press.

Lukes, Steven. 2005. *Power: A Radical View*. 2nd ed. New York: Palgrave Macmillan.

Lund, Emma. 2010. Dysfunctional Delegation: Why the Design of the CDM's Supervisory System Is Fundamentally Flawed. *Climate Policy* 10 (3): 277–88.

Lupia, Arthur, and Mathew D. McCubbins. 1994. Learning from Oversight: Fire Alarms and Police Patrols Reconstructed. *Journal of Law, Economics, and Organization* 10 (1): 96–125.

Lyne, Mona M., Daniel L. Nielson, and Michael J. Tierney. 2006. Who Delegates? Alternative Models of Principals in Development Aid. In *Delegation and Agency in International Organizations*, edited by Darren G. Hawkins, David A. Lake, Daniel L. Nielson, and Michael J. Tierney, 41–76. Cambridge: Cambridge University Press.

MacDicken, K. G. 1997. *A Guide to Monitoring Carbon Storage in Forestry and Agroforestry Projects*. Arlington, VA: Winrock International.

Majone, Giandomenico. 2001. Two Logics of Delegation: Agency and Fiduciary Relations in EU Governance. *European Union Politics* 2 (1): 103–22.

Martin, Lisa L. 1992. Interests, Power and Multilateralism. *International Organization* 46 (4): 765–92.

Mathews, Jessica T. 1997. Power Shift. *Foreign Affairs* 76 (January–February): 50–66.

Mattli, Walter, and Tim Büthe. 2003. Setting International Standards: Technological Rationality or Primacy of Power. *World Politics* 56 (1): 1–42.

———. 2005. Global Private Governance: Lessons from a National Model of Setting Standards in Accounting. *Law and Contemporary Problems* 68: 225–62.

Mattli, Walter, and Ngaire Woods. 2009a. In Whose Benefit? Explaining Regulatory Change in Global Politics. In *The Politics of Global Regulation*, edited by Walter Mattli and Ngaire Woods, 1–43. Princeton, NJ: Princeton University Press.

———. 2009b. *The Politics of Global Regulation*. Princeton, NJ: Princeton University Press.

Mayer, Frederick, and Gary Gereffi. 2010. Globalization: Prospects and Limits of Private Governance. *Business and Politics* 12 (3). Available from http://www.degruyter.com/view/j/bap.2010.12.3/bap.2010.12.3.1325/bap.2010.12.3.1325.xml?format=INT.

McCubbins, Matthew, Roger G. Noll, and Barry Weingast. 1987. Structure and Process, Politics and Policy: Administrative Procedures as Instruments of Political Control. *Journal of Law, Economics, and Organization* 3 (2): 243–77.

McDougal, Myres, and Harold Lasswell. 1970. Criteria for a Theory about Law. *Southern California Law Review* 44: 362–94.

McNamara, Kathleen. 2010. Constructing Authority in the European Union. In *Who Governs the Globe?*, edited by Deborah D. Avant, Martha Finnemore, and Susan K. Sell, 153–82. Cambridge: Cambridge University Press.

Meckling, Jonas. 2011. *Carbon Coalitions: Business, Climate Politics, and the Rise of Emissions Trading*. Cambridge, MA: MIT Press.

Meidinger, Errol. 2006. The Administrative Law of Global Private-Public Regulation: The Case of Forestry. *European Journal of International Law* 17 (1): 47–87.

Meijer, Ernestine, and Jacob Werksman. 2005. Keeping It Clean—Safeguarding the Environmental Integrity of the Clean Development Mechanism. In *Legal Aspects of Implementing the Kyoto Protocol*, edited by David Freestone and Charlotte Streck, 191–212. Oxford: Oxford University Press.

Merk, Jeroen. 2008. The Private Regulation of Labour Standards: The Case of the Apparel and Footwear Industries. In *Transnational Private Governance and Its Limits*, edited by Jean-Christophe Graz and Andreas Nölke, 115–26. New York: Routledge.

Meyer, David S., and Debra C. Minkoff. 2004. Conceptualizing Political Opportunity. *Social Forces* 82 (4): 1457–92.

Michonski, Katherine, and Michael Levi. 2010. *Harnessing International Institutions to Address Climate Change*. New York: Council on Foreign Relations. Available from http://www.cfr.org/publication/21609/harnessing_international_institutions_to_address_climate_change.html.

Milgrom, Paul A., Douglas North, and Barry Weingast. 1990. The Role of Institutions in the Revival of Trade: The Medieval Law Merchant, Private Judges, and the Champagne Fairs. *Economics and Politics* 2 (1): 1–23.

Milner, Helen V. 2009. Power, Interdependence, and Nonstate Actors in World Politics: Research Frontiers. In *Power, Interdependence, and Nonstate Actors in World Politics*, edited by Helen V. Milner and Andrew Moravcsik, 3–31. Princeton University Press.

Ministry of Economic Affairs of the Netherlands. 2000. *Operational Guidelines for Baseline Studies, Validation, Monitoring and Verification of Joint Implementation Projects*. Available from http://www.ecn.nl/fileadmin/ecn/units/bs/Kyoto/volume1.pdf.

Mitchell, Ronald B. 2002–13. *International Environmental Agreements Database Project*. University of Oregon. Available from http://iea.uoregon.edu/page.php?file=home.htm&query=static.

———. 2010. "Multilateral Environmental Agreements." Available from http://iea.uoregon.edu/images/Multilaterals.jpg.

Moe, Terry M. 1990. Political Institutions: The Neglected Side of the Story. *Journal of Law, Economics and Organization* 6: 213–53.

Mol, Arthur P. J., Frederick H. Buttel, and Gert Spaargaren. 2000. *Environment and Global Modernity*. London: Sage.

Moravcsik, Andrew. 1998. *The Choice for Europe*. Ithaca, NY: Cornell University Press.

———. 1999. A New Statecraft? Supranational Entrepreneurs and International Cooperation. *International Organization* 53 (2): 267–306.

Mosley, Layna. 2009. Private Governance for the Public Good? Exploring Private Sector Participation in Global Financial Regulation. In *Power, Interdependence, and Nonstate Actors in World Politics*, edited by Helen V. Milner and Andrew Moravcsik, 126–46. Princeton, NJ: Princeton University Press.

Moura-Costa, Pedro, and Marc Stuart. 1998. Forestry-Based Greenhouse Gas Mitigation: A Short Story of Market Evolution. *Commonwealth Forestry Review* 77: 191–202.

Moura-Costa, Pedro, Marc Stuart, Michelle Pinard, and Gareth Phillips. 2000. Elements of a Certification System for Forestry-Based Carbon Offset Projects. *Mitigation and Adaptation Strategies for Global Change* 5 (1): 39–50.

Moura-Costa, Pedro, Marc Stuart, and Eveline Trines. 1997. *SGS's Forest Carbon Offset Verification Service*. Vancouver: Elsevier.

Mufson, Steven. 2010. In China, Wal-Mart Presses Suppliers on Labor, Environmental Standards. *Washington Post*. Available from http://www.washingtonpost.com/wp-dyn/content/article/2010/02/26/AR2010022606757.html.

Muthien, Bernadette, and Ian Taylor. 2002. The Return of the Dogs of War? The Privatization of Security in Africa. In *The Emergence of Private Authority in Global Governance*, edited by Rodney Bruce Hall and Thomas J. Biersteker, 183–202. Cambridge: Cambridge University Press.

Nadvi, Khalid. 2008. Global Standards, Global Governance and the Organization of Global Value Chains. *Journal of Economic Geography* 8 (3): 323–43.

Najam, Adil. 2005. Developing Countries and Global Environmental Governance: From Contestation to Participation to Engagement. *International Environmental Agreements: Politics, Law and Economics* 5 (3): 303–21.

Newell, Peter. 2001. Environmental NGOs, TNCs, and the Question of Governance. In *The International Political Economy of the Environment: Critical Perspectives*, edited by Dimitris Stevis and Valerie J. Assetto, 85–110. London: Lynne Rienner.

Newell, Peter, Max Boykoff, and Emily Boyd, eds. 2012. *The New Carbon Economy: Constitution, Governance and Contestation*. Malden, MA: Wiley-Blackwell.

Newell, Peter, and Matthew Paterson. 2010. *Climate Capitalism: Global Warming and the Transformation of the Global Economy*. Cambridge: Cambridge University Press.

Newman, Abraham. 2008. Building Transnational Civil Liberties: Transgovernmental Entrepreneurs and the European Privacy Directive. *International Organization* 62 (1): 103–30.

Nielson, Daniel L., and Michael J. Tierney. 2003. Delegation to International Organizations: Agency Theory and World Bank Environmental Reform. *International Organization* 57 (2): 241–76.

Nye, Joseph S., Jr. 1990. *Bound to Lead: The Changing Nature of American Power*. New York: Basic Books.

———. 2011. *The Future of Power*. New York: PublicAffairs.

Oberthur, Sebastian, and Olav Schram Stokke, eds. 2011. *Managing Institutional Complexity*. Cambridge, MA: MIT Press.

O'Brien, Robert, Anne Marie Goetz, Jan Aart Scholte, and Marc Williams. 2000. Contesting Governance: Multilateralism and Global Social Movements. In *Contesting Global Governance: Multilateral Economic Institutions and Global Social Movements*, edited by Robert O'Brien, Anne Marie Goetz, Jan Aart Scholte, and Marc Williams, 1–23. Cambridge: Cambridge University Press.

OECD. 1999. *Codes of Corporate Conduct: An Inventory*. Paris: OECD.

Ohmae, Kenichi. 1995. *The End of the Nation State: The Rise of Regional Economies*. New York: Free Press.

O'Rourke, Dara. 2003. Outsourcing Regulation: Analyzing Nongovernmental Systems of Labor Standards and Monitoring. *Policy Studies Journal* 31 (1): 1.

Ostrom, Elinor. 2010. Beyond Markets and States: Polycentric Governance of Complex Economic Systems. *American Economic Review* 100 (3): 641–72.

Overdevest, Christine. 2010. Comparing Forest Certification Schemes: The Case of Ratcheting Standards in the Forest Sector. *Socio-Economic Review* 8 (1): 47–76.

Overdevest, Christine, and Jonathan Zeitlin. 2012. Assembling an Experimentalist Regime: Transnational Governance Interactions in the Forest Sector. *Regulation & Governance*. Available from http://onlinelibrary.wiley.com/doi/10.1111/j.1748-5991.2012.01133.x/abstract.

Oye, Kenneth A., and James H. Maxwell. 1994. Self-Interest and Environmental Management. *Journal of Theoretical Politics* 6 (4): 593–624.

Panayotou, Theodore. 1998. Six Questions of Design and Governance. In *Issues and Options: The Clean Development Mechanism*, edited by Jose Goldemberg, 45–52. New York: United Nations Development Programme.

Parson, Edward. 2003. *Protecting the Ozone Layer: Science and Strategy*. Oxford: Oxford University Press.

Pattberg, Philipp. 2005. The Institutionalization of Private Governance: How Business and Nonprofit Organizations Agree on Transnational Rules. *Governance* 18 (4): 589–610.

———. 2007. *Private Institutions and Global Governance: The New Politics of Environmental Sustainability*. Northampton, MA: Edward Elgar.

Pauly, Louis W. 2002. Global Finance, Political Authority and the Problem of Legitimation. In *The Emergence of Private Authority in Global Governance*, edited by Rodney Bruce Hall and Thomas J. Biersteker, 76–90. Cambridge: Cambridge University Press.

Peters-Stanley, Molly, Katherine Hamilton, Thomas Marcello, and Milo Sjardin. 2011. *Back to the Future: State of the Voluntary Carbon Market, 2011*. New York: Ecosystem Marketplace and New Carbon Finance. Available from http://www.ecosystemmarketplace.com/documents/cms_documents/StateOfThe VoluntaryCarbonMarkets_2009.pdf.

Pitkin, Hanna. 1967. *The Concept of Representation*. Berkeley: University of California Press.

Pollack, Mark A. 1997. Delegation, Agency, and Agenda Setting in the European Community. *International Organization* 51 (1): 99–134.

———. 2003. *The Engines of European Integration: Delegation, Agency and Agenda Setting in the EU*. Oxford: Oxford University Press.

Porter, Tony, and Karsten Ronit. 2006. Self-Regulation as Policy Process: The Multiple and Criss-crossing Stages of Private Rule-Making. *Policy Sciences* 39 (1): 41–72.

Potoski, Matthew, and Aseem Prakash. 2005. Covenants with Weak Swords: ISO 14001 and Facilities' Environmental Performance. *Journal of Policy Analysis and Management* 24 (4): 745–69.

Powell, Walter. 1990. Neither Market nor Hierarchy: Network Forms of Organization. *Research in Organizational Behavior* 12: 295–336.

Prakash, Aseem, and Matthew Potoski. 2006. *The Voluntary Environmentalists: Green Clubs, ISO 14001, and Voluntary Environmental Regulations*. Cambridge: Cambridge University Press.

PricewaterhouseCoopers. 2012. *Accelerating Progress toward a Lower-Carbon Future: Carbon Disclosure Report S&P 500 Climate Change Report*. New York: Carbon Disclosure Project. Available from https://www.cdproject.net /CDPResults/CDP-SP500-2012.pdf.

Rabkin, Jeremy. 2005. *Law without Nations? Why Constitutional Government Requires Sovereign States*. Princeton, NJ: Princeton University Press.

Ragin, Charles C. 2000. *Fuzzy-Set Social Science*. Chicago: University of Chicago Press.

———. 2004. Turning the Tables: How Case-Oriented Research Challenges Variable-Oriented Research. In *Rethinking Social Inquiry: Diverse Tools, Shared Standards*, edited by Henry Brady and David Collier, 123–38. Oxford: Rowman & Littlefield.

Raustiala, Kal. 1997. States, NGOs and International Environmental Institutions. *International Studies Quarterly* 41: 719–40.

Raustiala, Kal. 2001. Non-state Actors and Climate Change. In *International Relations and Global Climate Change*, edited by Urs Luterbacher and Detlef F. Sprinz, 95–118. Cambridge, MA: MIT Press.

———. 2002. The Architecture of International Cooperation: Transgovernmental Networks and the Future of International Law. *Virginia Journal of International Law* 43 (1): 2–92.

———. 2012. Institutional Proliferation and the International Legal Order. In *Interdisciplinary Perspectives on International Law and International Relations*, edited by Jeffrey L. Dunoff and Mark A. Pollack. Cambridge: Cambridge University Press.

Raustiala, Kal, and David G. Victor. 2004. The Regime Complex for Plant Genetic Resources. *International Organization* 58 (2): 277–309.

Raz, Joseph. 1990. Introduction. In *Authority*, edited by Joseph Raz, 1–19. New York: New York University Press.

Reinhardt, Eric. 2001. Adjudication without Enforcement in GATT Disputes. *Journal of Conflict Resolution* 45 (2): 174 –95.

Richardson, Alan J., and Burkard Eberlein. 2011. Legitimating Transnational Standard-Setting: The Case of the International Accounting Standards Board. *Journal of Business Ethics* 98 (2): 217–45.

Rosenau, James N., and Ernst Otto Czempiel. 1992. *Governance without Government: Order and Change in World Politics*. Cambridge Studies in International Relations, 20. Cambridge: Cambridge University Press.

Rosendorff, B. Peter, and Helen V. Milner. 2001. The Optimal Design of International Trade Institutions: Uncertainty and Escape. *International Organization* 55 (4): 829–57.

Ruggie, John Gerard. 1983. Continuity and Transformation in the World Polity: Toward a Neorealist Synthesis. *World Politics* 35 (2): 261–85.

———. 2002. The Theory and Practice of Learning Networks: Corporate Social Responsibility and the Global Compact. *Journal of Corporate Citizenship* 5 (Spring): 27–36.

———. 2004. Reconstituting the Global Public Domain—Issues, Actors, and Practices. *European Journal of International Relations* 10 (4): 499–531.

Sabel, Charles F., Dara O'Rourke, and Archon Fung. 2000. *Ratcheting Labor Standards: Regulation for Continuous Improvement in the Global Workplace*. Faculty Research Working Papers Series. Cambridge, MA: Harvard University.

Sabel, Charles F., and Jonathan Zeitlin. 2008. Learning from Difference: The New Architecture of Experimentalist Governance in the EU. *European Law Journal* 14 (3): 271–327.

———. 2010. *Experimentalist Governance in the European Union: Towards a New Architecture*. New York: Oxford University Press.

Sasser, Erika N., Aseem Prakash, Benjamin Cashore, and Graeme Auld. 2006. Direct Targeting as an NGO Political Strategy: Examining Private Authority Regimes in the Forestry Sector. *Business and Politics* 8 (3). Available from http://www.degruyter.com/view/j/bap.2006.8.3/bap.2006.8.3.1163/bap.2006.8.3.1163.xml?format=INT.

Schelling, Thomas. 1960. *The Strategy of Conflict*. Cambridge, MA: Harvard University Press.

Schreurs, Miranda. 2004. The Climate Change Divide: The European Union, the United States and the Future of the Kyoto Protocol. In *Green Giants? Environmental Policies of the United States and the European Union*, edited by Norman J. Vig and Michael G. Faure, 207–30. Cambridge, MA: MIT Press.

Scott, Colin. 2004. Regulation in the Age of Governance: The Rise of the Post-Regulatory State. In *The Politics of Regulation*, edited by Jacint Jordana and David Levi-Faur, 145–74. Cheltenham: Edward Elgar.

Singer, David Andrew. 2010. *Regulating Capital: Setting Standards for the International Financial System*. Ithaca, NY: Cornell University Press.

Singer, Peter. 2004. War, Profits and the Vacuum of Law: Privatized Military Firms and International Law. *Columbia Journal of Transnational Law* 42 (2): 521–49.

Siniscalco, Domenico, Alessandro Goria, and Josef Janssen. 1998. Outstanding Issues. In *Issues and Options: The Clean Development Mechanism*, edited by Jose Goldemberg, 91–98. New York: United Nations Development Programme.

Skjaerseth, Jon Birger, and Jorgen Wettestad. 2008. *EU Emissions Trading*. Aldershot: Ashgate.

Slaughter, Anne-Marie. 2004. *A New World Order*. Princeton, NJ: Princeton University Press.

Spar, Deborah. 1999. Lost in (Cyber)space: The Private Rules of Online Commerce. In *Private Authority and International Affairs*, edited by A. Claire Cutler, Virginia Haufler, and Tony Porter, 31–52. Albany: SUNY Press.

Spar, Deborah, and Lane T. LaMure. 2003. The Power of Activism: Assessing the Impact of NGOs on Global Business. *California Management Review* 45 (3): 78–101.

Starobin, Shana. 2009. List of Certification Schemes. Manuscript on file with the author.

Starobin, Shana, and Erika Weinthal. 2010. The Search for Credible Information in Social and Environmental Global Governance: The Kosher Label. *Business and Politics* 12 (3). Available from http://www.degruyter.com/view/j/bap.2010.12.3/bap.2010.12.3.1322/bap.2010.12.3.1322.xml?format=INT.

Steffek, Jens. 2010. Explaining Patterns of Transnational Participation: The Role of Policy Fields. In *Transnational Actors in Global Governance: Patterns, Explanations and Implications*, edited by Jonas Tallberg and Christer Jönsson, 67–87. New York: Palgrave Macmillan.

Stern, Nicholas. 2007. *The Economics of Climate Change: The Stern Review*. Cambridge: Cambridge University Press.

Stewart, Richard B., Dean Anderson, Malik Amin Aslam, Charles Eyre, Ged Jones, Philippe Sands, Marc Stuart, and Farhana Yamin. 2000. *The Clean Development Mechanism: Building Public Private Partnerships under the Kyoto Protocol: Technical, Financial and Institutional Issues*. New York: UNCTAD.

Stigler, George J. 1971. The Theory of Economic Regulation. *Bell Journal of Economics and Management Science* 2 (1): 3–21.

Stone, Randall W. 2002. *Lending Credibility: The International Monetary Fund and the Post-Communist Transition*. Princeton, NJ: Princeton University Press.

Stone, Randall W.. 2011. *Controlling Institutions: International Organizations and the Global Economy*. Cambridge: Cambridge University Press.

Strange, Susan. 1996. *The Retreat of the State*. Cambridge: Cambridge University Press.

Streck, Charlotte. 2004. New Partnerships in Global Environmental Policy: The Clean Development Mechanism. *Journal of Environment and Development* 13 (3): 295–322.

Suchman, Mark C. 1995. Managing Legitimacy: Strategic and Institutional Approaches. *Academy of Management: The Academy of Management Review* 20 (3): 571–610.

Sundin, Heidi, and Janet Ranganathan. 2002. Managing Business Greenhouse Gas Emissions: The Greenhouse Gas Protocol—A Strategic and Operational Tool. *Corporate Environmental Strategy* 9 (2): 137–44.

Tallberg, Jonas. 2006. *Leadership and Negotiation in the European Union*. Cambridge: Cambridge University Press.

Tarrow, Sidney. 1998. *Power in Movement: Social Movements and Contentious Politics*. Cambridge: Cambridge University Press.

Thompson, Alexander. 2006. Screening Power: International Organizations as Informative Agents. In *Delegation and Agency in International Organizations*, edited by Darren G. Hawkins, David A. Lake, Daniel L. Nielson, and Michael J. Tierney, 229–54. Cambridge: Cambridge University Press.

TRAFFIC. 2010. *TRAFFIC Bulletin* 22 (3): 93–146.

UNFCCC. 1992. United Nations Framework Convention on Climate Change. Available from http://unfccc.int/files/essential_background/background_publi cations_htmlpdf/application/pdf/conveng.pdf.

———. 1995. Activities Implemented Jointly under the Pilot Phase. FCCC/CP/ 1995/7/Add.1, Decision 5/CP.1. Available from http://unfccc.int/cop3/resource/ docs/cop1/07a01.pdf.

———. 1996a. Implementation of the Berlin Mandate. Proposals from Parties. Note by the Secretariat. FCCC/AGBM/1996/Misc.2/. Available from http:// unfccc.int/resource/docs/1996/agbm/misc02.pdf.

———. 1996b. Implementation of the Berlin Mandate. Proposals from Parties. Note by the Secretariat. Addendum. FCCC/AGBM/1996/Misc.2/Add.2. Available from http://unfccc.int/resource/docs/1996/agbm/misc02a02.pdf.

———. 1997. Implementation of the Berlin Mandate: Additional Proposals from Parties. FCCC/AGBM/1997/MISC.1/Add.3. Available from http://unfccc.int /cop4/resource/docs/1997/agbm/misc01a3.htm.

———. 1998a. Matters Related to Decision 1/CP.3 Paragraph 5, Activities Implemented Jointly: Compilation of Submissions by Parties. FCCC/CP/1998 /MISC.7. Available from http://unfccc.int/resource/docs/cop4/misc07.pdf.

———. 1998b. Matters Related to Decision 1/CP.3 Paragraph 5. Activities Implemented Jointly. Compilation of Submissions by Parties. FCCC/CP/1998/MISC.7 /Add.1. Available from http://unfccc.int/resource/docs/cop4/misc07a01.pdf.

———. 1998c. Preparatory Work Needed for the Fourth Session of the Conference of the Parties on the Items Listed in Decision 1/CP.3, Paragraph 5. FCCC/SB/1998 /MISC.1/Add.5. Available from http://unfccc.int/cop4/resource/docs/1998/sb /misc01a5.htm.

————. 1999a. Mechanisms Pursuant to Articles 6, 12 and 17 of the Kyoto Protocol: Further Proposals from Parties. FCCC/SB/1999/MISC.10. Available from http://unfccc.int/resource/docs/1999/sb/misc10.pdf.

————. 1999b. Mechanisms Pursuant to Articles 6, 12 and 17 of the Kyoto Protocol: Synthesis of Proposals by Parties on Principles, Modalities, Rules and Guidelines. FCCC/SB/1999/INF.2/Add.1. Available from http://unfccc.int/cop5/resource/docs/1999/sb/inf02a01.htm.

————. 1999c. Mechanisms Pursuant to Articles 6, 12 and 17 of the Kyoto Protocol: Synthesis of Proposals by Parties on Principles, Modalities, Rules and Guidelines. FCCC/SB/1999/MISC.10/Add.2. Available from http://unfccc.int/cop5/resource/docs/1999/sb/inf02a02.htm.

————. 2000a. Mechanisms Pursuant to Articles 6, 12 and 17 of the Kyoto Protocol. Additional Submissions from Parties. FCCC/SB/2000/MISC.4. Available from http://unfccc.int/resource/docs/2000/sb/misc04.pdf.

————. 2000b. Mechanisms Pursuant to Articles 6, 12 and 17 of the Kyoto Protocol. Additional Submissions from Parties. FCCC/SB/2000/MISC.4/Add.2. Available from http://unfccc.int/resource/docs/2000/sb/misc04a02.pdf.

————. 2000c. Mechanisms Pursuant to Articles 6, 12 and 17 of the Kyoto Protocol. Text for Further Negotiation on Principles, Modalities, Rules and Guidelines. Note by the Chairmen. FCCC/SB/2000/3. Available from http://unfccc.int/resource/docs/2000/sb/03.pdf.

————. 2001. Administrative and Financial Matters. FCCC/SBI/2001/16. Available from http://unfccc.int/resource/docs/2001/sbi/16.pdf.

————. 2002a. Funding under the Convention. FCCC/CP/2001/13/Add.1, Decision 7/CP.7. Available from http://unfccc.int/resource/docs/cop7/13a01.pdf.

————. 2002b. Guidance to an Entity Entrusted with the Operation of the Financial Mechanism of the Convention, for the Operation of the Least Developed Countries Fund. FCCC/CP/2001/13/Add.4, Decision 27/CP.7. Available from http://unfccc.int/resource/docs/cop7/13a04.pdf.

————. 2002c. Modalities and Procedures for a Clean Development Mechanism, as Defined in Article 12 of the Kyoto Protocol. FCCC/CP/2001/13/Add.2, Decision 17/CP.7. Available from http://unfccc.int/resource/docs/cop7/13a02.pdf.

————. 2012. Report of the Individual Review of the Annual Submission of Canada Submitted in 2011. CC/ERT/ARR/2012/11. Available from http://unfccc.int/files/kyoto_protocol/compliance/plenary/application/pdf/cc-ert-arr-2012-11_arr_2011_of_canada.pdf.

US EPA. 2009. Final Mandatory GHG Reporting Rule. US EPA. Available from http://www.epa.gov/climatechange/emissions/ghgrulemaking.html.

Usui, Mikoto. 2007. Business-Society Interaction towards Sustainable Development. In *The Politics of Participation in Sustainable Development Governance*, edited by Jessica F. Green and W. Bradnee Chambers, 62–89. Tokyo: United Nations University Press.

Victor, David G. 2011. *Global Warming Gridlock: Creating More Effective Strategies for Protecting the Planet*. Cambridge: Cambridge University Press.

Victor, David G., and Joshua House. 2004. A New Currency: Climate Change and Carbon Credits. *Harvard International Review* (2): 56–59.

Vine, Edward, and Jayant Sathaye. 1997. *The Monitoring, Evaluation, Reporting and Verification of Climate Change Mitigation Projects: Discussion of Issues and Methodologies and Review of Existing Protocols and Guidelines*. Berkeley: Lawrence Berkeley National Laboratory.

Vogel, David. 2008. Private Global Business Regulation. *Annual Review of Political Science* 11: 261–82.

———. 2009. The Private Regulation of Global Corporate Conduct. In *The Politics of Global Regulation*, edited by Walter Mattli and Ngaire Woods, 151–99. Princeton, NJ: Princeton University Press.

Wapner, Paul. 1996. *Environmental Activism and World Civic Politics*. Albany: State University of New York Press.

Wara, Michael W. 2007. Measuring the Clean Development Mechanism's Performance and Potential. *UCLA Law Review* 55 (6): 1759–1804.

Wara, Michael W., and David G. Victor. 2008. *A Realistic Policy on International Carbon Offsets*. Stanford, CA: Program on Energy and Sustainable Development, Stanford University.

Weber, Max. 1978. *Economy and Society*. Translated by Guenther Roth and Claus Wittich. Berkeley: University of California Press.

Weiss, Linda. 1998. *The Myth of the Powerless State*. Ithaca, NY: Cornell University Press.

Wendt, Alexander. 1992. Anarchy Is What States Make of It: The Social Construction of Power Politics. *International Organization* 46 (2): 391–425.

Werksman, Jacob. 1998. The Clean Development Mechanism: Unwrapping the Kyoto Surprise. *Review of European Community and International Environmental Law* 7 (2): 147–58.

Whytock, Christopher A. 2010. Private-Public Interaction in Global Governance: The Case of Transnational Commercial Arbitration. *Business and Politics* 12 (3). Available from http://www.degruyter.com/view/j/bap.2010.12.3 /bap.2010.12.3.1324/bap.2010.12.3.1324.xml?format=INT.

Williams, Phil. 2002. Transnational Organized Crime and the State. In *The Emergence of Private Authority in Global Governance*, edited by Rodney Bruce Hall and Thomas J. Biersteker, 161–82. Cambridge Studies in International Relations, 85. Cambridge: Cambridge University Press.

Wilson, James Q. 1980. *The Politics of Regulation*. New York: Basic Books.

Wolf, Klaus Dieter. 2005. Governance and Democracy Comparing National, European and International Experiences. In *Private Actors and the Legitimacy of Governance beyond the State: Conceptual Outlines and Empirical Explorations*, edited by Arthur Benz and Yannis Papadopolous, 200–227. London: Routledge.

Wolff, R. P. 1990. The Conflict between Authority and Autonomy. In *Authority*, edited by Joseph Raz, 20–31. New York: New York University Press.

Wood, Stepan. 2005. Three Questions about Corporate Codes: Problematizations, Authorizations and the Public/Private Divide. In *Ethics Codes, Corporations and the Challenge of Globalization*, edited by Wesley Cragg, 245–89. Cheltenham: Edward Elgar.

World Resources Institute. 2001. *GHG Protocol Update, September 2001*. Washington, DC: World Resources Institute. Available from http://www.ghgprotocol

.org/downloads/newsletter_archive/GHG_Protocol_Newsletter_Sept_2001
.pdf.

———. 2007. *Measuring to Manage: A Guide to Designing GHG Accounting and Reporting Programs.* Washington DC: World Resources Institute.

World Resources Institute and LMI. 2011. *The Greenhouse Gas Protocol for the U.S. Public Sector.* Washington DC: World Resources Institute.

World Resources Institute and World Business Council on Sustainable Development. 2001. *The Greenhouse Gas Protocol: A Corporate Accounting and Reporting Standard.* Washington, DC: World Resources Institute.

———. 2004. *The Greenhouse Gas Protocol: A Corporate Accounting and Reporting Standard.* Rev. ed. Washington, DC: World Resources Institute.

Yamin, Farhana. 1998. Operational and Institutional Challenges. In *Issues and Options: The Clean Development Mechanism*, edited by Jose Goldemberg, 53–80. New York: United Nations Development Programme.

———, ed. 2005. *Climate Change and Carbon Markets: A Handbook of Emission Reduction Mechanisms.* London: Earthscan.

Young, Oran, ed. 1999. The Effectiveness of International Environmental Regimes. In *The Effectiveness of International Environmental Regimes: Causal Connections and Behavioral Mechanisms*, 1–32. Cambridge, MA: MIT Press.

———. 2001. Inferences and Indices: Evaluating the Effectiveness of International Environmental Regimes. *Global Environmental Politics* 1 (1): 99–121.

———. 2002. *The Institutional Dimensions of Environmental Change: Fit, Interplay, and Scale.* Cambridge, MA: MIT Press.

———. 2009. Governance for Sustainable Development in a World of Rising Interdependencies. In *Governance for the Environment: New Perspectives*, edited by Magali A. Delmas and Oran Young, 12–40. Cambridge: Cambridge University Press.

Zapfel, Peter, and Matti Vainio. 2002. *Pathways to European Greenhouse Gas Emissions Trading: History and Misconceptions.* Venice: Fonazione Eni Enrico Mattei.

Zelli, Fariborz. 2011. The Fragmentation of the Global Climate Architecture. *Wiley Interdisciplinary Reviews: Climate Change* 2 (2): 255–70.

Index

Abbott, Kenneth W., 57, 59n31, 83, 89, 173n25
accountability, 20, 46, 46n90, 48, 177–78
Activities Implemented Jointly (AIJ), 109, 109n20, 110, 123, 160; support of by the UNFCCC, 117–18, 138
adjudication, 61, 67, 69, 72
"agency slack," 17, 48, 49, 51
agents: agents of validation and verification used by states in the CDM, 114–22, 166–67; as "atmospheric police," 24, 105, 107–8, 130; control of, 34, 171; delegation to private agents by states, 54, 55, 105–6, 164, 166, 177, 179–80; private actors as *sole* agents, 69–70, 74, 78; role of private agents, 69, 173
Agreement on Administrative Arrangements for the Prek Thnot Power and Irrigation Development Project, 64
Alchian, Armen A., 71n59
"ally principle," 46, 48. See also delegation
Ambrosi, Philippe, 143n39
Arthur Andersen, 121
Asia-Pacific Fishery Commission, 71
Australia, 148n55, 174
Austria, 104
authority, 27–28; and consent, 27–28, 29; *de facto* authority, 33, 34n38, 36, 52; definition of, 6, 27; *de jure* authority, 33, 34, 34n38, 36, 52; exercise of as an institutionalized activity, 30; multiple loci of, 5, 6, 14, 55, 65, 103, 164, 165, 174; as mutually constituted, 28; as a non-zero sum, 5, 9, 11, 70, 163, 165; as a right granted by the ruled, 30; as a type of power, 27. See also delegated authority; entrepreneurial authority; private authority
autonomy, loss of, 45. See also sovereignty costs
Avant, Deborah D., 9, 38

"Baptist and bootlegger" coalitions, 175
Bartley, Tim, 37, 85
Berlin Mandate, 123

Bernstein, Steven, 38, 142n34
Betsill, Michele M., 148nn55–56
Bhopal disaster, 82
Biersteker, Thomas J., 38
biodiversity, 75, 169, 174
Bird Friendly coffee, 89
Bolivia, 128
B&Q, 18
Bradley, Curtis A., 33n35, 59, 66n52
branding, 15
Brazil, 119, 129, 154; proposal of for a "Clean Development Fund," 125
Bent Spar, sinking of, 157
Brewster, Michael, 50n104
British Petroleum (BP), development of emissions trading scheme by, 138–39
Broz, J. Lawrence, 50n104
bureaucracies, public, 46n93
Bush, George W., 159
Büthe, Tim, 40, 59

Cafaggi, Fabrizio, 59
California, 148n55
California Climate Action Registry, 148, 152
Canada, 87, 100, 104–5
Canadian Chemical Producers Association, 35, 82
Capoor, Karan, 143n39
carbon: carbon accounting, 98, 100; carbon certification schemes, 99, 169; and entrepreneurial authority, 99. See also carbon offsets; greenhouse gases (GHG), GHG accounting
Carbon Disclosure Project, 99, 99n77, 144, 144n40, 145, 174, 175; as global user of the GHG Protocol, 146–47
"Carbon Offset Verification Service," 110
carbon offsets, 99–100, 105–6, 108, 114, 131; bilateral carbon offset mechanism, 105–6; "certified tradeable offsets," 110; measuring of, 109; monitoring of, 106; offset credits, 110–11; opposition to, 124; third-party monitoring of, 106, 107
Carrefour, 12

focal institutions (*continued*)
  Convention on Climate Change (UNFCCC) Secretariat, as a focal institution
Food and Agriculture Organization's Code of Conduct for Responsible Fisheries, 93
Forest Stewardship Council (FSC), 13, 31, 32, 44, 85
forestry, 83, 109, 110, 169, 176; regulations concerning, 108; third-party verification protocol for forestry offset projects, 120
forum shopping, 50
Framework Convention. *See* UN Framework Convention on Climate Change (UNFCCC) Secretariat
Fransen, Luc, 83
free-rider problem, 56
Friends of the Earth, 18

General Motors Corporation, 139
Gereffi, Gary, 35
Global Climate Coalition, 175
Global Compact, 85n38
Global Environment Facility (GEF), 109, 114, 116–17
Global Invasive Species Program, 76
Global Reporting Initiative, 81
globalization, 37, 38, 84, 164; management of, 178–79
Gold Standard, 101, 174
governance, 163–64; carbon governance, 131; climate governance, 131; definition of, 26n2; global environmental governance, 26, 30, 130, 180; "governance by disclosure," 81n9; "governance trilemma," 178; growth in the amount of governance, 181; increase in total amount of, 54–55; "institutional density" of global governance, 55; as a "social function," 181. *See also* nonstate market driven governance
governments (national), as agents of validation and verification, 114, 116
governors, 9, 11, 28, 32–33, 34, 35, 45–46, 164; global governors, 38, 80, 174n30; and the governed, 29, 30, 32–33, 34, 35, 45–46; potential governors (those that aspire to authority), 29–30, 29n17
Graz, Jean-Christophe, 37
Green, Jessica, 59n27, 83, 84n32

"green club," 157
Green Mark (Taiwan), 88
Greenhouse Gas Protocol (GHG Protocol), 13, 15, 24, 99, 100, 101, 175, 180; adoption of GHG Protocol standards, 142–45, 143nn38–39; adoption of the GHG Protocol in emissions trading schemes, 148, 150–51, 148n55; adoption of GHG Protocol by GHG registries, 145–48; authority of, 151–54; and "baseline protection," 155; creation of as a multi-stakeholder process, 141–42; definition of, 136–37; and the division of GHG emissions into different "scopes," 136; effect of on outputs, 171; good faith negotiations of the members of, 140–41; as a management tool for emissions mitigation, 166–67; proportion of GHG registries that use the GHG Protocol, 144; as a successful case of entrepreneurial authority, 161–62; voluntary nature of, 136n10. *See also* Greenhouse Gas Protocol (GHG Protocol), explaining the emergence of
Greenhouse Gas Protocol (GHG Protocol), explaining the emergence of, 154–57; and the focal institution, 160–61; and heterogeneous state preferences, 157–60
greenhouse gases (GHG): *de facto* standards for GHG emissions, 132; GHG accounting, 132, 133, 134–35, 141, 157; GHG emissions, 72, 105; international regulation of GHG emissions, 133, 134; mandatory GHG emissions trading, 135, 135n4; reduction in GHG emissions, 3–4
greenwashing, 99, 177
Group of 77 (G-77), 123, 125, 126, 127, 129; opposition to the delegation of rule-making authority, 128; opposition to North-South cooperation through carbon offset projects, 124
Grubb, Michael, 125n82
Guide to Monitoring Carbon Storage in Forestry and Agroforestry Projects (Winrock International), 109
Gupta, Aarti, 81n9
Gutner, Tamar, 170

Haas, Peter, 170
Hall, Rodney Bruce, 38